I0419184

CIRCA 1958: BREAKING GROUND IN AMERICAN ART

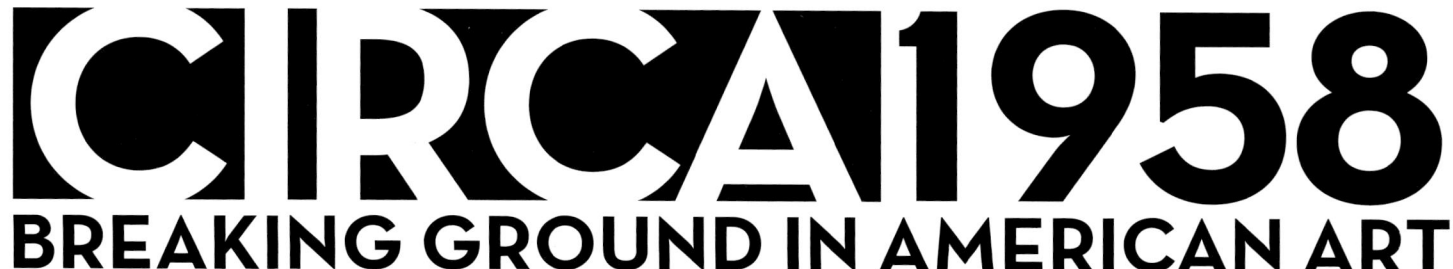

CIRCA 1958
BREAKING GROUND IN AMERICAN ART

Roni Feinstein

Ackland Art Museum
The University of North Carolina at Chapel Hill • 2008

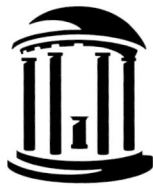

Publication of *Circa 1958: Breaking Ground in American Art* is scheduled in conjunction with an exhibition of the same name. The exhibition, publication, and programming are made possible by the generosity of friends of the Ackland in honor of the Museum's fiftieth anniversary.

Circa 1958: Breaking Ground in American Art
Ackland Art Museum
The University of North Carolina at Chapel Hill
Chapel Hill, North Carolina
September 21, 2008 - January 4, 2009

© 2008 Ackland Art Museum
The University of North Carolina at Chapel Hill

All rights reserved.
No part of this publication may be reproduced or transmitted in any form or by any means, electronic or mechanical, including photocopying, recording, or any information storage or retrieval system, without permission in writing from the publisher.

Library of Congress Control Number: 2008932650

ISBN: 978-0-8078-5949-0

Published in the United States by:
Ackland Art Museum
The University of North Carolina at Chapel Hill
Campus Box 3400
Chapel Hill, North Carolina 27599-3400

Designed by:
The Splinter Group
Carrboro, North Carolina

Printed in the United States by:
Classic Graphics
Morrisville, North Carolina

Distributed by:
The University of North Carolina Press
116 Boundary Street
Chapel Hill, North Carolina 27514-3803
www.uncpress.unc.edu

TABLE OF CONTENTS

Artists

Richard Anuszkiewicz
Darby Bannard
Romare Bearden
Larry Bell
Billy Al Bengston
Karl Benjamin
Wallace Berman
Ronald Bladen
Lee Bontecou
George Brecht
John Chamberlain
Chryssa
Bruce Conner
Beauford Delaney
Jim Dine
Lorser Feitelson
Red Grooms
Al Held
Robert Indiana
Alfred Jensen
Jess
Jasper Johns
Ray Johnson
Allan Kaprow
Ellsworth Kelly
Ed Kienholz
Gabriel Kohn
Nicholas Krushenick
Alexander Liberman
Roy Lichtenstein
Morris Louis
Robert Mallary
Marisol
Agnes Martin
John McLaughlin
Robert Morris
Louise Nevelson
Kenneth Noland
Claes Oldenburg
Yoko Ono
George Ortman
Robert Rauschenberg

James Rosenquist
Ed Ruscha
Robert Ryman
Lucas Samaras
George Segal
Leon Polk Smith
Tony Smith
Richard Stankiewicz
Frank Stella
Myron Stout
Lenore Tawney
Alma Thomas
Andy Warhol
Tom Wesselmann
Jack Youngerman

Donors

The University of North Carolina at Chapel Hill

William R. Kenan Jr. Charitable Trust

Nathan Cummings Foundation
Randleigh Foundation Trust

Arthur F. and Alice E. Adams Foundation

Mr. James-Keith Brown and Mr. Eric G. Diefenbach
Dr. J. Kenneth and Mrs. Ellen T. Chance
Mr. C. Perry Colwell and Ms. Betty Neese
Ms. Shirley Drechsel and Mr. Wayne Vaughn
Mr. W. Howard Holsenbeck Jr.
Mr. Thomas S. Kenan III
The Estate of William O. Livingstone
Mrs. Beatrice Cummings Mayer
Dr. Charles W. Millard III
Ms. Elizabeth Kenan Morton
Ms. Paula Davis Noell
Mr. and Mrs. James Richard Patton Jr.
Ms. Josephine Ward Patton
Drs. Leena and Sheldon Peck
Ms. Katharine Lee Reid
Mr. and Mrs. Herbert F. Shatzman
Mr. Michael and Ms. Gayle Sheppard
Mr. and Mrs. John L. Townsend III
Mr. Charles Weinraub
Mr. Charles J. Wolfe and Ms. Sandra Roth
Ms. Ann Bondurant Young

Acknowledgments

On behalf of the Ackland Art Museum I want to express my deep appreciation to the individuals and organizations who have contributed to the success of this exhibition. First, I extend sincerest thanks to guest curator Roni Feinstein who responded magnificently to the challenge of developing an exhibition that would showcase the artistic ambitions and innovations of the late 1950s. The resulting exhibition and publication capture the spirit and vitality of this extraordinary time within a meaningful context.

Many generous gifts made this exhibition possible. Former Chancellor James Moeser generously allocated a special grant from The University of North Carolina at Chapel Hill for the exhibition. The William R. Kenan Jr. Charitable Trust extended a major challenge grant and I am particularly grateful to Richard Krasno, president of the Kenan Trust, and Tom Kenan for their enthusiasm. The Ackland National Advisory Board and friends of the Ackland provided generous financial support for the exhibition, publication, and programs. The early confidence of these funders enabled us to secure agreements with public and private collections across the country and to plan for this publication.

A number of UNC-Chapel Hill colleagues have been invaluable resources, from participating in early discussions about potential themes and artists, to offering expertise and resources in the planning of related programming on the theme of "circa 1958." These include David Sontag, Joy Kasson, John Kasson, Juan Logan, Bob Cantwell, Jay Garcia, Peter Filene, Beth Grabowski, Emil Kang, Rosemary Holland, Julie Fishell, Karen Hagerman, Tim Carter, Jim Ketch, Stefan Litwin, Cary Levine, Joe Haj, and Hassan Melehy.

I am very grateful to Lane Wurster, Steve Balcom, and Phillip Dwyer at The Splinter Group for the design of this handsome catalogue, and to J. W. Photo Labs for the masterful handling of images. I am also delighted to be entering a new partnership with The University of North Carolina Press who will distribute this catalogue on behalf of the Ackland Art Museum.

Finally, without the generosity of the artists, collectors, museums, and galleries who made their works available and who kindly provided recollections and other observations, this exhibition would not have been possible. Thank you.

Emily Kass
Director, Ackland Art Museum

My enthusiasm for this project grew in large part out of my devotion to the art of Robert Rauschenberg, which has been a major part of my professional life for over three decades and has long fostered my preoccupation with the art of the fifties and sixties as a whole. The exhibition is devoted to the memory of this remarkable man whose art opened my eyes and mind, greatly enriched my life, and will live on forever in its brilliance and vitality.

At the Ackland Art Museum, I extend my gratitude to Director Emily Kass, for having granted me the opportunity to guest curate this exhibition and to Barbara Matilsky, curator of exhibitions, who has been the most remarkable advisor, supporter, and collaborator in every phase of the exhibition's organization and in the realization of this publication. The gracious assistance and organizational skills of Christine Huber, assistant curator of exhibitions, have been invaluable and Kate Arpen, graduate student intern, has been a wonder, helping to compile the selected bibliography and photographic images. Many additional Ackland Art Museum staff members worked tirelessly on *Circa 1958*: Scott Hankins, assistant registrar; Joseph Gargasz, chief preparator; Carolyn Wood, assistant director for art and education; Nic Brown, director of communications, and Lauren Sanford, curatorial assistant. Ulrike R. Guthrie proved a most able editor. Amanda M. Hughes, director of external affairs, served as managing editor for this publication. Her grasp of the project's scope and attention to every detail were heroic and admirable.

Numerous artists, representatives of artist's estates, dealers, collectors, and museum directors were not only exceedingly generous in lending us their treasures, but were extremely forthcoming with their time, recollections, and expertise. In this regard, special thanks are owed to Robert Indiana and Ellsworth Kelly, as well as to Ramon Alcolea of the Estate of Ronald Bladen; Richard Armstrong of the Carnegie Museum of Art, Pittsburgh; Sylvia Bandi of Hauser and Wirth, Zurich; Jack Cowart of the Roy Lichtenstein Foundation; David Mirvish; Michael Findlay of Acquavella Gallery; Samuel Freeman; Mrs. Robert B. Mayer and Marla Hand of the Robert B. Mayer Family Collection; Mara Held of the Al Held Foundation; Jon Hendricks; Michael Kohn of the Michael Kohn Gallery; Kathleen Nugent Mangan of the Lenore G. Tawney Foundation; Michael Rosenfeld and halley k. harrisburg of the Michael Rosenfeld Gallery; Lynda Shield of the Jacobson Howard Gallery; Louis Stern of Louis Stern Fine Arts; and Donald and Linda Schlenger. I am grateful to The Museum of Contemporary Art, Los Angeles, for making not one, but two significant Rauschenberg Combines available to us.

Finally, I extend my deepest gratitude to Don, Olivia, and Ivan Blaustein for their love and support during the many phases of this project and always.

Roni Feinstein

FOREWORD

Foreword

Emily Kass

Circa 1958: Breaking Ground in American Art is presented to coincide with the Ackland Art Museum's fiftieth anniversary. When we initially began discussing an anniversary exhibition, we hypothesized a show that would survey the artists and styles—emerging and dominant—around the time the brand new William Hayes Ackland Memorial Art Center opened at the University of North Carolina at Chapel Hill in 1958. Soon it became clear that no single show could do justice to the complexity of the era.[1] However, by concentrating on the year 1958, albeit with a liberal dose of "circa," we might be able to zero in on key trends that were to become highly influential in the 1960s and beyond.

One tends to look back at the late 1950s with some degree of nostalgia, remembering a time of peace, prosperity, relative innocence, or perhaps inertia: a time of calm before the storm of the sixties. In reality, world events in 1958 offered significant and sobering reminders of the fragility of peace and the prevalence of the Cold War in the American consciousness. Khrushchev became premier of the Soviet Union. After the USSR launched Sputnik in 1957, the "space race" began when in 1958, the United States successfully launched the first satellite, Explorer I, and Eisenhower established NASA. The collapse of the Batista government in Cuba in 1958 and Fidel Castro's triumphant takeover of Havana in January 1959 set fears and actions in motion that escalated to the Bay of Pigs crisis and a standoff that continues to this day. With the threat of nuclear annihilation not far from people's minds—Hiroshima had occurred only thirteen years previously and tests of atomic and even more powerful hydrogen bombs continued— scientists from forty-three nations petitioned the United Nations to create the first Nuclear Test Ban Treaty. The Campaign for Nuclear Disarmament began in England and spread to the United States, and along with it, the Peace Symbol, designed in 1958, which would become the emblem of the antiwar movement of the 1960s.

Recalled through the lens of television, America of the 1950s was filled with *Donna Reed*, *Ozzie and Harriet*, and *Father Knows Best*—all portraits of white, well-to-do families living in suburbia. Television did little by way of nightly programming to suggest that this was a time when social and political protests were beginning to emerge. For example, it was in 1958 that the Supreme Court mandated that the Little Rock, Arkansas, Public Schools integrate immediately rather than wait until 1961. Little Rock responded by closing public schools for a year. It would take years of marches and sit-ins, by courageous protesters starting in Greensboro, North Carolina in 1960 and reaching a crescendo with the 1963 March on Washington, DC with Martin Luther King Jr.'s *"I have a dream"* speech heard by 200,000 to effect the societal changes that ultimately secured legal recourse for those who did not live in the world of *Ozzie and Harriet*.

In 1958, a frequent contributor to "women's magazines" named Betty Friedan was unable to find a publisher for an article that described the discontent of her former college classmates, women who felt trapped in the role of homemaker and for whom society allowed few other options. Five years later, this article was expanded into a book: *The*

Feminine Mystique, and became an important "call to arms" of the Women's Rights Movement of the 1960s. The early successes of individual women and African Americans that allowed them to move beyond the narrow, traditional roles defined by the white, male dominated society were generally achieved without any strong societal support. The mass cultural movements that would become known as the Civil Rights Movement and the Women's Movement were still some years away.

It was also a time of debate among intellectuals about high culture vs. popular culture, with critics lining up on both sides. In a recent essay "1958: The War of the Intellectuals", Rachel Donadio writes, "Much has been made of 1968 . . . But what of its more unassuming antecedent? Fifty years ago, Eisenhower was in the White House, the country was in a recession and the American intellectual scene was crackling with energy."[2] Donadio then describes ". . . the attempt by some influential critics to preserve the quickly dissolving distinctions among highbrow, middlebrow, and lowbrow culture." At the same time, the distinction between artistic achievement and commercial success, which American intellectuals had long assumed to be mutually exclusive, was losing its hold. In a 1939 essay, "Avant-Garde and Kitsch," Clement Greenberg set forth the criteria that he believed should be applied to all great works of art, music, and literature, and which he would apply to the work of the artists he championed: "A pure preoccupation with the invention and arrangement of spaces, surfaces, shapes, colors, etc., to the exclusion of whatever is not necessarily implicated in these factors."[3] In contrast, to the avant-garde, he railed against the rear guard: "*Kitsch*: popular, commercial art and literature with their chromeotypes, magazine covers, illustrations, ads, slick and pulp fiction, comics, Tin Pan Alley music, tap dancing, Hollywood movies, etc. etc."[4] Among other concerns, visual artists of the time took up the challenges raised by the critics of both high culture and popular culture and moved to a new visual vocabulary.

Throughout the twentieth century, the fine arts as avant-garde had been viewed as a succession of movements: Fauvism, Cubism, Surrealism, and other "isms." Most of these movements had thrived in Paris—with some offshoots such as German Expressionism and Futurism popping up elsewhere—until the center moved to New York after World War II. By 1958, Abstract Expressionism had dominated the New York art world for most of the decade. Jackson Pollock's 1956 death in a car crash, tragic though it was, fit in with the mythology of the romantic, rebel artist (a la James Dean who had similarly been killed in 1955). The subsequent high prices for Pollock's work and growing success of some of the other Abstract Expressionists changed the dynamics of the New York art market. While Abstract Expressionism would continue to be a viable style for some years, and one of great beauty and originality in the hands of a few artists, sensibilities were shifting. Art that was actively conscious of itself as "art" or incorporated the banalities of the world around the artist began to replace the existential, frequently angst-ridden persona and subject matter of the Abstract Expressionists.

Although not included in this exhibition, it is important to note that photography, film, and printmaking were also undergoing as radical a transformation as painting and sculpture in 1958. Photography was rarely included in art galleries, despite the presence of The Museum of Modern Art's photography program. Documentary photography and photo essays, such as those featured in *Look* and *Life*, were prominent. Some photographers began to respond to the prevailing glossy, optimistic images (notably in MoMA's 1955 exhibition *The Family of Man*—a massive photography show that celebrated peace and "oneness") by casting a critical eye on the edges and detritus of society instead. In 1956, Robert Frank, received a Guggenheim Fellowship to travel around the United States and document life. While superficially in the tradition of, for example, Walker Evans' and Dorothea Lange's documentary photographs during the Depression, Frank's view was far more cynical than that of his predecessors. He captured not just the vitality of America, but also poverty, segregation, and often bleakness sitting just to the side of the mainstream. These photographs were first published in 1958, with an essay by Beat writer Jack Kerouac whose novel *On the Road* had been published the year before. Other photographers at the time, such as William Klein, similarly captured the grittiness of the urban experience using awkward cropping, blurry images, and grainy film quality. These techniques would become the standard of "street" photography in the 1960s and emphasized the transient nature of their point of view.

In many of the same ways that photographers broke the rules for new expressive purposes, filmmakers also questioned the role and nature of film through editing techniques, abstraction, found footage, and by upending traditional narrative formats. The American Independent Film Movement was initiated in 1958 with Stan Brakhage's *Anticipation of the Night*, an "autobiography" which abandoned traditional sequence, narrative, editing, and camerawork. Bruce Conner presented *A Movie* as part of his first exhibition of Assemblages in 1958. The film is a montage of re-edited snippets of found footage from educational and scientific films and newsreels, with an equally unrelated but striking musical soundtrack. This tendency toward film as an individual, highly subjective expression prefigured video art which became possible only with the advent of more portable and available equipment beginning in 1964 with Fluxus artist Nam June Paik.

Elsewhere in the arts, printmaking was to begin a renaissance with the establishment of Universal Limited Art Editions (ULAE), started by Tatyana and Maurice Grossman in a small house on Long Island. In 1957, ULAE published its first work with Larry Rivers and the writer Frank O'Hara in a series of twelve lithographs. From its beginnings, the hallmark of ULAE was to nurture collaboration among artists and master printers and to encourage creative and technical experimentation. A relatively small group of artists were invited to work at ULAE over the years. Among them, Rauschenberg, Johns, Rosenquist, Dine (all represented in this exhibition and catalogue) would subsequently create some of the most innovative prints of their time.

From our 2008 vantage point, it is hard to imagine a time when so many constraints were imposed on artists and that a serious debate raged over abstraction. That photography, pop images, recycled materials, and advertising were ever considered inappropriate for art seems quaint. There is no single center of the art world today, as artists and collectors globe trot to art fairs, galleries, and museums world wide. In our cyber-world with instant access to information and images, with blogs and YouTube that allow any voice to be an authority, it is hard to fathom that fifty years ago a relatively small group of tastemakers could so dominate the art world.

Much is owed to this time, and to the pioneer artists, circa 1958, who were breaking new ground in American art. This exhibition and catalogue gather these artists together for a kind of retrospective. In it we find reminders of the world as it appeared and suggestions of what the world would become. It is a privilege to bring these works—and these artists— together again, to consider their influence, their vision, and the remarkable accomplishment and beauty of their artistic moment.

————

NOTES

1. Other recent exhibitions also explore aspects of the art of the fifties and sixties. These include, *Birth of the Cool: California Art, Design, and Culture at Midcentury* (Orange County Museum of Art); *Color as Field: American Painting, 1950 – 1975* (The American Federation of Arts); and *New York Cool: Painting and Sculpture from the NYU Art Collection* (Grey Art Gallery).

2. A recent essay by Rachel Donadio in the *New York Times Book Review*, "1958: The War of the Intellectuals" (Sunday, May 11, 2008, 39)

3. Reprinted in *Art and Culture: Critical Essays*, by Clement Greenberg (Boston: Beacon Press, 1971), 7.

4. Ibid., 9.

CIRCA 1958: BREAKING GROUND IN AMERICAN ART

Circa 1958: Breaking Ground in American Art

Roni Feinstein

This exhibition explores a transitional moment in American art that occurred around the year 1958. It was at this point that two major alternatives to Abstract Expressionism, which had been dominant and triumphant since the beginning of the 1950s, first made themselves evident: Assemblage on the one hand and Post-painterly Abstraction on the other. Each of these tendencies was both an outgrowth of and reaction to Abstract Expressionism. In each, literal attitudes about art, the world, and the materials and processes of art making replaced emotional and mythic content. Each assumed a wide variety of manifestations, flourished for a number of years, and then gave rise to offshoots such as Pop Art, Fluxus, and Minimalism. Assemblage and Post-painterly Abstraction each in its own way not only introduced new methods for creating art, but new definitions of what art could be. Together they were groundbreaking and redirected the course of American art.

Abstract Expressionism was born of a particular set of historical and cultural circumstances. With the outbreak of World War II, many leading artists and intellectuals were among the European expatriates who sought refuge in the United States and particularly in New York. Among them were the Surrealists André Breton, Max Ernst, Yves Tanguy, André Masson, and Roberto Matta. The Surrealists brought with them a predilection for organic and biomorphic form and the practice of automatism, an improvisational manner of working that was said to tap into the artist's unconscious, both ideas that were quickly embraced by the Americans in the late thirties and early forties.

By the late forties, world events like the United States' bombing of Hiroshima and Nagasaki and the revelations of the Holocaust's horrors led American artists to create an art of social conscience responsive to the anxieties of the age. In the work of those Abstract Expressionists whom the critic Harold Rosenberg was to dub "Action Painters"[1]—Jackson Pollock, Willem de Kooning, Franz Kline, and others—the life and inner feelings of the artist were expressed through the ostensibly unpremeditated act of manipulating paint over the surface of a large canvas in a highly physical way, either through dripping or through the use of broad brushes (fig. 1). Others, who belonged to what later came to be called the "Color Field School"—Barnett Newman, Mark Rothko, and Clyfford Still—reached beyond the self in a less autographic, more purely color-based art to express the tragic, timeless, and sublime (fig. 2).

As there was as yet little public audience for this new art, the artists came together in a show of mutual support to form "the community of the New York School." Its base was Eighth Street in Greenwich Village, the locus of many of the artists'

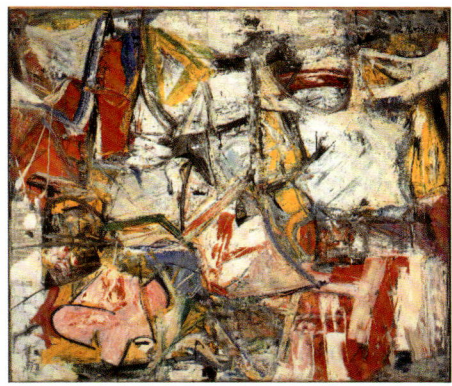

Fig. 1
Willem de Kooning (1904 - 1997), *Gotham News*, 1955. Oil on canvas, framed Albright-Knox Art Gallery, Buffalo, New York, Gift of Seymour H. Knox, Jr.

Barnett Newman (1905 - 1970), *Vir Heroicus Sublimis*, 1950-51. Oil on canvas, 7' 11 3/8" x 17' 9 1/4". The Museum of Modern Art, New York, Gift of Mr. and Mrs. Ben Heller, 240.1969.

Fig. 2

studios, a number of galleries devoted to their work, Hans Hofmann's school,[2] the Cedar Street Tavern (a favorite watering hole), and the Eighth Street Club (sometimes called simply "the Club," a gathering place and site for lectures and panels on the new art). Because their work was largely ignored by the art establishment (i.e., the museums), the artists often organized exhibitions of their own, such as the *Ninth Street Show* of 1951 and the subsequent *New York Painting and Sculpture Annuals* held at the Stable Gallery.[3] Beginning with the *Ninth Street Show* members of the so-called "second-generation"—younger artists who seemed to share the style and something of the content of the work of their elders—became part of the expanding circle as participants at the Club and in the exhibitions. At this point, younger artists did not find inspiration in the flat, color-based painting of Newman, Rothko, and Still, which were largely misunderstood and did not come into prominence until the end of the decade.[4] In contrast, the younger generation of Abstract Expressionists—among them Helen Frankenthaler, Joan Mitchell, Grace Hartigan, Alfred Leslie, Larry Rivers, and Michael Goldberg—were overwhelmingly gesture painters assuming the improvisational manner of Jackson Pollock, Willem de Kooning, Hans Hofmann, and others.

By the late 1950s, the period of this exhibition's works, gesture painting had become a mass manner and was regarded by many observers and participants in the New York scene to have grown academic and stale.[5] So pervasive was this manner by 1958 that while participating on a panel at the Club on January 19 entitled, "Has the Situation Changed?," Alfred Barr, director of The Museum of Modern Art (MoMA) in New York, bemoaned

the fact that a "rebellion" against Abstract Expressionism's dominance had not yet occurred and he called upon younger artists to reject their elders with greater vehemence. "I look forward to a rebellion, but I don't see it. Am I blind or does it exist? Are painters continuing a style when they should be bucking it?"[6] He concluded, "I hope that I am wrong [and] that something new is happening . . ."[7] Indeed it was.

The very next day, Jasper Johns' first solo show opened at the Leo Castelli Gallery, an exhibition to which Barr responded with enthusiasm. He purchased three of the works for the MoMA collection, one for his own, and, fearing repercussions due to the politically-loaded nature of the image, had Philip Johnson buy *Flag*, with the idea that it would later be donated to the museum, which it was. One of the works Barr purchased for MoMA, Johns' *Target with Four Faces* (1955), appeared on the January 1958 cover of *ARTnews* (fig. 3).[8] As art historian and critic Robert Rosenblum was to note, "Johns put a stake through the heart of Abstract Expressionism,"[9] presumably for having toppled the ascendancy of the preceding movement

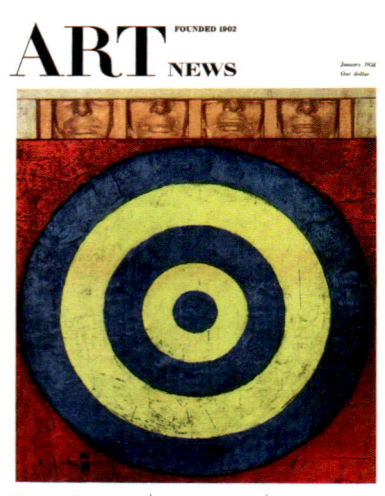

Fig. 3

Cover of *ARTnews*, January 1958, with Jasper Johns' *Target with Four Faces* (1955).

through elevating intellect over emotion. In paintings rendered in encaustic and collage, he focused upon literally flat, found images derived from the culture, "things," as he said, "the mind already knows." And Johns was not alone in departing from Abstract Expressionism at this time. Looking back, it appears that 1958 was a pivotal year, the moment when any number of artists emerged whose work announced the arrival of new sensibilities and fresh modes of art making. In addition to Johns, 1958 was the year in which Jack Youngerman, Agnes Martin, and Marisol had their first solo exhibitions in New York. It was the same year in which Robert Rauschenberg unveiled a large group of Combines (signature works that combined aspects of painting and sculpture), John Chamberlain showed sculptures made with automobile parts, Louise Nevelson exhibited her first installation, Allan Kaprow presented his first Happening, and Frank Stella, Kenneth Noland, and Robert Ryman turned their attention to painting stripes, targets, and monochromes, respectively. At around the same moment in California (where the San Francisco School of Abstract Expressionism was dominant), Wallace Berman and Billy Al Bengston had their first solo shows, Ed Kienholz began making freestanding sculptures, and Ed Ruscha started to create a word-based art. The exhibition *Sixteen Americans*, curated by Dorothy Seckler, which opened at New York's MoMA in mid-December 1959, featured a host of artists who were emerging as leaders of the avant-garde, among them Johns, Rauschenberg, Nevelson, Richard Stankiewicz, Robert Mallary, Ellsworth Kelly, Stella, and Jack Youngerman.[10]

The Emergence of Assemblage and Post-painterly Abstraction

While these and other artists whose work came to light at this time embraced a wide range of styles, sources, and intentions, each can be absorbed into one of two general artistic directions that emerged as alternatives to Abstract Expressionism: Assemblage and Post-painterly Abstraction.

Assemblage artists extended the physicality and immediacy of their art into the real world by incorporating actual materials in real space. They translated the painterliness of Abstract Expressionist canvases into an expressionistic handling of paint and objects, or of objects alone; the raw, unfinished look of these canvases led the Assemblagists to include the worn and decayed, the literally scrappy and junky.

This focus on the stuff of life also led many of the Assemblage artists to infuse their work with a sense of whimsy, play, and humor that had been largely absent in the high seriousness of Abstract Expressionism. When compared to the heroic grandeur of the preceding movement, Assemblage was often condemned in the early fifties for its lack of decorum. In fact, it was initially

referred to as "Neo-Dada," the label typically being assigned as an act of derision, since Dada was then generally seen as a nihilistic, anti-art strain with no possibilities for extension or renewal.[11] However, as Assemblage became more prevalent, the "shock" of its tawdry, found materials began to subside. The term "Assemblage," which came to be widely applied to this art of found materials, originated with the French post-war artist Jean Dubuffet, who used it to refer to an art that went beyond collage. *The Art of Assemblage* was the title that curator William Seitz gave to a major exhibition at MoMA in 1961 that defined this tendency and gave the term popular usage.

The term "Post-painterly Abstraction" derives from the title of an exhibition devoted to the new abstract art organized by the critic Clement Greenberg for the Los Angeles County Museum in 1964.[12] Compared to the Assemblagists, the artists involved with Post-painterly Abstraction tended to avoid the older avant-garde generation's gestural and expressive handling in favor of a controlled application of paint and an emphasis on the formal aspects of picture making: line, shape, color, form, and edge.

Not all Post-painterly Abstraction was a response to Abstract Expressionism; a few of the artists sidestepped it altogether, having found inspiration in European Modernism, particularly the art of Piet Mondrian, Hans Arp, and Henri Matisse. Most of those who came to be associated with Post-painterly Abstraction, however, began their careers as gesture painters working in a "de Kooningesque" mode or at least began their careers in the milieu in which Abstract Expressionism flourished. Widespread recognition of their work began with the exhibition *American Abstract Expressionists and Imagists*, organized by H. H. Arnason and presented at the Solomon R. Guggenheim Museum in 1961, a counterpart of sorts to MoMA's *The Art of Assemblage* of the same year. While Post-painterly Abstraction is often categorized into "Hard-edge Painting" and "Stained Color Field Abstraction," among others, in this essay the artists are considered both as part of a larger entity and as individuals in order to better clarify both their shared characteristics and their unique contributions and aims.

While Assemblage and Post-painterly Abstraction represented two very different means of art making, those associated with each were united in seeking alternatives to the painted gestures and romantic rhetoric surrounding the work of their precursors. They favored more literal (or factual) attitudes about the materials and processes of art making in response to both the art world and American life in the 1950s, which was generally more practically minded, less angst-ridden, and more politically complacent than during the formative years of Abstract Expressionism.

Although the fifties were by no means trouble free—the Cold War was a continuing concern, the McCarthy trials were underway, and the Korean War raged from 1950–53—it was not a time of crisis in the manner of the preceding decade. The younger artists who embraced Assemblage and Post-painterly Abstraction grew up free of the concerns and deprivations suffered by those who had experienced the Great Depression. Their art, if not the artists themselves, tended to be largely apolitical, although certain Assemblage artists embraced countercultural attitudes, as we see later. It was a time of prosperity in America and consumer culture was on the rise: it was the "golden age of television," the mass media played an increasing role in American life, and Elvis dominated rock and roll (his army service beginning with great fanfare in 1958).

Artists associated with Assemblage and Post-painterly Abstraction belonged to the first generation of Americans able to attend college on the GI Bill, initiated in 1944. In the late forties and early fifties, several of the artists who were later to become leaders of the new art, among them Robert Rauschenberg, Ray Johnson, Kenneth Noland, and John Chamberlain, attended Black Mountain College, an experimental college and center for avant-garde art and activity situated in Asheville, North Carolina. Although Black Mountain closed in 1956 after 23 years, its influence in the fields of art, architecture, and poetry was to extend over decades.[13] While artists of a wide range of sensibilities attended the college, for many, their time at the school resulted in a career-long openness to experimentation and to extending art in new directions.

The tight, insular "community of the New York School" dissipated over the course of the 1950s as the art world expanded, artists splintered into smaller groups, and a variety of support systems emerged including a larger number of galleries and museums, which began to play a more active role in supporting avant-garde art. Likewise, more art journals were paying attention to the new art, as were numerous mass media publications, like *Life*, *Time*, and *Newsweek* magazines. Yet despite art patronage being on the rise at this time, few artists made money through the sale of their art until the art market began to boom in the mid-sixties.[14]

Although 1958 may be identified as the year in which Assemblage and Post-painterly Abstraction emerged, the seeds of the "rebellion" had been sown some years before. Individual artists had begun to posit alternatives to the mass manner of Abstract Expressionism early in the decade, but they were viewed as lone wolves or went largely unrecognized.

The following two essay sections—the first devoted to Assemblage and the second to Post-painterly Abstraction—suggest the rich variety of forms and approaches taken by the artists featured in *Circa 1958: Breaking Ground in American Art*. Each section considers how these artists contributed to the essential character and development of each movement, while developing their own individual styles. The essay also explores the roots of Pop Art, Fluxus, and Minimalism in Assemblage and Post-painterly Abstraction.

Assemblage

Although the first group presentation of Robert Rauschenberg's Combines, the body of work with which he was to establish his influence and reputation, did not take place until March 1958 at the Leo Castelli Gallery, the artist was already a prominent figure in New York. Often referred to as the "*enfant terrible* of the New York scene," Rauschenberg's irreverent approach to art making was summarized in 1953 with a symbolic act that in many ways epitomized the ambition of his generation, whatever their stylistic orientation: he took a drawing that was given to him expressly for this purpose by de Kooning, erased it, then put it in a gold leaf frame with the handwritten label, "*Erased de Kooning Drawing*, Robert Rauschenberg, 1953." This was an iconoclastic gesture on the order of Duchamp's famed *L.H.O.O.Q.*, in which a moustache and goatee were drawn on a reproduction of the *Mona Lisa*: both works sought to topple art world heroes and ideals. The *Erased de Kooning Drawing* served as a literal manifestation of the desire to wipe the slate clean to begin anew.

In the early fifties, Rauschenberg had begun to cover his canvases with newspaper and then with other found papers and fabrics, painting over them with monochromatic black, or, slightly later, with red paint. During the course of 1954, the range of materials that he attached to his paintings' surfaces began to multiply and extend into the space of the room, until some of the works were freestanding, the found matter no longer covered over with paint but exposed. In these works, which typically hung upon the wall, everything from articles of clothing to taxidermically stuffed animals, automobile tires, plain and printed papers and fabrics, and reproductions of Old Master paintings were intermingled with expressionistic (but not self-expressive) paint touches and marks. With regard to his use of found materials, Rauschenberg said, "I don't want a picture to look like something it isn't, I want it to look like something it is. And I think a picture is more like the real world when it's made out of the real world."[15]

Rauschenberg's extroverted, high spirited works in which gestural mark making was integrated with the world of objects significantly influenced artists who were to be associated with Assemblage later in the fifties.[16] Many critics, however, initially dismissed Rauschenberg's work as mere sensationalism and declared the artist to be an imitator of the Dadaist Kurt Schwitters, who had also made extensive use of found materials beginning in the late teens. As the fifties progressed, however, an increasing number of writers recognized that Rauschenberg gathered cultural artifacts into his art so as to reflect the multiplicity and variety of contemporary experience, while operating on deeper symbolic levels of content. Among the materials found in *Painting with Grey Wing* (1959) in the current exhibition (Plate 25), for example, are several that evoke themes of flight and containment (which tellingly surround a photograph of his then estranged, pregnant wife).

Jasper Johns' "Flag" and "Target" paintings, which he began late in 1954, are also covered with newspaper collage. But Johns made a giant leap out of Rauschenberg's aesthetic in the development of his own by focusing upon a single, recognizable image. The newspaper in Johns' paintings was buried under a layer of encaustic paint (a wax-based medium) which meant that unlike the juicy, lush paint strokes found in the gestural painting of the time, Johns' were hard and quick-drying (although, given Johns' unfailingly masterful touch, they were imbued with a sensuality of their own). Also unique in Johns' art was the fact that his subjects were not "found" in the process of working, but preconceived. As Johns famously said, "I like to work with something already designed, because it gives me room to work on other levels." It was with his "Flag" and "Target" paintings that Johns made an indelible impact upon the art of the late fifties and early sixties, the impersonal, repetitive nature of his motifs being a primary influence upon Frank Stella's stripe paintings begun in 1958 and the focus on singular, found images providing inspiration for Andy Warhol, Roy Lichtenstein, and other artists who were to be associated with the emergence of Pop Art.

Other works by Johns incorporated found objects, as in the paintings, *Canvas* (1956), *Book* (1957), *Thermometer* and *Hanger* (both 1959), and the sculpture *Flashlight I* (1958), each of which featured the actual thing that was named. These works followed in the tradition established by Marcel Duchamp in his Readymades—manufactured objects that Duchamp selected and turned into art by placing them, unaltered, into an art gallery or museum so that they could be reconsidered anew. Johns' works departed from the precedent offered by Duchamp by not isolating but rather absorbing into the conventions of paintings and sculpture the things he was portraying.

While the found materials used by Rauschenberg and Johns were not necessarily of junk origins (some having been store bought or derived from everyday use), sculptors Richard Stankiewicz and Louise Nevelson pioneered true junk sculpture in the early 1950s. Beginning in 1953, Stankiewicz welded and soldered discarded, rusted metal machine parts found in railroad yards, vacant lots, and the like into works of figurative reference, as indicated by *Railroad Urchin* (1959) in *Circa 1958* (Plate 31).

While his sculpture found sources ranging from so-called primitive art to Picasso to Surrealism to the work of sculptor David Smith, the immediacy of his work tied it inextricably to the urban industrial world. Nevelson made use of cast-off wooden elements, also drawn from the contemporary environment, which, although painted uniformly in black (and later white or gold), retained their original identities. Nevelson's sculptures of the early and mid-fifties, which tend to be of tabletop scale, generally evoke altars and places of the spirit, as seen in *Distant Cathedral* (1955) (Plate 20). In 1958, she extended this concept to room-size installations whose enveloping nature and mood suggested a link to the paintings of Mark Rothko.

In the late 1950s, several other sculptors emerged whose improvisationally assembled work found a source or point of reference in Abstract Expressionism. John Chamberlain's sculptures, composed of sheets of painted steel derived from automobile bodies, and Robert Mallary's mixed media works both translated the gestures of Abstract Expressionist painters like de Kooning and Franz Kline into real materials and actual space. However, Chamberlain's *Nutcracker* (1958) and Mallary's untitled, undated piece reveal muscular rather than existentialist intention (Plate 5, Plate 17). Around 1959, Lee Bontecou (Plate 3) began to insert pieces of found cloth (often from old laundry bags) into specially constructed wire armatures, producing mysterious reliefs whose evocative and sexually provocative forms recall those found in the paintings of Robert Motherwell and Adolph Gottlieb, Abstract Expressionist artists who worked with a similarly allusive abstract imagery.

The acceptance of these artists' work within the tradition of "high" (or museum) art was not necessarily the case for another group of New York Assemblagists that emerged in the late fifties whose art was junkier still (in that it was less formally composed) and had a distinct counter-cultural edge (meaning that it violated preconceptions about what a work of art can be, traditional notions of art ownership and collecting, etc.). Many of these artists expanded their work beyond a single sculpture to entire rooms and events, generally known at the time as Environments and Happenings. These were ephemeral manifestations that challenged the commodity status of the art object and conventional definitions of art.

In his 1958 article, "The Legacy of Jackson Pollock," Allan Kaprow, an art historian and leading artist in this trend, placed this new art in context by clarifying its roots in Action Painting:

"Pollock . . . left us at the point where we must become preoccupied with and even dazzled by the space and objects of our everyday life either our bodies, clothes, rooms, or, if need be, the vastness of Forty-second Street. Not satisfied with the suggestion through paint of our other senses, we shall utilize the specific substances of sight, sound, movements, people, odors, touch. Objects of every sort are materials for the new art: paint, chairs, food, electric and neon lights, smoke, water, old socks, a dog, movies, a thousand other things which will be discovered by the present generation of artists. Not only will these bold creators show us, as if for the first time, the world we have always had about us but ignored, but they will disclose entirely unheard of happenings and events, found in garbage cans, police files, hotel lobbies; seen in store windows and on the streets . . . . "[17]

Kaprow's desire to embrace the viewer in sensory stimulation ("we shall utilize . . . sight, sound, movements, people, odors . . . ") so as to show "the world we have always had about us but ignored," had largely been motivated by his exposure to the Zen- and Dada-inspired artistic philosophy of the composer, John Cage. In the mid-forties, Cage had become involved with Zen Buddhism, which inspired him to move away from an art of self-expression towards a wholly impersonal aesthetic, often involving chance procedures, like flipping coins—rather than taste or aesthetic considerations—to determine the sequence of sounds. Cage believed that art should have its source in the everyday world, in the "facts" of the physical environment as they are perceived by the senses. His conception of art as "purposeless play" involved with the stuff of life aligned his sensibility with that of Duchamp and other Dadaists, who were among the first visual artists to engage in art performances.[18] In the early fifties, Cage became close friends with Rauschenberg and Johns. In the late fifties, the composer taught a class on experimental music at the New School for Social Research in New York that attracted not only musicians, but poets and visual artists as well, among them Kaprow and George Brecht.

Kaprow became a spokesperson for the new art and a conduit for Cage's ideas. He carried them first to the Hansa Gallery, a New York cooperative founded in 1952 by several former Hans Hofmann students, that under Kaprow's aegis in the late fifties

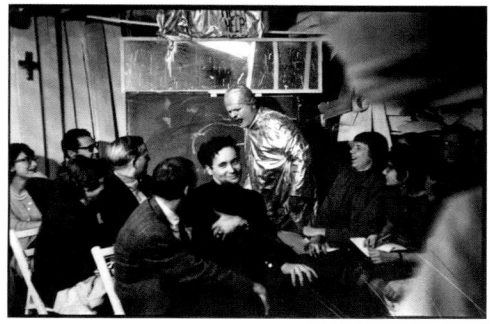

Fig. 4
Jim Dine performing *Car Crash* at the Reuben Gallery, November 1, 1960. Artist Robert Indiana seated center, art writer Jill Johnston center right.

became a locus for the new art. In 1957, Kaprow exhibited at the Hansa Gallery his first Environment: a maze-like structure formed by strips of fabric and plastic sheets suspended from the ceiling and incorporating lights and electronic sounds. His first Happening occurred a year later at the New Jersey chicken farm of his friend, the artist George Segal, during a picnic for gallery members. Kaprow and Segal were then both teaching at Rutgers University, in New Brunswick, New Jersey, which Kaprow helped transform into a major center of avant-garde activity.[19] Segal was motivated to move from figurative painting to an art of life-sized plaster figures (Plate 30) in large part because of his exposure to Kaprow's ideas and Happenings. Lucas Samaras (Plate 29), who was then a student at Rutgers, moved to Assemblage under Kaprow's and Segal's tutelage.

These and other like-minded artists gravitated to the short-lived, highly adventurous Reuben Gallery, lasting from October 1959 to April 1961, which also presented Assemblages, Environments, and Happenings by George Brecht, Robert Rauschenberg, Ray Johnson, Claes Oldenburg, Red Grooms, and Jim Dine (fig. 4).[20] Another important space for the showing of the new, experimental art was the Judson Gallery established in 1959 by Tom Wesselmann, Claes Oldenburg, and others and located in the basement of Judson Church.

George Brecht, who attended Cage's class with Kaprow at the New School and showed with him at Rutgers and the Reuben Gallery, was one of the originators of a more conceptual strain of Assemblage. By 1958–59, motivated by Cage's Zen-inspired acceptance of things of the everyday world in their natural state, he rejected the materialism and physicality of his colleagues in favor of an art involved with acts of appropriation on the order of Duchamp's Readymades, displacing objects and events to the realm of art with little or no alteration. His *Three Chair Events* (1961) (fig. 5), recreated for the current exhibition (Plate 4), for example, consists of three everyday chairs that have been variously situated within the space of the museum. Brecht's concept-based art anticipated the 1962 establishment of Fluxus, a loosely affiliated group of artists, in Weisbaden, West Germany.[21] Like Brecht, Fluxus artists like Yoko Ono and Fluxus-affiliated artists like Robert Morris subscribed to a Duchampian spirit of wit and irony and devoted themselves to involving the spectator in the work of art. The economical nature of Fluxus objects and events was to find a parallel in the Minimalist sensibility that emerged in the mid-sixties, of which Morris was a leading exponent, his *Box with the Sound of Its Own Making* (1961), a simple wooden box that encloses a real-time tape recording of its construction, being a prime transitional object in this regard (Plate 19).

In extreme contrast to the formal economy of Fluxus was the excessive and often deliberately junk-laden work of the California Assemblagists. While the New York artists may have used cast-off materials to imply a critique of America's culture of waste, cultural criticism became more explicit in the work of their California contemporaries.

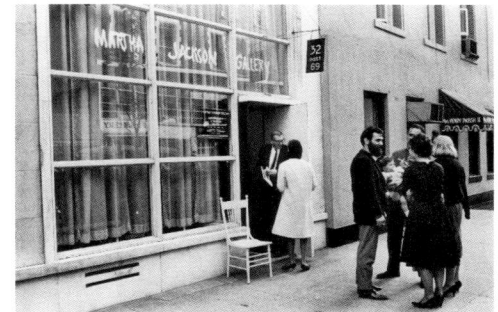

Fig. 5
George Brecht, *Three Chair Events*, 1961, with one chair placed outside the Martha Jackson Gallery, New York.

California Assemblage was decidedly oppositional and often embraced pointed political and social commentary. Its rise is generally linked to that of Beat poetry and prose (at least some of which was written in New York City), known for its deliberate engagement with life and yet also with spiritual transcendence. It was in the San Francisco Bay Area that Allen Ginsberg's *Howl and other Poems* (1956), Jack Kerouac's *On the Road* (1957),

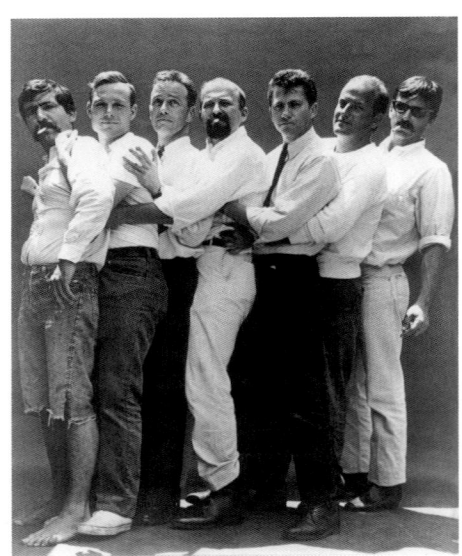

William Burrough's *Naked Lunch* (1959) and other works encompassing distinctly anti-bourgeois attitudes first achieved success. An inspirational figure in the visual arts was the artist and poet Wallace Berman, whose maxim was "Art is Love is God." Berman believed that art and life were both part of a spiritual quest and that artists should use their art to teach others about the need to free themselves from material things. His anti-

Fig. 6
Ferus Gallery members, left to right: John Altoon, Craig Kauffman, Allen Lynch, Ed Kienholz, Ed Moses, Robert Irwin, Billy Al Bengston, Los Angeles, 1958.

materialist philosophy was manifested in his first solo show at the Ferus Gallery in 1957, which was closed by the police on an obscenity charge for the inclusion of a close-up image of a copulating couple.[22] This Los Angeles gallery, which became a breeding ground for California's avant-garde, had been founded earlier that year by Walter Hopps (an art historian who was later to become a highly influential museum curator) and self-taught artist Ed Kienholz (fig. 6).

In many ways, California Assemblage is more easily understood as an independent manifestation than as an outgrowth or reaction against Abstract Expressionism.[23] Much of this work has its root in indigenous folk traditions employing found objects as well as in Dada, Surrealist Art, and New York "Neo-Dada," particularly the art of Robert Rauschenberg. However, Jess Collins, better known simply as Jess, studied with Clyfford Still at the California School of Fine Arts (now the San Francisco Art Institute) and briefly worked in an abstract painting style before

experimenting with collage. In works he called "paste-ups," a multitude of found images drawn from mass media and other sources reflect on the complexities of the human condition, as seen in the title figure and swarming multitudes in *The Hang'd Man: Tarot XIII* (1959) (Plate 10).

Ed Kienholz was apparently inspired to move from paintings and reliefs to freestanding Assemblages in 1959 after having seen reproductions of Rauschenberg's work in art magazines.[24] In *John Doe* (1959), his first significant work in this mode, which is included in the Ackland exhibition, the head and torso of a male mannequin mounted on a baby carriage offers a biting parody of the "typical" modern man (Plate 15 a,b). In 1961, Kienholz expanded his work into Environments, which he referred to as "*tableaux.*" The first was *Roxy's* (1961), an evocation of a Nevada brothel with strong emotional and moral overtones. Living and working in San Francisco, in 1959 Bruce Conner began to produce Assemblages in which ripped nylon stockings were filled with a wide array of found objects and materials—broken dolls, brocade and lace, fur, mirrors, cigarette butts, and photographs, many of them of pornographic origin. These works evoked both a fetishistic content and a commentary on America's materialistic culture.

During the late fifties and early sixties, the trend toward Assemblage was established and defined by an important group of exhibitions held in New York. *Sixteen Americans*, which opened in December 1959, featured work by Rauschenberg, Johns, Stankiewicz, and Mallary as well as Louise Nevelson's *Dawn's Wedding Chapel*, her first white-painted Environment.[25] This was followed in June and September 1960, by *New Forms-New Media*, a two-part exhibition held at the respected uptown Martha Jackson Gallery; this was the first major exhibition to acknowledge Assemblage as a group style. *The Art of Assemblage*, curated by William Seitz at MoMA in late 1961, marked the culmination of the trend. Like the Martha Jackson show, *The Art of Assemblage* was international in scope, featuring work by California and European Assemblagists as well as those based in New York. Both also had "historical sections" of work by Picasso, Duchamp, Schwitters, and others, a didactic approach used to help legitimize Assemblage, which continued

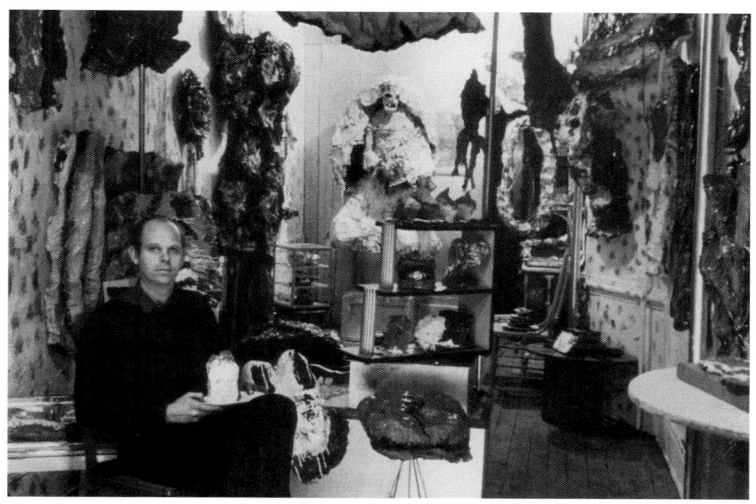

Fig. 7
Claes Oldenburg seated in *The Store*, 1961.

to be viewed by many as offensive and vulgar due to a more informal use of junk materials.[26]

The Emergence of Pop Art

While Assemblage never ceased to be controversial during the brief period of its flowering, which extended from about 1958 to 1962, it nevertheless had become, like gestural expressionism before it, a mass manner with any number of practitioners. In consequence, it too spawned a "rebellion," both from without and within. Shortly after the beginning of the new decade, a shift in orientation had begun to occur: many of the artists who had been associated with highly experimental work in the preceding period started, literally, to "clean up their act," thereby anticipating the impending emergence of Pop Art. This transition is exemplified in the two very different installations of Claes Oldenburg's *The Street*, presented first at the Judson Gallery in January and then at the Reuben Gallery in May, both in 1960. In the first, Oldenburg's ragged, silhouetted figures made of charred cardboard, burlap, and similar materials were distributed helter-skelter in a trash-strewn environment, which was used as the setting for his decidedly gritty performance piece, *Snapshots from the City*; in the second, they were isolated as discrete forms in an otherwise spic-and-span gallery. Oldenburg's Environment, *The Store*, which opened in

December 1961 in an actual storefront on New York's Lower East Side, was filled with glossy, brightly painted plaster sculptures of food, clothing, and other consumer items, his first Pop creations (fig. 7).

In late fall 1962, the emergence of Pop Art on the New York scene was announced in an enormous, two-gallery group exhibition entitled *The New Realists* presented at the Sidney Janis Gallery.[27] It included work by Jim Dine, Claes Oldenburg, George Segal, Tom Wesselmann, and Robert Indiana, all of whom were associated with Assemblage, although their work was now uniformly less junky and expressionistic and more upbeat and even celebratory in feel. Even Andy Warhol and Roy Lichtenstein, whose work was featured in the show and who were to be leading Pop artists, had recently moved their art away from casual messiness and towards greater formal control, while preserving a sense of fun. Artists in general had become less interested in found materials than in found images and in a subject matter focused on the mass media and consumer culture. For many artists, painting replaced object making and much of the painting that came to be associated with Pop Art was based on commercial models. As seen in the billboard-inspired work of James Rosenquist (Plate 27), the look was flat, cool, and spanking new, making the gestural, often shoddy-looking work of the Assemblagists seem a thing of the past.[28] That this work was impersonal in handling and formally controlled found a parallel in Post-painterly Abstraction.

Post-painterly Abstraction

Having left the United States for Paris two years before to study at the École des Beaux-Arts on the GI Bill, by 1950 Ellsworth Kelly had arrived at his own distinctive brand of abstraction free of New York School influence. Although he explored a range of interests at this time, all of the resulting work featured flatly rendered surfaces and clearly defined shapes. In 1954, he read an article in *ARTnews* about Ad Reinhardt's purist abstractions and decided to move to New York, thinking that such art had become prevalent and that his own work would be readily accepted. Reinhardt was included as a member of the Abstract Expressionists circle beginning in the 1940s, but he vehemently rejected their art of expressive content (fig. 8). His insistence on "art for art's sake" and on the formal elements of picture making—line, form, color, etc.—was singular among this group.[29] Reinhardt, however, was not alone. A number of artists—like Ellsworth Kelly, Leon Polk Smith, and Lorser Feitelson (working independently in Paris, New York, and Los Angeles respectively)—had also pursued this direction but, like Reinhardt, they did not receive recognition until later.

Kelly's first solo show in New York, held at the Betty Parsons Gallery in 1956, included work executed in Paris as well as paintings created since his return. Many of these paintings (among them *Two Blacks, White and Blue* [Plate 47]) were multipart works consisting of individual, flatly painted, monochrome panels set side by side that dealt with issues of shape and proportion and referred to the architectural space (the blank, white wall) in which they were shown. While its controlled and reductive form made this art radical for the time, it attracted little notice. For several years after this, Kelly pursued a direction in his art that he had initiated in France, but now began to explore in earnest: shape and ground paintings, which often found sources in the real world as well as in the abstract nature of the art of Henri Matisse (particularly his volumetric contours). It is on the basis of these works that in the late fifties Kelly came to be grouped with Jack Youngerman, Alexander Liberman, Myron Stout, Leon Polk Smith, and several other artists under the label "Hard-edge Painters." Kelly and Youngerman greatly objected to the term, insisting that they were interested in shape, not edge.

Jack Youngerman, who had spent several years with Kelly in Paris, moved to New York in 1956 and soon after began to create large, striking paintings featuring color shapes that often resemble flowers, his works distinctive for their loosely

Fig. 8
Ad Reinhardt (1913 - 1967), *Abstract Painting (Blue)*, 1952. Oil on canvas, 9' 1/4" x 40' 1/8". The Museum of Modern Art, New York, Given anonymously (by exchange) and purchase, 427.1981.

brushed, textural surfaces and craggy (rather than hard-edged) forms. Alexander Liberman, an older artist of Russian birth, arrived at a reductive, geometric style of painting in the early fifties through influences derived from Russian Constructivism. Both Myron Stout and Leon Polk Smith developed non-painterly modes of abstraction focused upon clearly defined forms in the early 1950s. Both had been profoundly influenced by Mondrian, but in their mature aesthetics worked with organic, rather than rectilinear forms and often confined themselves to vivid contrasts of black and white. The most notable among the many differences between them was the matter of size, with Smith working big in the New York School manner and Stout confining himself to intimately-scaled easel painting.

The term "hard-edge painting" had actually originated in the catalogue for the 1959 exhibition *Four Abstract Classicists*, curated by Jules Langsner for the Los Angles County Museum of Art.[30] Langsner used the term to describe the clearly articulated abstractions of the Los Angeles-based painters Lorser Feitelson, John McLaughlin, and Karl Benjamin, which these artists had begun to produce a few years before. Like the New York artists discussed above, their work derived from a range of sources. McLaughlin's paintings, in which white, black, gray, and color blocks are organized with formal austerity, are indebted both to Mondrian and to McLaughlin's preoccupation with Asian art. Benjamin created Cubist-inspired compositions of flatly rendered, sharp edged, overlapping, and interlocking shapes and colors that engage in animated spatial play. Feitelson's paintings often consisted of fields of clearly defined, vertical stripes whose monumental rhythms, unexpected spatial ambiguities, and evocations of psychological tension betray a kinship with the artist's earlier, Surrealist-inspired paintings. Most prominent among the characteristics that separate the work of all three California artists from that of their New York counterparts are their remarkable non-prismatic colors.

Unlike the work of the individuals discussed above, which had various points of origin, most Post-painterly Abstraction grew directly out of Abstract Expressionism, as was the case with the work of Morris Louis and Kenneth Noland. In 1953, the art critic Clement Greenberg brought these artists, who were then working in heavily pigmented expressionist styles, to Helen

Frankenthaler's studio to view her "breakthrough" painting, *Mountains and Sea* (fig. 9). A few years before, Greenberg had brought Frankenthaler to Jackson Pollock's studio to watch him paint. Observing Pollock drip paint upon his canvas gave rise to her gestural "stain paintings" in which diluted pigment was poured onto unprimed canvas to produce broad lines and

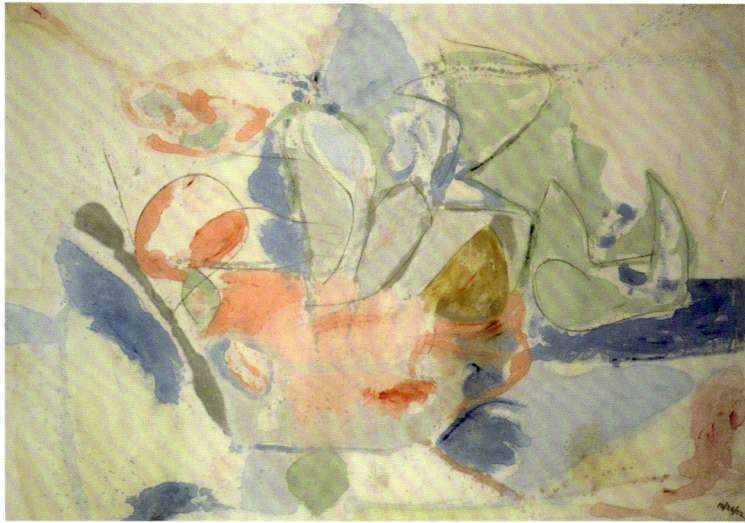

Fig . 9

Helen Frankenthaler, *Mountains and Sea*, 1952. Oil on canvas, 7' 2 5/8" x 9' 9 ¼". Collection of the artist, on extended loan to the National Gallery of Art, Washington, DC.

spreading pools of paint. She thus became, as Morris Louis was later to declare, "the bridge between Pollock and what was possible."[31]

By 1958, Morris Louis and Kenneth Noland had each arrived at the characteristic format of his first extended series of paintings using a stain technique. In the "Veils," which Louis produced from 1958–59, broad pours of thinned pigment flooded what were often enormous expanses of unsized, unprimed canvas, producing striated veils of blended color. Noland's "Circle Paintings" featured concentric bands of stained color centered on unprimed canvas; each painting of the series, which was to total about 175 by 1963, varied according to the width, number, placement, and color of the circles, among other things. The "Circle Paintings" of 1958 featured gesturally-rendered outer circles, as a vestige of Noland's Abstract Expressionist roots (Plate 54); by 1961, generally only clean-edges were seen.

While Noland's concentric circles recall Johns' "Targets," a more significant influence was offered by the example of Josef Albers with whom Noland, a North Carolina native, studied at Black Mountain College in 1948–49. Albers had come to Black Mountain to teach from the Bauhaus, the German art school devoted to abstract geometric art and design, after it was closed by the Nazis in 1933. At Black Mountain, Albers taught a foundations course and color theory, using principles he had taught at the Bauhaus.[32] Around 1950, Albers began to teach at Yale and initiated his "Homage to the Square" series: flat, painted canvases in which squares were set in a roughly concentric format. The paintings varied only in the colors of the squares. This interest in the "interaction" of color, how colors change, and how they are differently perceived when set in new juxtapositions, had impact upon Noland and many other students during Albers' career.[33]

Clement Greenberg, who had been instrumental in steering the development of Morris Louis' and Kenneth Noland's art, developed a cohesive and brilliantly-argued Formalist theory during the course of the 1950s that, although controversial, dominated the art and thought of the late fifties and sixties and greatly affected the rise and spread of Post-painterly Abstraction.[34] In the mid-fifties, he had embarked on a campaign to denigrate the Abstract Expressionist "Action Painters" in favor of the "Color Field Painters" (Newman, Rothko, and Still).[35] In doing so, he intentionally ignored the professed "sublime" content of their work, focusing instead upon those formal properties (i.e., flatness of surface and subtly modulated color) that suited his Formalist agenda. Greenberg asserted that Modernism involved a progression whereby each art moved increasingly towards greater self-purification. (His focus on purity also meant Greenberg dismissed Assemblage out-of-hand.) Painting, he believed, should aspire to two things—flatness of the picture plane and "opticality," a term he used as the opposite of tactile, thickly applied pigment. For Greenberg, Noland and Louis, each of whom had arrived at paintings filled with optical color of such literal flatness that the weave of the canvas remains visible throughout, had achieved perfection.[36] That their art lacked content and was purely decorative in nature he viewed as a Formalist ideal.

It was ironically not one of the artists Greenberg championed, but Frank Stella, whom he largely chose to ignore, whose paintings best realized some of Greenberg's ideas. Frank Stella was an undergraduate art student at Princeton University when he saw Jasper Johns' first exhibition at the Leo Castelli Gallery in January 1958. Stella has said he went back to school and kept thinking about the rhythm and repetition of the stripes. It was not Johns' use of such representational images as flags and targets that impressed him, but the inherent abstraction of the motifs. For the rest of the year, Stella executed paintings filled with stripes, increasingly covering the whole of his canvas with repetitive patterns and working in monochrome, as seen in *Blue Horizon* (1958) exhibited here (Plate 59). In 1959, Stella began his extended series of "Black Paintings," in which he replaced improvisation with predetermined patterns and methodical paintwork (fig. 10). He drew straight lines with

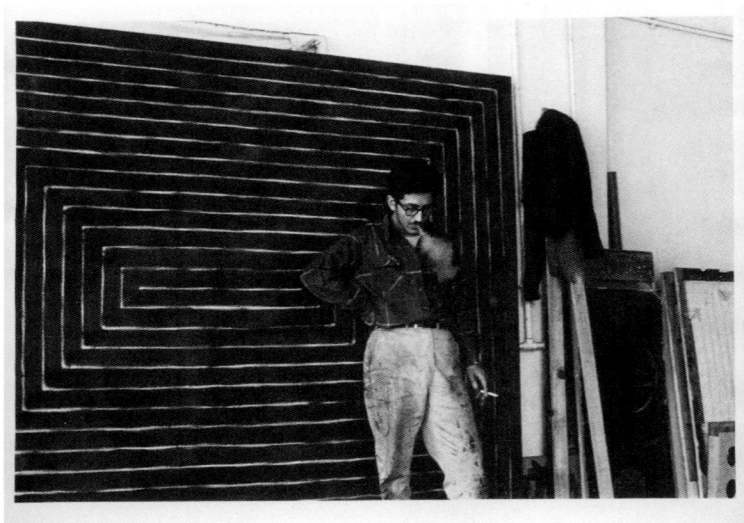

Fig. 10
Hollis Frampton (1936 - 1984), *Untitled* from *The Secret World of Frank Stella*, 1958-62. Black-and-white photograph, 8 x 10". Collection Walker Art Center, Minneapolis. Painting shown is *Tomlinson Court Park*, 1959.

black housepainter's enamel, covering the entire surface of each of his predominantly large-scale canvases with a regular, symmetrical pattern. Using stretchers that were a bit thicker than normal and approximated the width of the black stripes, the whole had what has been called, an "object quality," functioning as a single unit.[37]

While Stella epitomized the younger generation's "rebellion" against Abstract Expressionism, during the late fifties and early sixties a number of somewhat older artists began to abandon the thickly pigmented surfaces and gestures of their earlier Abstract Expressionist works in favor of greater clarity of color, form, and design. In 1957, Alfred Jensen replaced the expressionist imagery of his early work with thickly painted, brightly colored geometric diagrams, often in checkerboard configurations, which were of symbolic intent. This is conveyed by the plotted organization of cryptic forms and title of *Magic 2 and 6* (1960) in the Ackland show (Plate 46). Al Held, Ronald Bladen, and Nicholas Krushenick had been leading gesture painters at Krushenick's Brata Gallery on Tenth Street, founded in 1957. By 1960, Held had moved to an art focused on the interaction of geometric shapes, Bladen to an interest in the controlled gestures of simple relief forms (which he carried into space in the monumental forms of his Minimalist sculpture a few years later) and Krushenick to thickly outlined forms in bright, clean colors. Sculptors Gabriel Kohn and Tony Smith were friends with the first generation of Abstract Expressionists and shared some of their philosophical ideals. By the late 1950s in the case of the former and 1961 in the case of the latter, their work was characterized by precisely controlled forms and a modular quality that found a parallel in Post-painterly Abstraction and anticipated Minimal Art.

Minimalism

The roots of Minimalism, which emerged as a dominant movement in the mid-sixties, are apparent in the reductive aspects of much Post-painterly Abstraction—the use of repetitive formats and structures, the anonymous and economical handling of materials, the "object quality," and the lack of traditional content. Minimal Art was further characterized by greater formal severity and often involved factory fabrication or industrial processes. It is generally considered less an art of painting and sculpture than object-making, largely because the primary spokespersons (Robert Morris, Donald Judd, and Sol LeWitt) worked in this mode. Whereas Assemblage, an object-based art, transitioned into Pop, which was primarily an art of painting, Post-painterly

Abstraction, a painted art, gave way to Minimalism, a predominantly object-based art.

However, several painters who developed their personal aesthetics in the context of Post-painterly Abstraction later came to be recognized as leading Minimalists. In the late 1950s, Agnes Martin began to produce highly reductive work utilizing square formats, simple geometric forms and grids, and a nuanced neutral palette. Robert Ryman's career-long preoccupation with all-white square paintings, which had its inception in 1958, also anticipated Minimalism. In his works, Ryman explored permutations involving tones of white, paint application, and the nature of the support. While California artist Larry Bell alternated between painting and sculpture in the late fifties and early sixties, the framed cubic constructions that he began to produce at this time (Plate 38) anticipated his own Minimalist box pieces of the mid-sixties made of manufactured, vacuum-coated glass.

Whereas MoMA's *The Art of Assemblage* exhibition of 1961 marked the apogee of Assemblage (most shows featuring work that used found objects and images organized in the following years were devoted to Pop rather than Assemblage), *American Abstract Expressionists and Imagists* presented at the Guggenheim in the same year marked the beginning of an expansive period for Post-painterly Abstraction.[38] Both Post-painterly Abstraction and Minimalism were seen to offer a parallel to the bright colors, clean forms, impersonality, and commercially-derived processes of Pop. The Guggenheim show was followed by *Geometric Abstraction in America*, organized for the Whitney Museum of American Art by John Gordon in 1962, which appears to have been the first New York exhibition to include work by the California painters Karl Benjamin, Lorser Feitselson, and John McLaughlin along with the east coast artists. Clement Greenberg's *Post Painterly Abstraction*, which opened at the Los Angeles County Museum of Art in 1964, traveled to the Walker Art Center in Minneapolis and the Art Gallery of Ontario in Toronto, effectively spreading Greenberg's influence. The tendency continued to be appreciated in 1965 with MoMA's exhibition *The Responsive Eye* organized by William Seitz, which focused on "Op Art"—work in which forms and colors generate optical vibrations in the eye of the

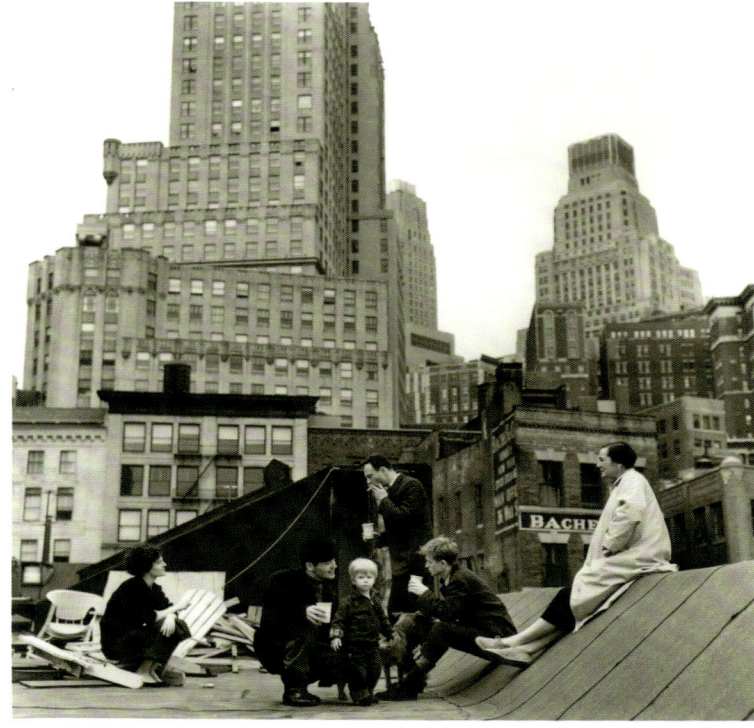

Fig. 11

Agnes Martin, Jack Youngerman, Ellsworth Kelly, Robert Indiana, and others on a Coenties Slip rooftop, 1957.

viewer—but included work by leading figures in Post-painterly Abstraction. In 1966, *Primary Structures: Younger American and British Sculptors*, organized by Kynaston McShine for the Jewish Museum, and *Systemic Painting*, curated by Lawrence Alloway for the Guggenheim Museum, were the first exhibitions to offer a comprehensive view of Minimal Art.

Conclusion

While the two primary directions that emerged circa 1958 have been divided into the two separate categories of Assemblage and Post-painterly Abstraction for discussion, no such clear-cut schism existed in the art world at that time. Apart from the exhibitions mentioned above, which were significant in defining and calling attention to each tendency, many shows, like Dorothy Seckler's continuing series of "Americans" exhibitions at MoMA, the Whitney Museum of American Art's Annuals and others, exhibited the work in tandem. Similarly, although groups of like-minded artists gathered around particular galleries, like the short-lived Reuben Gallery, the artists intermingled, as was clearly seen in the Coenties Slip neighborhood in lower Manhattan, where artists of different "schools" came together as friends and colleagues (fig. 11).[39] Living in close proximity to each other in the late fifties and early sixties were Ellsworth Kelly, Agnes Martin, Robert Indiana, Jack Youngerman, Lenore Tawney, Richard Anuszkiewicz, James Rosenquist, and many others. Johns and Rauschenberg lived a few blocks away from this waterfront artists' neighborhood (fig. 12).

While Robert Indiana's art is generally associated with Pop, his work in the late fifties and early sixties alternated between wooden totems incorporating painted passages and found elements and paintings made up of brightly colored, flatly painted words and signs that find counterparts in the post-gestural work of Kelly and others. Likewise, some of Agnes Martin's early abstractions incorporated such found elements as bottle caps, wire, metal boat spikes, and wooden planks. Outside of Coenties Slip, Frank Stella is known to have experimented with Assemblage while at Princeton in the late fifties.[40] Further, the Minimal artist Donald Judd, who worked as an art critic and painter during the late fifties and early sixties, found inspiration for his evolving concept of "Specific Objects" (what he would later call his Minimalist sculpture) in the "object quality" of much Assemblage Art, from the Combines of Rauschenberg to the constructed works of Bontecou and others.

The Leo Castelli Gallery, which opened in a townhouse on East Seventy-seventh Street in 1957, was a further "melting pot" for artists working in a range of avant-garde styles, including Assemblage, Post-painterly Abstraction, Pop, and Minimal Art.[41] While a few of Castelli's first exhibitions showcased established European and American artists, the *New Work* show of May 1957, which included work by a number of younger, emerging artists like Johns, Rauschenberg, and Marisol, set the course for the future. During the next few years, Castelli established himself not only as a leading international dealer, but also, as Irving Sandler has said, as "the most influential critic-impressario of the half-century following World War II"[42] because of his selection of artists. Among the artists he represented in the late fifties and early sixties, in addition to those mentioned

above, were Frank Stella, Roy Lichtenstein, Andy Warhol, James Rosenquist, Claes Oldenburg, Ellsworth Kelly, John Chamberlain, Gabriel Kohn, and Robert Morris. Many of these artists stayed with the Castelli Gallery for several decades. Castelli, who died in 1999, once suggested in an interview that the gallery was so successful because it functioned as a kind of living "organism" and "coterie" in which artists and their work interacted, influenced one another, and gave rise to subsequent work, as in the manner in which Johns' and Rauschenberg's art anticipated that of Stella and Pop.[43]

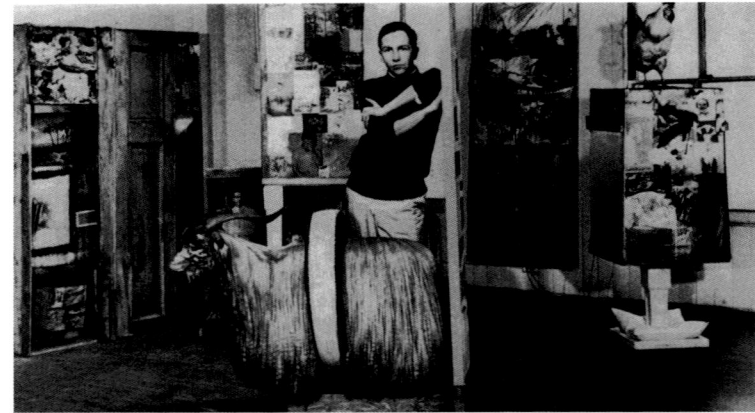

Fig. 12
Robert Rauschenberg in his Front Street Studio, 1958.

Assemblage and Post-painterly Abstraction were in many ways polar opposites, one a sculptural and object-based art encompassing a wide range of materials drawn from the everyday world, the other primarily an art of painting devoted to formal properties. One was an art of fullness and excess, the other of spareness and economy of means. Despite their many differences, Assemblage and Post-painterly Abstraction emerged from Abstract Expressionism at the same moment—the year 1958—and while both reacted against it, each retained vestiges of the earlier movement.

In their manipulation of worn and decayed objects, Assemblage artists tended to convey the messy randomness and feel of the city, often exploiting the poignancy of rejected matter, so that the gestural look and emotive feel of Abstract Expressionism persisted. At the same time, the Assemblagists challenged conventions of (good) taste. They expanded definitions of what art could be to include constructions, environments, and actions made up of commonplace things and replete with meaning, humor, and sometimes beauty. With the rise of Pop's upbeat sensibility, Assemblage's heyday passed; Assemblage appeared old hat, while Pop appeared vital and new.

Initially, much work associated with Post-painterly Abstraction also retained evidence of its ties to Abstract Expressionism. While aiming at greater clarity of form and impersonality, the hand of the artist was often revealed, the work "soft" around the edges, as found in the irregularities of the stripes in Stella's early paintings, the freehand gestures of Al Held and Noland's ragged outer rings in his circle paintings. By the early sixties, however, most such evidence of personal touch had disappeared. Artistic production evolved into a cool, machine-like aesthetic, the soft edges replaced by hard, which were to become harder still in the manufactured objects of the Minimalists.

Looking back after half a century, the work in the present exhibition remains significant because it represents a groundbreaking moment in the history of art in which artists rebelled against a prevailing trend while extending their work in new directions, opening up a multitude of possibilities for their own time and the future. Many of the artists who had their first exhibitions or developed characteristic modes of working that established their influence and reputations circa 1958 remain towering presences in the art world a full fifty years later, which stands as a testament both to the enduring nature of their contributions and to their continued pursuit of an art expressive of themselves and contemporary existence.

————

About the author:
Guest Curator Roni Feinstein (Ph D 20th-Century European and American Art, Institute of Fine Arts, New York University) is a corresponding editor of *Art in America* and an instructor in the Department of Education at The Museum of Modern Art in New York. Formerly Branch Director of the Whitney Museum of American Art in Stamford, Connecticut, and Visiting Professor at the University of Miami in Coral Gables, Florida, Feinstein has over thirty years of museum experience. She has organized numerous exhibitions, including *Robert Rauschenberg: The Silkscreen Paintings, 1962-64* at the Whitney Museum of American Art in New York, and *The "Junk" Aesthetic: Assemblage of the 1950s and Early 1960s*, *American Print Renaissance 1958-1988*, and *With the Grain: Contemporary Panel Painting* at the Whitney's Stamford Branch.

————

NOTES

1. Harold Rosenberg, "The American Action Painters," *ARTnews,* December 1952, 22-23, 48-50. A noteworthy recent study of the roles Rosenberg and "rival" critic Clement Greenberg played in American art and thought beginning in the 1940s is found in Norman L. Kleeblatt, ed., *Action/Abstraction: Pollock, de Kooning, and American Art, 1940-1976*, The Jewish Museum in Association with Yale University Press, 2008.

2. Hans Hofmann, a German-born artist who was associated with the first generation of Abstract Expressionists (although he was a generation older), moved his school from Munich to New York in the early thirties after its closing by the Nazis. Hofmann taught the majority of artists associated with the American Abstract Artists group, founded in New York in 1936, as well as any number of "second generation" artists (among them Helen Frankenthaler, Joan Mitchell, Larry Rivers, and Wolf Kahn) as well as Allan Kaprow, Richard Stankiewicz, Louise Nevelson (who studied with him in Munich), Myron Stout, Marisol, and Red Grooms who were associated with the next wave and are featured in this exhibition. In 1958, Hofmann closed his New York school and summer school in Provincetown in order to devote himself to painting full time. It is widely felt that for the next eight years of his life, when he was in his 70s and 80s, he produced his best work.

3. For information on these artist-organized exhibitions, see Marika Herskovic, ed., *New York School Abstract Expressionists: Artists Choice by Artists: A Complete Documentation of the New York Painting and Sculpture Annuals; 1951-1957* (New York: New York School Press, 2000).

4. Barnett Newman was so devastated by the negative criticism received by his solo show at the Betty Parsons Gallery of April 23-May 12, 1951, which included his first eighteen-foot-long painting, *Vir Heroicus Sublimis* (Fig. 12), that he did not exhibit again in New York for eight years. In 1959 (March 11-April 5), the art critic Clement Greenberg organized the watershed exhibition, *Barnett Newman: A Selection 1946-1952*, to inaugurate the new French & Company contemporary gallery.

5. As early as 1955, Clement Greenberg wrote that Abstract Expressionist gesture painting was "nearing exhaustion," in "American-Type Painting," *Partisan Review* (Spring 1955), 179-96, reprinted in Clement Greenberg, *Art and Culture: Critical Essays* (Boston: Beacon Press, 1971), 220. In 1958, Allan Kaprow declared that gestural paintings influenced by Abstract Expressionism had become "clichés of college art departments," in "The Legacy of Jackson Pollock," *ARTnews* (October 1958), 24-25, 55-57, reprinted in Ellen G. Landau, ed., *Reading Abstract Expressionism: Context and Critique* (New Haven: Yale University Press, 2005), 183. William Rubin, "Younger American Painters," *Art International I* (January 1960), 26, wrote that such work had become "formulaic and decorative."

6. Irving Sandler, *A Sweeper-Up After Artists: A Memoir* (London: Thames and Hudson, 2003), 229.

7. Irving Sandler and Amy Newman, eds., *Defining Modern Art: Selected Writings by Alfred Barr* (New York: Harry N. Abrams, Inc., 1986), 41.

8. Barr had apparently wanted to buy Johns' whole show, but Castelli wouldn't sell it to him, probably because Castelli sought to "share the wealth" and wanted to cultivate the interest of private collectors in Johns' art.

9. Interview with Robert Rosenblum, November 17, 1982.

10. The presentation of *Sixteen Americans* at MoMA followed that of *The New American Painting, as shown in Eight European Countries 1958-59*, an exhibition of work by the leading Abstract Expressionist painters, curated by Dorothy Miller, that had traveled under the auspices of the museum's newly formed International Program. This exhibition, which was composed of fifteen older artists and two members of the "second generation" (Grace Hartigan and Sam Francis), was presented at MoMA from May 28-September 8, 1959. *Sixteen Americans* extended from December 16, 1959-February 14, 1960. *The New American Painting* represented the old guard, *Sixteen Americans* the new.

11. Dadaism was an active movement after WW I, whose followers in art and literature cynically expressed their revulsion at a civilization that could produce such conflict and destruction by embracing nonsense and the extra-aesthetic (or non-art) concerns—concerns generally regarded as residing outside the realm of "high" art. According to Jeffrey S. Weiss, "Chronology" in *Jasper Johns: Allegory of Painting, 1955-65* (New Haven: Yale University Press, 2007), 264, the term "Neo-Dada" was first used in Robert Rosenblum's review of the May 1957 *New Work* show at the Leo Castelli Gallery. Rosenblum spoke of the Readymades of Duchamp and coined the term "Neo-Dada" in his discussion of Johns. Susan Hapgood, "Neo-Dada," in *Neo-Dada: Redefining Art, 1958-62*, exhibition catalogue (New York: American Federation of the Arts, 1995), dates the first use of the term to *ARTnews* (January 1958), 1 and 5, where it is used in reference to Johns' *Target with Four Faces*, which appeared on the journal's cover. For an extended discussion of the use of the term see Hapgood 11-12 and 58-59, footnotes 1-4.

12. Greenberg's exhibition, whose title was written as *Post Painterly Abstraction*, included Frankenthaler and others who continued to work within a gestural mode. In this essay, the term is applied to artists who worked (or were moving toward) an art of clean edges and centralized compositions and away from a pushing manipulation of paint. The artists in the Ackland's show that were included in the 1964 show are: Darby Bannard, Al Held, Alfred Jensen, Ellsworth Kelly, Nicholas Krushenick, Alexander Liberman, Morris Louis, Kenneth Noland, and Frank Stella.

13. For information on Black Mountain College see Martin Duberman, *Black Mountain: An Exploration in Community* (New York: W. W. Norton & Co. Inc.,

1973) and May Emma Harris, *The Arts at Black Mountain College* (Cambridge: MIT Press, 2002).

14. Among the exceptions in the late 1950s were Jasper Johns (as noted above), Willem de Kooning, and Frank Stella. Irving Sandler pointed out in *American Art of the 1960s* (New York: Harper & Row, 1988), 90, that whereas de Kooning had previously struggled with sales, his 1959 show at the Sidney Janis Gallery "sold out on its first day for a total of $150,000, establishing a new high in prices for living American painters." Irving Sandler also notes that in 1960, The Museum of Modern Art's acquisition of Frank Stella's *Marriage of Reason and Squalor* (1959) that had been included in *Sixteen Americans* "made a big impression, particularly because he was only twenty-three at the time and had not yet had a one-person show." Sales to David Rockefeller, Philip Johnson, the Tremaines, and other leading collectors soon followed.

15. Rauschenberg quoted by Calvin Tomkins in *The Bride and the Bachelors: Five Masters of the Avant Garde* (New York: Penguin Books, 1968), 193-94.

16. Rauschenberg's status as a leading and influential figure was acknowledged in his being the only young artist included in the symposium William Seitz, curator and moderator, organized for *The Art of Assemblage* exhibition. The panel consisted of writers Lawrence Alloway and Roger Shattuck, Dadaists Marcel Duchamp and Richard Huelsenbeck, and Rauschenberg.

17. Kaprow, "The Legacy of Jackson Pollock," *ARTnews* (October 1958), 24-25, 55-57, reprinted in Ellen G. Landau, ed., *Reading Abstract Expressionism: Context and Critique* (New Haven: Yale University Press, 2005).

18. Kaprow and other artists associated with Happenings and similar manifestations (like Fluxus) are known to have read *The Dada Painters and Poets: An Anthology*, Robert Motherwell, ed., (Cambridge: Belknap Press, 1952), which contains descriptions of Dada performances. At Black Mountain College during the summer of 1952, Cage organized what is often referred to as the first Happening, *Theatre Piece #1*. Its participants—Robert Rauschenberg, Merce Cunningham, Cage, David Tudor, Mary Caroline Richards, and Charles Olsen—did whatever he or she wanted within a prescribed time frame. There are many descriptions of this historic piece; one is found in Tomkins, *The Bride and the Bachelors*, 117.

19. For information on the art scene at Rutgers in this period, see Joan Marter, ed., *Off Limits: Rutgers University and the Avant-Garde, 1957-1963* (New Brunswick, NJ: Rutgers University Press in conjunction with the Newark Museum,1999). Also, Geoffrey Hendricks, *Critical Mass: Happenings, Fluxus, Performance, Intermedia, and Rutgers University, 1958-1972* (New Brunswick: Rutgers University Press, 2003).

20. For more on the Reuben Gallery see Lawrence Alloway, *Eleven from the Reuben Gallery*, exhibition brochure, (New York: Solomon R. Guggenheim Museum, 1965).

21. Among the many texts on Fluxus is Elizabeth Armstrong and Joan Rothfus, *In the Spirit of Fluxus,* exhibition catalogue, (Minneapolis: Walker Art Center, 1993).

22. Berman's Ferus Gallery exhibition featured multiple reproductions, some scattered about the gallery floor, of the "lewd" drawing by his friend, Marjorie Cameron Parsons Kimmel, better known simply as Cameron. Berman was jailed and fined after the vice squad raided and closed his exhibition. For the next seven years, he largely devoted himself to the publication of a small, unbound poetry, text, and image magazine called *Semina*, which he printed in quantities of 150-300 and chiefly distributed to friends. For more on Berman and his influence see Michael Duncan and Kristine McKenna, *Semina Culture: Wallace Berman and His Circle*, exhibition catalogue (New York: D.A.P./Distributed Art Publishers in conjunction with the Santa Monica Museum of Art, 2005).

23. See Anne Ayers, "Directions in California Assemblage," in *Forty Years of California Assemblage*, exhibition catalogue (Los Angeles: Wight Art Gallery, University of California Los Angeles, 1989), 52.

24. See Susan Hapgood, "Neo-Dada," in *Neo-Dada: Redefining Art, 1958-62*, exhibition catalogue (New York: American Federation of the Arts, 1995) 53n144 and 65 for confirmation that Kienholz was looking at Rauschenberg's art.

25. Among the sixteen Americans were Jay DeFeo and Wally Hedrick, two California-based painters who were strongly associated with California Assemblage, although the work included in the MoMA show did not represent this aspect of their art. An early state of DeFeo's monumental piece *The Rose* (or *Deathrose*), which she was to work on from 1958-1966, was reproduced in the exhibition catalogue. The piece, which was to total 2,300 pounds in weight, was composed of thickly encrusted house paint and other pigments, wood, stones, beads, and other objects. It is now in the collection of the Whitney Museum of American Art.

26. It is interesting to note that of the young New York artists then gaining prominence, Allan Kaprow, Jim Dine, Claes Oldenburg, and Red Grooms were excluded from the MoMA show, probably because their work was among the most "anti-formalist" of the time. George Brecht and Lucas Samaras, whose works were more neatly organized, not only had pieces included in the show, but purchased by the museum: Brecht's compartmentalized *Repository* (1961) and Samaras' *Untitled* (1960-61), a wall piece with plaster-covered feathers and assorted hardware arranged in a centered format.

27. The first museum exhibition devoted to Pop, *New Paintings of Common Objects*, organized by Walter Hopps, opened at the Pasadena Museum of Art (now the Norton Simon Museum) a few months earlier, in September 1962. Unlike the Sidney Janis show, it included both California (Ed Ruscha, Joe Goode) and New York Pop artists. It may be recalled in the context of noting California's fervent response to Pop that the first solo show of Andy Warhol's Pop-related work—an exhibition consisting of 32 small silkscreen paintings of Campbell's soup cans—took place in July 1962 at the Ferus Gallery in Los Angeles. That the arrival of Pop was by no means universally "celebrated" in New York is evidenced by the fact that Mark Rothko, Robert Motherwell, Adolph Gottlieb, and William Baziotes were so angered by *The New Realists* exhibition that they withdrew from the Sidney Janis Gallery's representation in protest; Willem de Kooning remained.

28. Helping to situate Assemblage in the past was the fact that *The New Realists* exhibition brought the American Pop artists together with a large group of Europeans (among them the Nouveaux Réalistes) whose work corresponded more closely to Assemblage than Pop. Although probably unintentional, the exhibition thereby accentuated the gulf that separated the old (Assemblage) from the new (Pop).

29. Reinhardt's call for pure painting—for art free of illusions, representations, heroics, anguish, structure, paint qualities, and more—was clearly stated in his statement "Abstract Art Refuses," in *Contemporary American Painting*, exhibition catalogue, (Urbana: University of Illinois, 1952), n.p., reprinted in Barbara Rose, *Art as Art: The Selected Writings of Ad Reinhardt (Documents of Twentieth Century Art)* (University of California Press, 1991), 50. While Reinhardt had been working in near-monochrome using symmetrical, cruciform formats for several years, he did not arrive at the format of his "ultimate picture" until 1960: a five-foot-square canvas composed of nine squares that formed an internal cruciform pattern rendered in a palette so low-register as to appear almost uniformly black. He painted exclusively in this format until his death in 1967.

30. The fourth "abstract classicist" was Frederick Hammersley, whose work is not included in the present show. *Four Abstract Classicists* traveled to the San Francisco Museum of Art and then a revised version, retitled *West Coast Hard Edge* by writer/critic Lawrence Alloway, traveled to the Institute of Contemporary Art, London, and Queens College, Belfast, in 1960. It may be noted that all four "abstract classicists" were excluded from Clement Greenberg's 1964 exhibition *Post Painterly Abstraction,* which took place in their home city. Apparently, Greenberg selected all of the work for the show with the exception of the California artists, who were chosen by James Elliott, the curator at LACMA who organized the exhibition. California-based artists Sam Francis, Ron Davis, and Ludwig Sander were featured in the show. All four "abstract classicists," however, were previously included in John Gordon's *Geometric Abstraction in America*, held at the Whitney Museum in 1962, and subsequently featured in William Seitz's *The Responsive Eye*, presented at the Museum of Modern Art in 1965.

31. Gerald Nordland, *The Washington Color Painters*, exhibition catalogue, (Washington DC: Washington Gallery of Art, 1965), 12.

32. Although Albers' own painting focused on abstract geometric design, the "materials class" he taught at Black Mountain, which originated at the Bauhaus, led students to investigate the inherent properties of a wide range of found materials. This had particular impact on Robert Rauschenberg and Ray Johnson, both of whom studied with him at Black Mountain in the late forties.

33. Among those influenced by Albers' theories on the interaction of colors was Richard Anuszkiewicz, who studied with Albers at Yale.

34. Greenberg's ideas gained widespread impact through the publication of a compendium of his essays, *Art and Culture: Critical Essays* (Boston: Beacon Press, 1971), first published in 1961. It is interesting to note that this is the same year Cage's *Silence: Lectures and Writings*, which embodied a wholly opposing artistic philosophy, was first published by Wesleyan, Middletown, CT.

35. See note 34 above. Greenberg, "American-Type Painting," 179-196.

36. Clement Greenberg, "Louis and Noland," *Art International 4*, no. 5 (1960), 26-29; reprinted in *Clement Greenberg: The Collected Essays and Criticism*, John O'Brien, ed., vol. 4 (Chicago, 1986)

37. Stella's friend, the sculptor Carl Andre, whom he knew from prep school, wrote the following statement on Stella's Formalism that was published in Dorothy C. Miller, ed., *Sixteen Americans*, exhibition catalogue, (New York: The Museum of Modern Art, 1959), 76.
    Preface to Stripe Painting
    Art excludes the unnecessary. Frank Stella has found it necessary to paint stripes. There is nothing else in the painting.
    Frank Stella is not interested in expression or sensitivity. He is interested in the necessities of painting.
    Symbols are counters passed among people. Frank Stella's painting is not symbolic. His stripes are the paths of the brush on the canvas. These paths lead only to painting.
    —CARL ANDRE.
It may be noted that while Stella's Black Paintings were not personally expressive, the artist gave the works titles that he associated with the idea of "blackness," ranging from references to death (Nazi slogans, major disasters) to African American and jazz tunes, clubs and musicians that he greatly admired.

38. *American Abstract Expressionists and Imagists* featured a small background section of works by artists no longer living (like Jackson Pollock and Arshile Gorky) as well as a few early paintings by Barnett Newman, Clyfford Still, and Roberto Matta. The bulk of the exhibition, however, consisted of paintings completed either in 1960 or 1961 by about sixty artists, about a quarter of whom worked in non-gestural styles.

39. For further information see Mildred Glimcher, *Indiana, Kelly, Martin, Rosenquist, Youngerman at Coenties Slip*, exhibition catalogue, (New York: Pace Gallery, 1993).

40. See Harry Cooper and Megan R. Luke, *Frank Stella 1958* (New Haven: Yale University Press in conjunction with the Fogg Art Museum, Harvard University, 2006), 12-13 and plates 30-34.

41. The Ferus Gallery, which operated in Los Angeles from 1957 to 1966, was also a "melting pot" for artists working in different styles. While it played a highly significant role in the California art scene, it did not affect late twentieth-century art on an international scale with the same force as the Leo Castelli Gallery. The Ferus, which was operated by Walter Hopps (from its inception through 1962, when he departed to serve as curator of the Pasadena Museum of Art) and Irving Blum (from 1958, when Ed Kienholz sold him his share, to its demise), exhibited the work of the following California artists included in *Circa 1958*: Kienholz, Wallace Berman, Bruce Conner, Billy Al Bengston, Larry Bell, and Ed Ruscha. In the sixties, the Ferus Gallery exhibited the work of several artists in Castelli's stable, among them Roy Lichtenstein, Frank Stella, Jasper Johns, Ellsworth Kelly, and Robert Morris. See note 27 above.

42. See note 6 above. Sandler, 262.

43. Paul Cummings, "Interview with Leo Castelli: May 14, 1969," *Archives of American Art*, Smithsonian Institution, transcript on Internet www.aaa.si.edu/collections/oralhistories/transcripts/castel69may. htm#Interview1.

ABOUT THE PLATES

All plates are presented with the following information: artist's name, place of birth, birth year – death year, place of death (living artists include current place of residence), title, date, medium, dimensions in inches only (height x width x depth), and lender. On pages with multiple plates, the sequence is indicated with the object description (as in plates 21, 22, 23) or reads left to right to correspond with the first and second description (as in plates 12, 13).

ASSEMBLAGE INTO FLUXUS AND POP ART

Any incentive to paint is as good as any other. There is no poor subject.
. . . . Painting relates to both art and life. Neither can be made. (I try to act in that gap between the two.)
A pair of socks is no less suitable to make a painting with than wood, nails, turpentine, oil and fabric.
A canvas is never empty.

Robert Rauschenberg

from
Sixteen Americans
Exhibition catalogue
The Museum of Modern Art, New York, 1959

Romare Bearden
Charlotte, North Carolina
1911 – 1988
New York, New York

Jacob and the Angel Tree, 1961
collage of printed papers
(magazine stock)
13 x 9 inches
The Estate of Nanette Bearden

Though a member of the Abstract Expressionist generation whose paintings were predominantly abstract and gestural in the 1950s, in 1961 Romare Bearden moved to a figurative, collage-based practice that focused on African American experience. Born in Charlotte, North Carolina, but raised in New York City in the midst of the Harlem Renaissance (his parents were friends with Langston Hughes, Duke Ellington, Paul Robeson, W.E.B. du Bois, and many other prominent figures), Bearden's work reflected the African American community while at the same time embracing a complex, humanistic world view. His collages, which consist largely of photographic images derived from newspapers and magazines, find sources in the Dada photo-collages of his one-time teacher George Grosz, as well as in a wide range of art drawn from African, Asian, European, and American cultures.

In *Jacob and the Angel Tree* (1961), the biblical story of Jacob and the Angel is enacted in the upper left of the piece, set in the midst of a beautiful and fanciful wild kingdom of plants and animals. Although the work's structure is that of twentieth-century collage, it also harkens back to Chinese landscape painting, a discipline Bearden had studied in the mid-fifties.

Suggested Reading:
Fine, Ruth. *The Art of Romare Bearden*. Exhibition catalogue. Washington, DC: National Gallery, 2003.

Plate 1

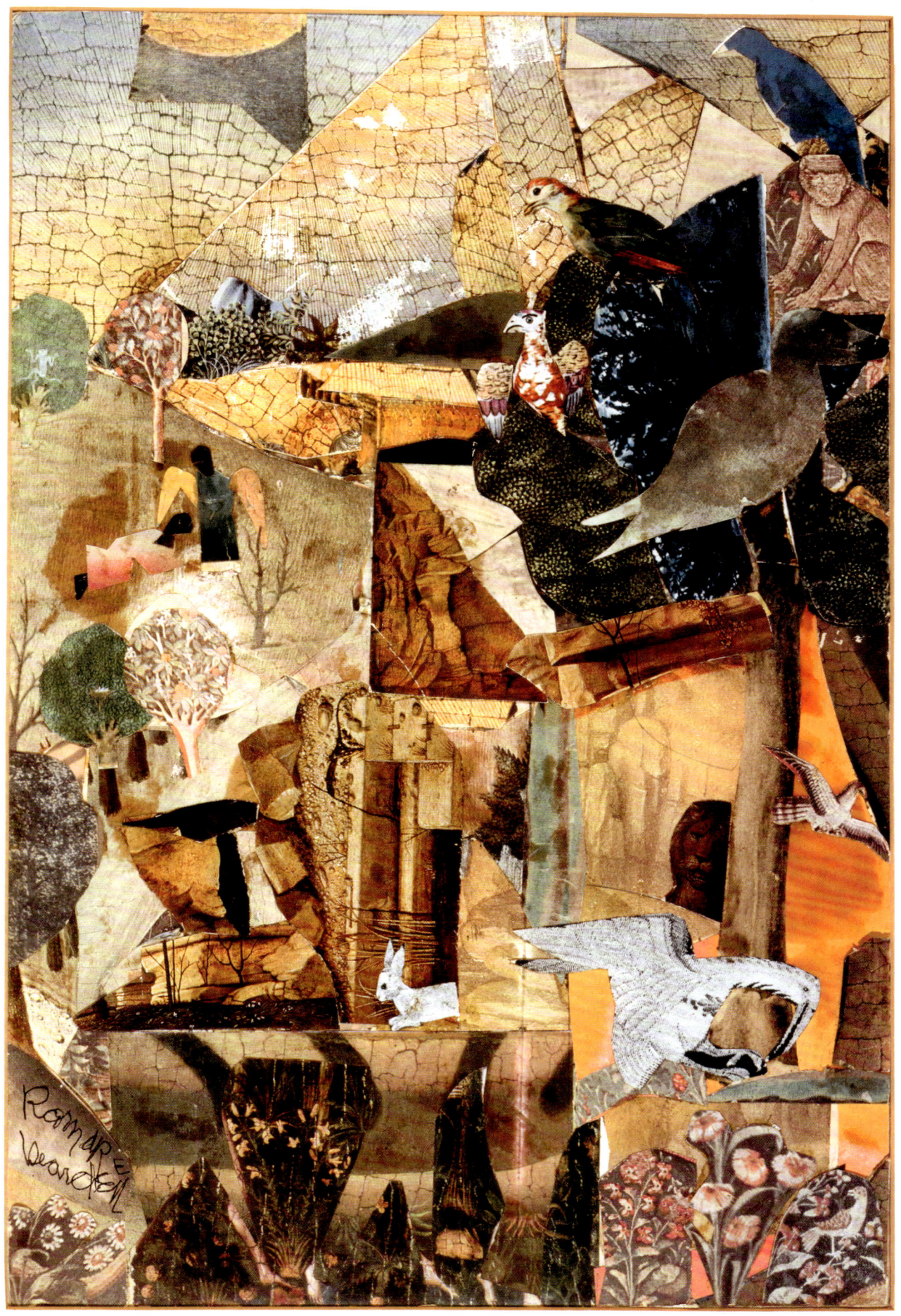

Wallace Berman
Staten Island, New York
1926 – 1976
Los Angeles, California

Untitled, 1956–57
collage on canvas: ink and
shellac on torn parchment paper
on primed canvas
19 1/2 x 19 1/2 inches
Private Collection

Wallace Berman's *Untitled* (1956–57), a parchment printed with Hebrew letters deliberately made to look old and stained like an historic relic (perhaps like a fragment of the Dead Sea Scrolls), was one of twelve such works that appeared in the artist's first solo show at the Ferus Gallery in Los Angeles in 1957. This exhibition put forth Berman's artistic philosophy, which had considerable impact upon the development of California Assemblage—"Art is Love is God"—which called for artists to reject material possessions in favor of a spiritually-based art. The show, however, was closed by the vice squad for its inclusion of a large wooden cross from one of whose arms hung what was considered to be a pornographic image. For the next seven years, Berman devoted himself to the publication of his hand-printed Beat poetry journal, *Semina*. In 1964, he reemerged on the national art scene with his extended series of grid-format works made using a Verifax, an early photocopying machine. Most of these works featured the repeated image of a hand holding a communications device—a transistor radio—upon which were superimposed both mass media images and Hebrew letters of the sort seen here, demonstrating Berman's continued preoccupation with spiritual thought.

Suggested Reading:
Duncan, Michael and Kristine McKenna. *Semina Culture: Wallace Berman & His Circle*. Exhibition catalogue. Santa Monica, CA: Santa Monica Museum of Art, 2005.

Plate 2

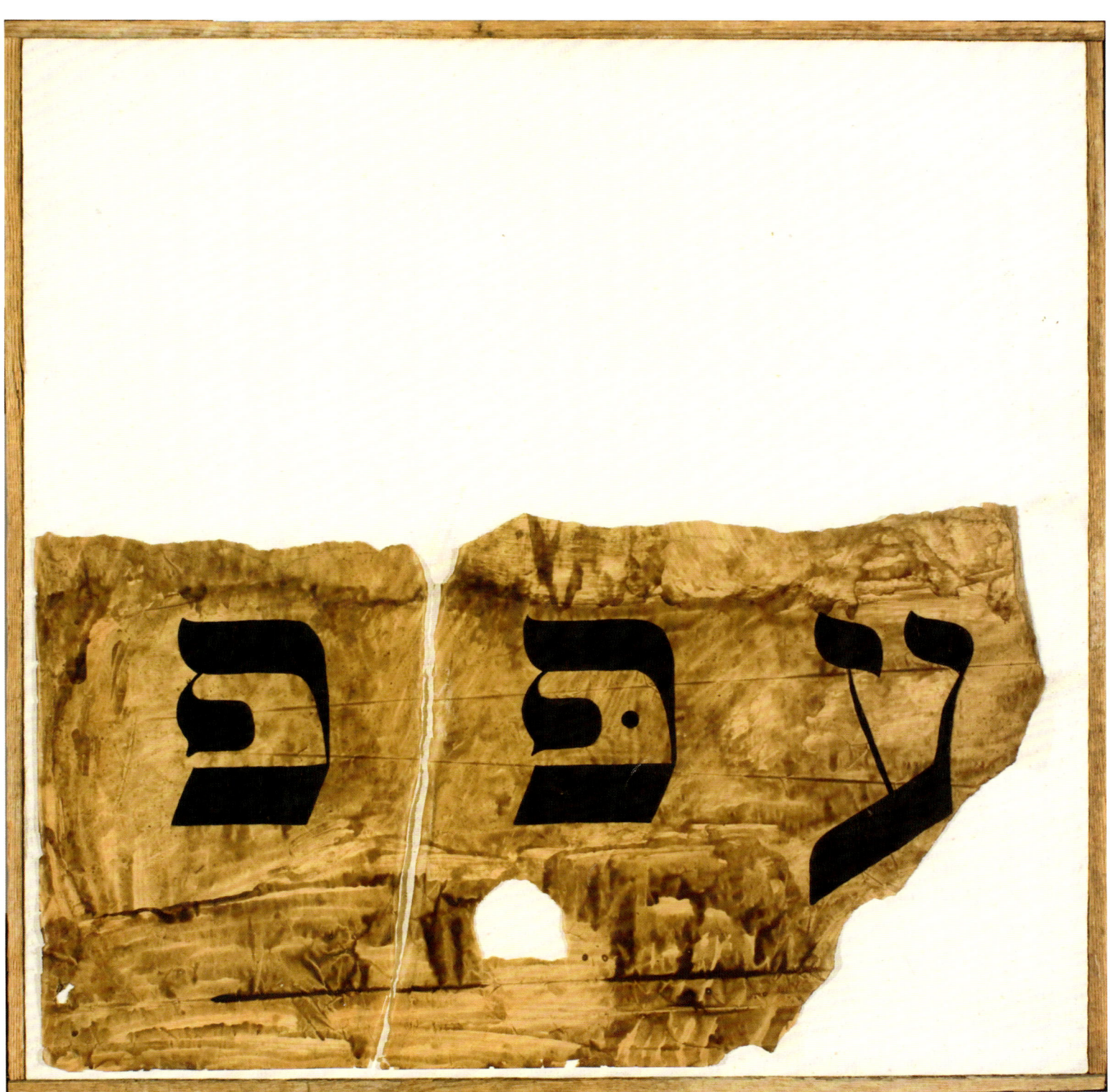

Lee Bontecou

Born in Providence, Rhode
Island 1931; lives in Orbisonia,
Pennsylvania

Flit, 1959
welded iron, canvas, wire, and
black velvet
65 x 65 inches
Anonymous Gift, courtesy of the
Herbert F. Johnson Museum of
Art, Cornell University

In 1959, Lee Bontecou began to produce the Assemblages that established her reputation: wall-mounted relief sculptures in which fragments of canvas and found fabrics are fastened onto welded metal armatures in configurations that provoke a range of organic and mechanistic associations. To create these works, Bontecou scavenged old laundry bags, knapsacks, and army surplus items. In *Flit* (1959), the letters that form the work's title are printed on a found fragment of canvas that appears to the upper right. A single gaping hole projects from the surface of the work at its center, framing a dark, receding (black velvet) inset. Its roughly concentric circular format suggests at once an eye, a bodily orifice, a nest or hive, a camera aperture, among a host of other things. The overall effect of Bontecou's work is generally described as "mysterious" and "menacing." This series of work, which preoccupied the artist until 1967, was presented first in a solo exhibition at the Leo Castelli Gallery in 1960.

Suggested Reading:
Smith, Elizabeth A. T. *Lee Bontecou: A Retrospective*. Exhibition catalogue. Chicago: Museum of Contemporary Art; Los Angeles: UCLA Hammer Museum; New York, in association with Harry N. Abrams, Inc., 2003.

Plate 3

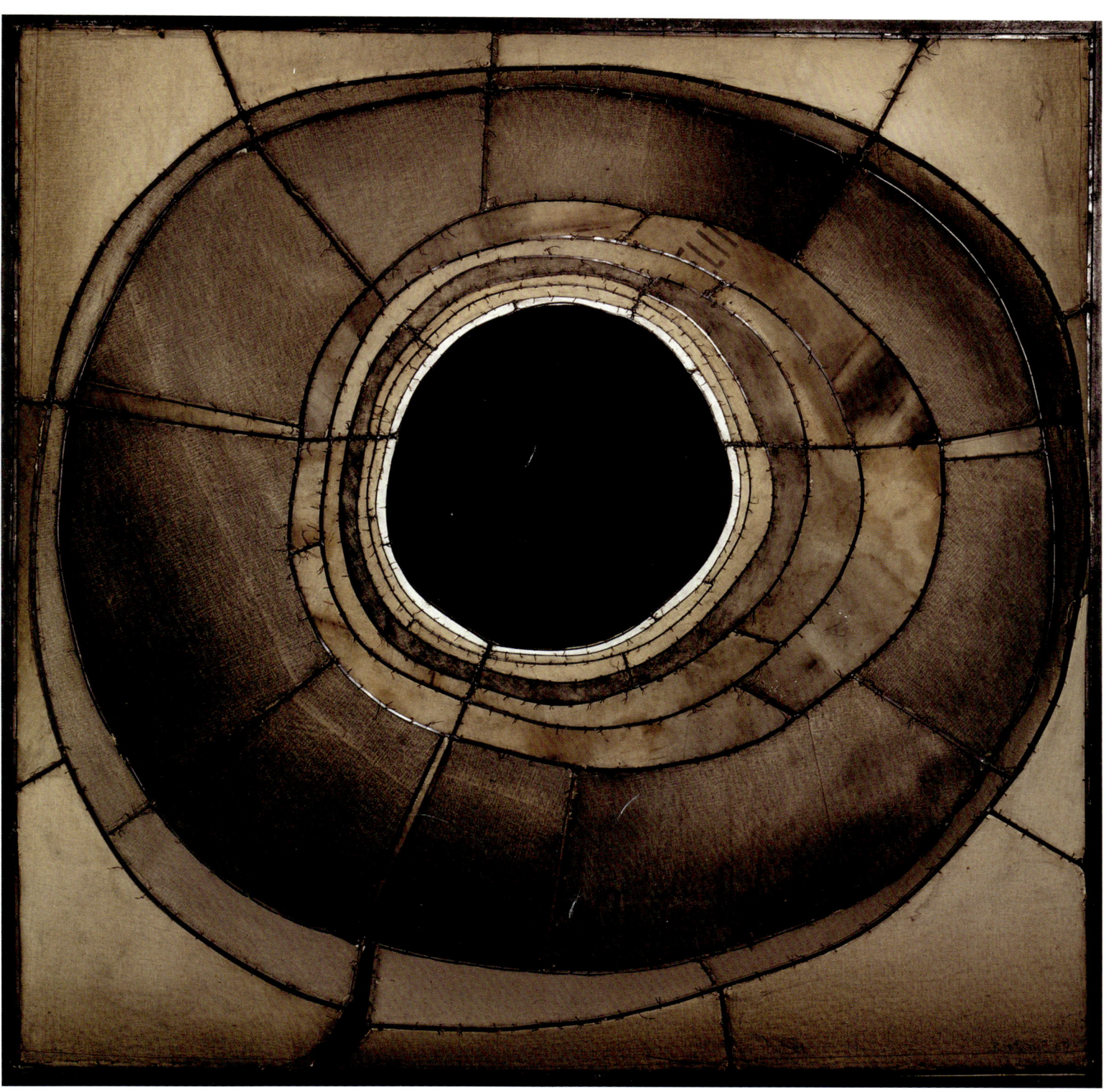

George Brecht
Born in Halfway, Oregon 1926;
lives in Cologne, Germany

Three Chair Events, 1961
three chairs in differing contexts
dimensions variable
Realized in 2008 with permission
of the artist

George Brecht began his artistic career in the late fifties while working as a research chemist in New Jersey. It was at this time that he developed friendships with Allan Kaprow, Robert Watts, and others on the art faculty at Rutgers University and wrote *Chance Imagery*, a book completed in 1957. Not published until a decade later, the book explored the use of chance in art from Dada to Jackson Pollock to John Cage. In 1958, Brecht (and Kaprow) began taking a class in experimental music with John Cage at the New School for Social Research in New York. This is where Brecht first developed his concept of the "Event Score," a verbal cue that would frame an experience for the viewer in time and space (*Exit*, 1961, for example, consisted of the single word and its corresponding act). His first solo exhibition, *Towards Events: An Arrangement*, held at New York's Reuben Gallery in 1959, featured Assemblages and event scores whose economical nature and embrace of chance anticipated the emergence of the artistic movement officially christened "Fluxus" in Wiesbaden, West Germany, in 1962.

Brecht's *Three Chair Events*, recreated here, was first presented in the group exhibition *Environments, Situations, Spaces*, held at New York's Martha Jackson Gallery in 1961. Three different chairs (one black, one white, and one yellow) were each set in a different situation: one outside the gallery on the street, the second in a hall, and the third in a bathroom (page 7, fig. 5). The "events" consist of all occurrences that take place in the vicinity of the chairs, including sitting on them. Brecht's "Event Score" for the piece reads:

"Sitting on a black chair.
Occurrence.
Yellow chair.
(Occurrence.)
On (or near) a white chair.
Occurrence."

Suggested Reading:
Fischer, Alfred, ed. *George Brecht Events*. Exhibition catalogue. Cologne: Museum Ludwig; Walter König Publishers, 2006.

Plate 4 a, b, c

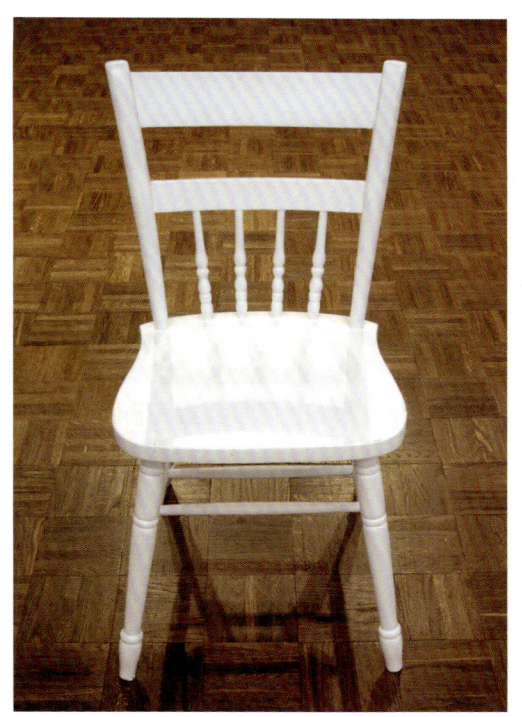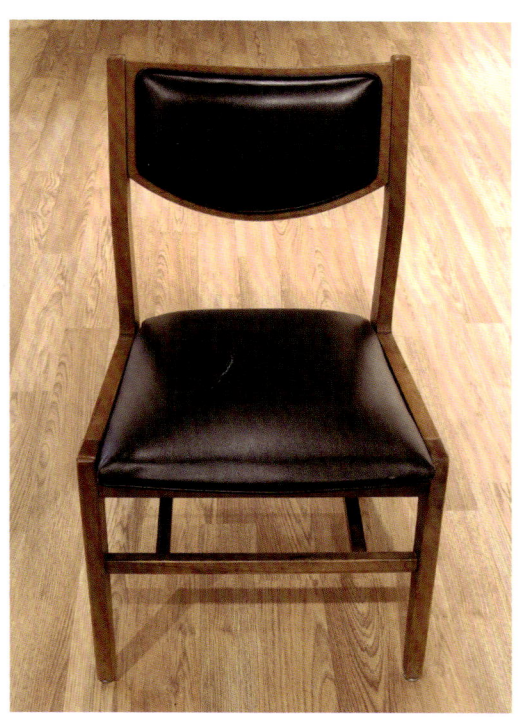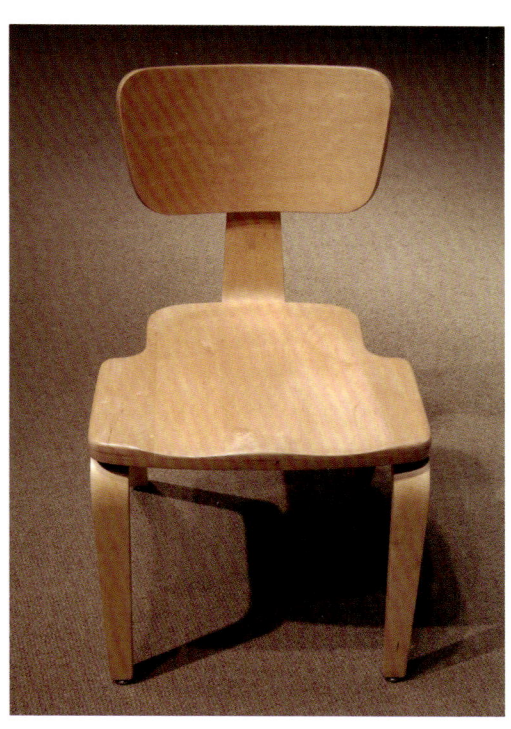

John Chamberlain

Born in Rochester, Indiana 1927;
lives on Shelter Island, New York

Nutcracker, 1958
painted steel
47 x 39 x 30 inches
Private Collection, courtesy Allan
Stone Gallery, New York

John Chamberlain attended the Art Institute of Chicago in the early fifties and then studied and taught sculpture at Black Mountain College in Asheville, North Carolina, from 1955-56, where most of his friends were poets, among them Robert Creeley and Charles Olson. At this time, he was producing energetic, largely flat and open-form welded iron sculptures influenced by the Abstract Expressionist sculptor David Smith. In 1957, he began to include scrap metal from automobiles in his work and *Nutcracker* (1958) is among his first works built entirely of automobile parts welded together. It is a fully three-dimensional work in which self-colored, irregularly-shaped planes and a seemingly endless variety of linear elements that bend, crinkle, and zig-zag are pieced together to form a quasi-volumetric core. *Nutcracker*'s muscular energy and fundamentally Cubist structure recall the Abstract Expressionist paintings of Willem de Kooning. Chamberlain's translation of de Kooning's gestures into real space through the use of rusted, castoff industrial materials, made him a leading figure in late fifties Assemblage.

Suggested Reading:
Sylvester, Julie. *John Chamberlain: A Catalogue Raisonné of the Sculpture, 1954-1985*. New York: Hudson Hills Press, 1986.

Plate 5

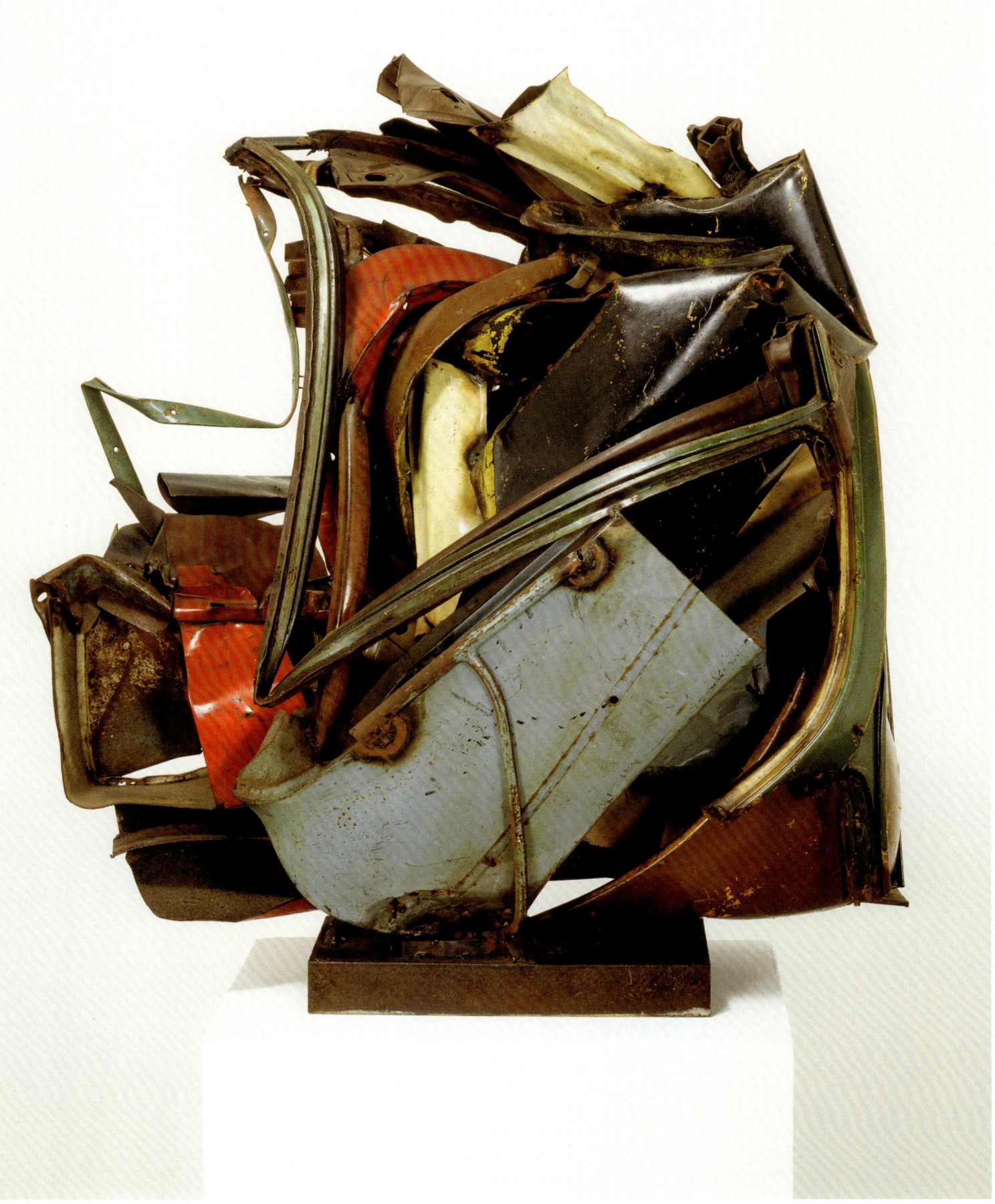

Bruce Conner
McPherson, Kansas
1933 – 2008
San Francisco, California

Walkie-Talkie, 1959
mixed media
32 7/8 x 11 1/4 x 13 1/4 inches
Hirshhorn Museum and
Sculpture Garden, Smithsonian
Institution, Washington DC,
Joseph H. Hirshhorn Purchase
Fund, 2008

Based in San Francisco, Bruce Conner was a leading figure in California Assemblage. In 1959, he developed his characteristic manner of working, which was related to but distinct from the work then being produced in New York, as its roots were planted in Surrealism rather than Abstract Expressionism and its content was both politically-motivated and fetishistic. The artist sought to expose the materialism and hypocrisy of American society while indulging in the erotic and seamy side of the culture. Pornographic images and ripped nylon stockings, which exude an aura of lust and disgust, were mainstays of his early art. Contorted and dismembered baby dolls made frequent appearances as well.

In *Walkie-Talkie* (1959), the painted head, arm, and body of a child's doll are enclosed in a bulky box form made of corrugated cardboard that also comprises plain and printed papers, charred fabric, metal washers and staples, thumb tacks, heavy wire, various types of string, and sprayed and brushed paint. The overall shape and telescoping antenna connote the communication device suggested by the work's title. Conner's intention might have been to contrast the preverbal (the baby) with the verbal (the walkie-talkie)* or to imbue an inanimate object with a life force and capacity for independent speech. Additionally, he might have been seeking to comment on the foolhardiness of the consuming public, as hard plastic "Walkie-Talkie" dolls began to be marketed in the 1950s.

Suggested Reading:
Boswell, Peter, Bruce Jenkins, and Joan Rothfuss. *2000 BC: the Bruce Conner Story, Part II*. Exhibition catalogue. Minneapolis, MN: Walker Art Center, 1999.

*This was suggested by Michael Kohn of the Michael Kohn Gallery, Los Angeles, who represents Conner's art.

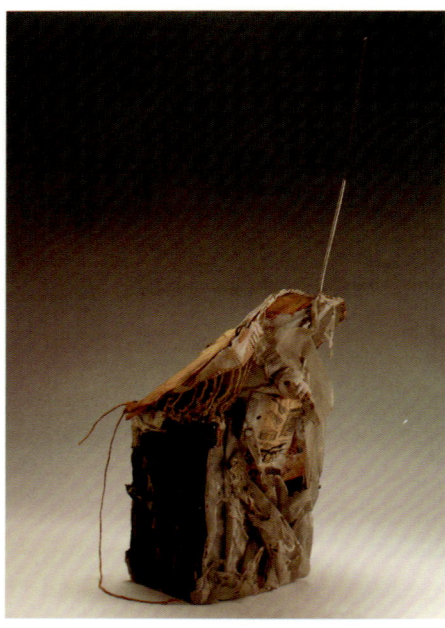

Plate 6 a, b

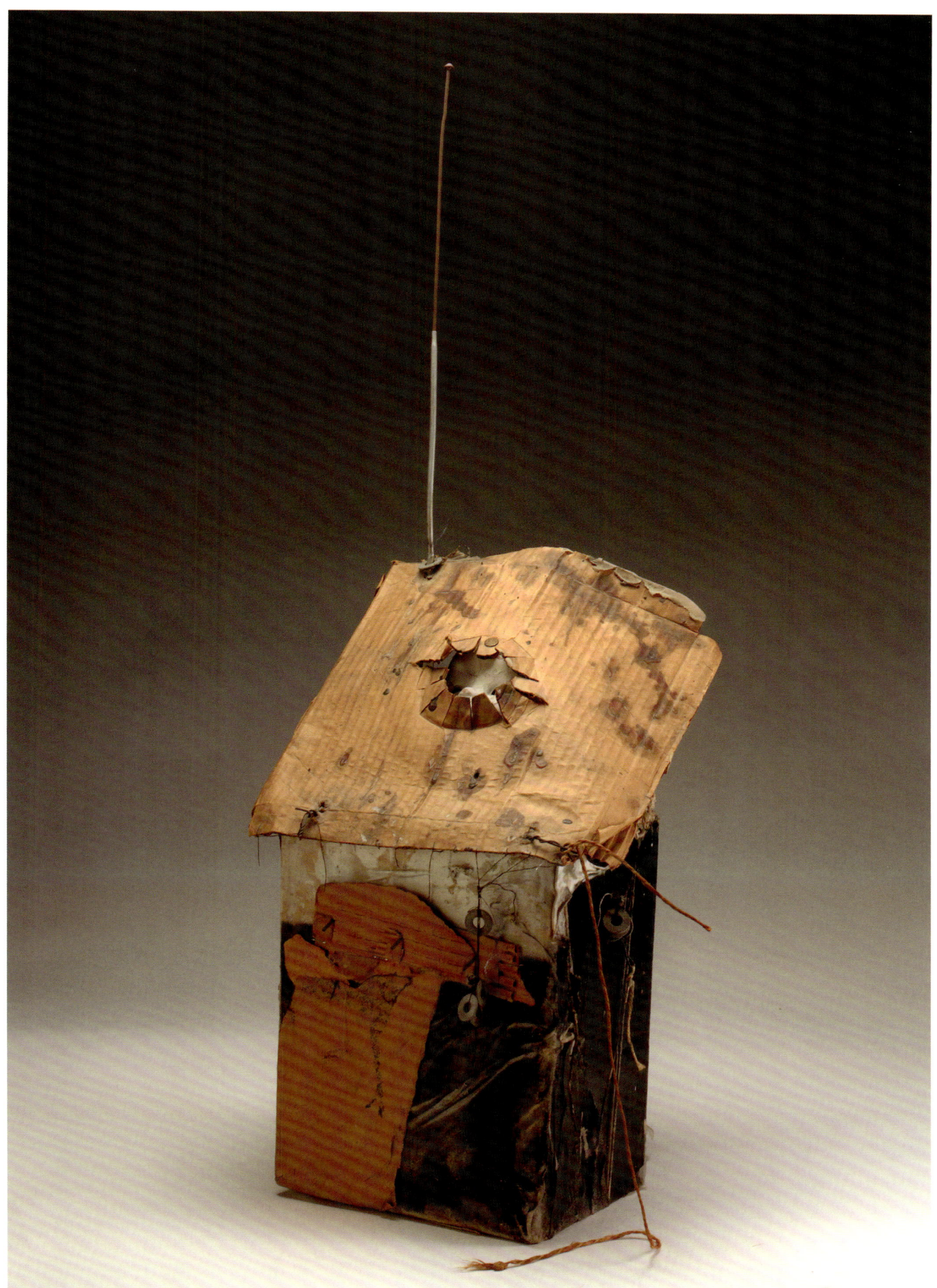

Jim Dine
Born in Cincinnati, Ohio 1935;
lives in New York City and
Putney, Vermont

Study for *The Car Crash: Man in
Woman's Costume and Woman
in Man's Costume*, 1960
ballpoint pen, brush and ink,
chalk, watercolor, colored pencil,
pencil, and cut-and-paste paper
on paper
16 3/4 x 21 3/4 inches
The Museum of Modern Art,
New York, Gift of the Artist,
122.1965

After seeing Robert Rauschenberg's Combines reproduced in *ARTnews* magazine, Jim
Dine resolved to move to New York, which he did in 1958 after his graduation with a B.F.A.
from Ohio University. Almost immediately, he met Allan Kaprow, Claes Oldenburg, Red
Grooms, Lucas Samaras, and others and began to produce Assemblages and
Happenings, among the most significant of which was *Car Crash*, a dramatic, 15-minute
piece that was performed at the Reuben Gallery in early November 1960 (page 7, fig. 4).
Spectators entered an enclosed space entirely covered either with white paint or cloth.
Dine, dressed in silver with a silver-painted face and red lipstick, drew cartoonish cars on
a blackboard with white chalk, which kept breaking. He seemed to want to speak, but
merely grunted, growing increasingly frantic at his inability to communicate. An eight-foot-
tall woman (a woman standing on a ladder draped in white cloth) recited words associated
with cars, many with sexual overtones, while recorded sounds of running car engines,
screeching tires, and honking horns were heard. A woman dressed in a man's white suit
and a man dressed in an evening dress also appeared, as seen in the drawing shown here.
When the light from flashlights carried under their arms hit Dine in his silver suit, he cried
out as if in pain.

Inspired by two car accidents in which Dine had personally been involved during the
previous year and possibly by a crash involving the death of a friend, the "Car Crash"
theme, with its focus on bloody red crosses, violence, and death, appeared in Dine's art
not only in his performance piece and related studies, but in an extended series of
drawings in various media as well as in his first suite of prints. Though Dine was soon to
focus on painting and to become a leading figure in Pop Art, his work was never cool and
impersonal, but remained expressive and even autobiographical, his handling of paint
retaining a gestural virtuosity.

Suggested Reading:
Celant, Germano and Clare Bell. *Jim Dine: Walking Memory*. Exhibition catalogue. New York: Solomon R.
Guggenheim Museum, 1999.

Plate 7

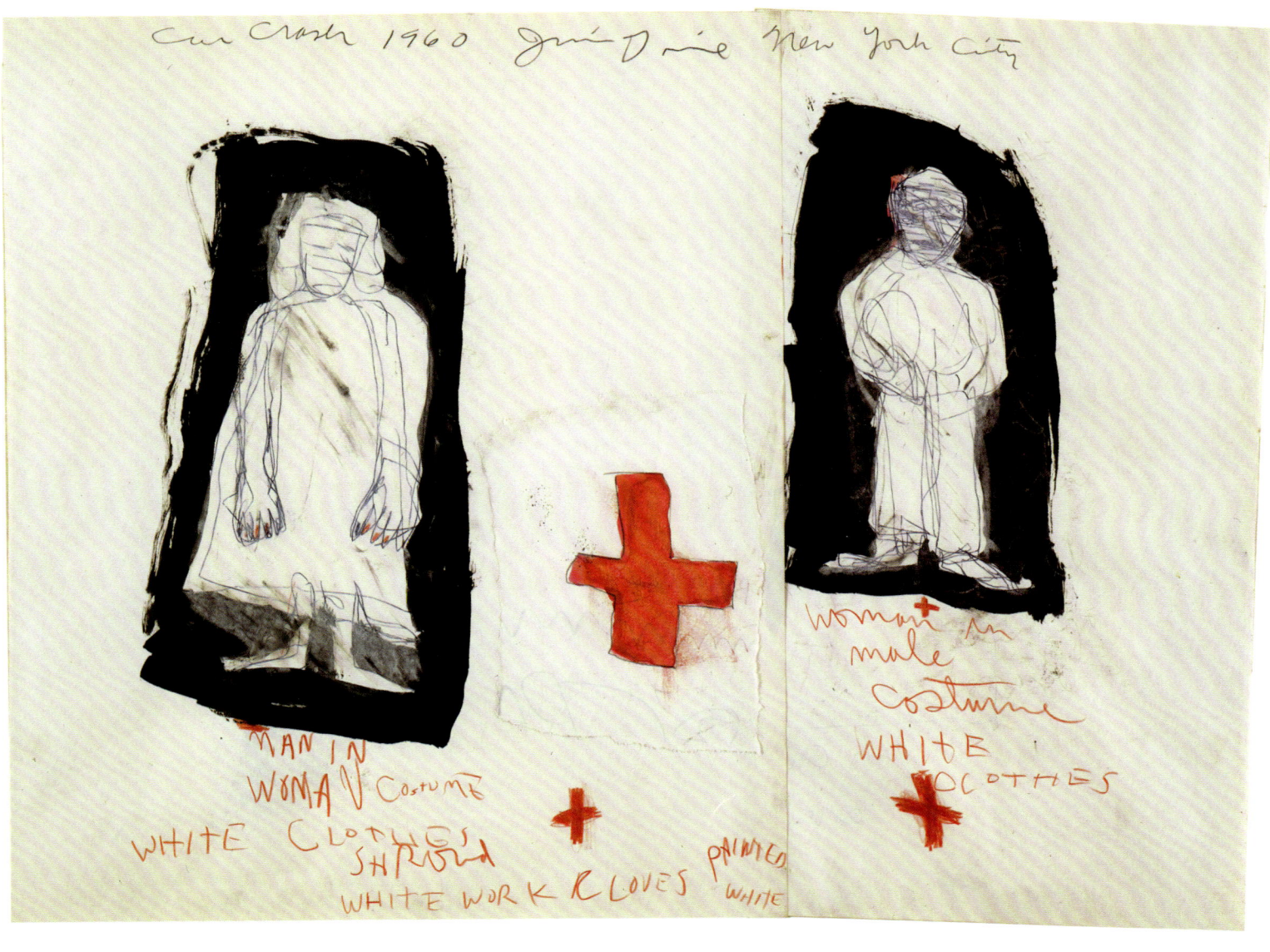

Red Grooms
Born in Nashville, Tennessee
1937; lives in New York City

Policewoman, 1959
wood and metal on wood
45 x 29 x 10 inches
University at Buffalo Art Galleries,
Gift of David K. Anderson, 2000

Born Charles Rogers Grooms in Nashville, Tennessee, Grooms was nicknamed "Red" during the summer of 1957 while working as a dishwasher in Provincetown, Massachusetts, and studying art with Hans Hofmann. He had his first solo show of paintings at a Provincetown gallery a year later and opened a part of his New York loft as the City Gallery where he showed his own work as well as that of friends Lester Johnson, Alex Katz, Bob Thompson, Claes Oldenburg, and others. He staged his best known Happening, *The Burning Building (1959),* in his next loft/studio, which he called The Delancey Street Museum. This performance piece was distinct from those of Kaprow in that it followed a quasi-linear narrative and was comedic in nature. Grooms was a consummate showman by nature, as his later work both in art and film reveal. It was also in 1959 that Grooms moved from painting to Assemblage, as seen in the charming, stick-figure *Policewoman* (1959) made of found bits of wood and metal. Although modest and unassuming, this work anticipates Grooms' vibrant and often colossal "sculpto-pictoramas," such as *Ruckus Manhattan* (1975), a mixed media, environmental construction that can be entered and explored by the viewer, executed in collaboration with his wife of the time, Mimi Gross. It features colorful, cartoon-like representations of the buildings and varied characters found in lower Manhattan and exudes a carnival-like atmosphere.

Suggested Reading:
Danto, Arthur C., Timothy Hyman, and Marco Livingstone, *Red Grooms*. New York: Rizzoli, 2004.

Plate 8

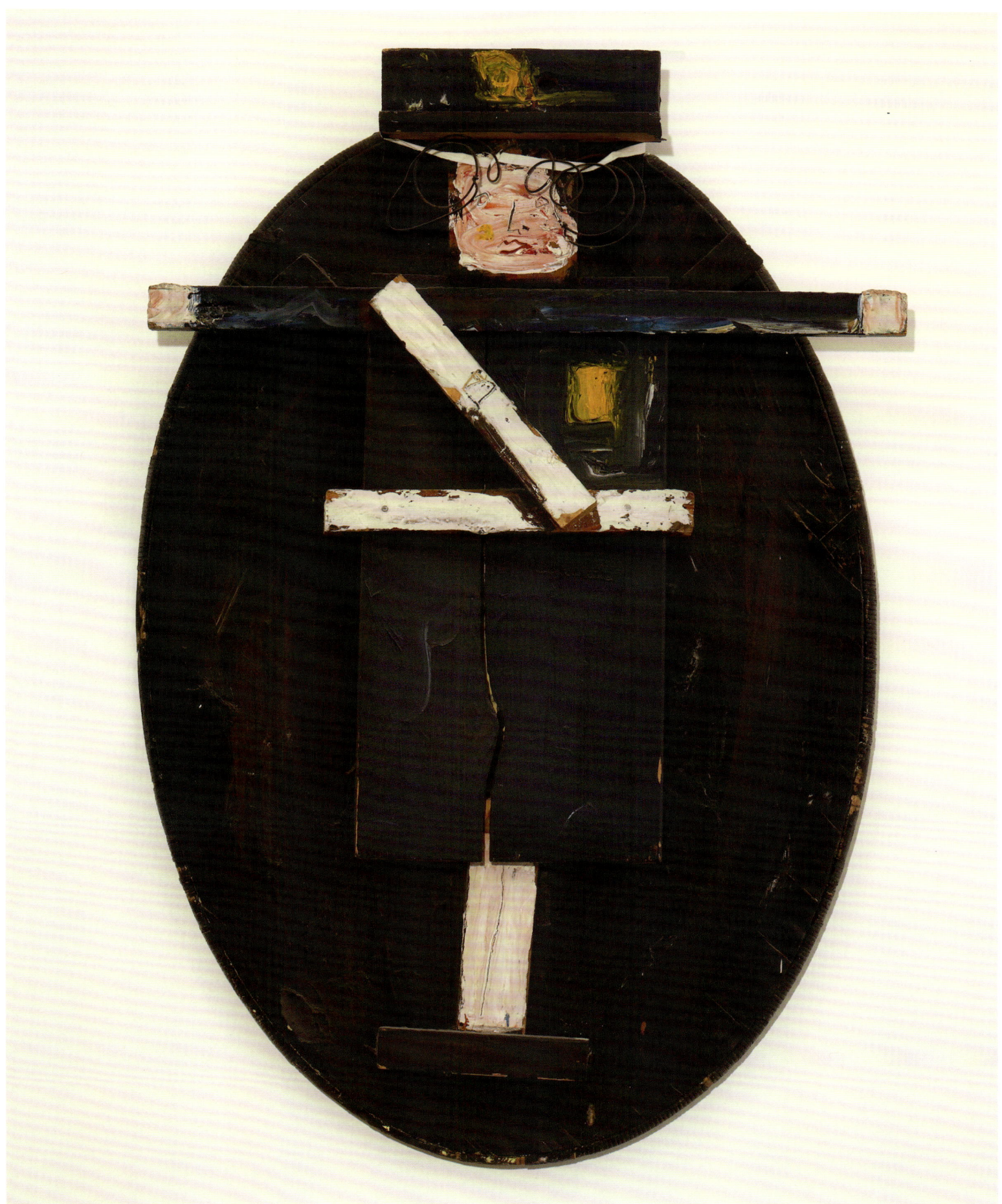

Robert Indiana
Born in New Castle, Indiana,
1928; lives in Vinalhaven, Maine

Eat, 1962
graphite on paper
25 1/8 x 19 1/16 inches
Ackland Art Museum,
purchased with the aid of funds
from the National
Endowment for the Arts and the
Ackland Associates, 77.20.1

While the Ackland Art Museum's graphite drawing *Eat* (1962) may appear to be a modest and unassuming work by this major figure associated with Pop Art, it was of monumental importance in Robert Indiana's *oeuvre*. According to the artist,* when he moved into his loft studio at 25 Coenties Slip in lower Manhattan in 1956, he found a brass stencil for The American Hay Company that had been left behind by a previous tenant. Intrigued by the manner in which it combined words with an abstract, iconic design, Indiana decided to make a rubbing (or *frottage*) of the stencil, although he changed the word "Hay" to "Man," so that it now read "The American Man Company." He also added "EAT" horizontally and vertically at its center. This was one of the first uses in his art of the word "eat," which was to become a kind of trademark (slightly less famed than his exploitation of the word "LOVE"). Although "eat" is a commonplace word often seen as a sign in the American landscape, the artist claims it to be of personal significance, as it refers both to a diner his mother operated and to the last word she uttered before she died. Indiana has also said that his career-long use of words inscribed within flatly painted circular forms derives not from pinball machine graphics, as has often been thought, but from the stencil used to make the Ackland's drawing. The original brass stencil, which he says "was very important to my whole life," currently hangs in the kitchen of his home in Vinalhaven, Maine.

Suggested Reading:
Wilmerding, John and Joachim Pissarro. *Robert Indiana: the Artist and his Work, 1955-2005*. New York: Rizzoli, 2006.

*Telephone conversation between the artist and Roni Feinstein, April 22, 2008.

Plate 9

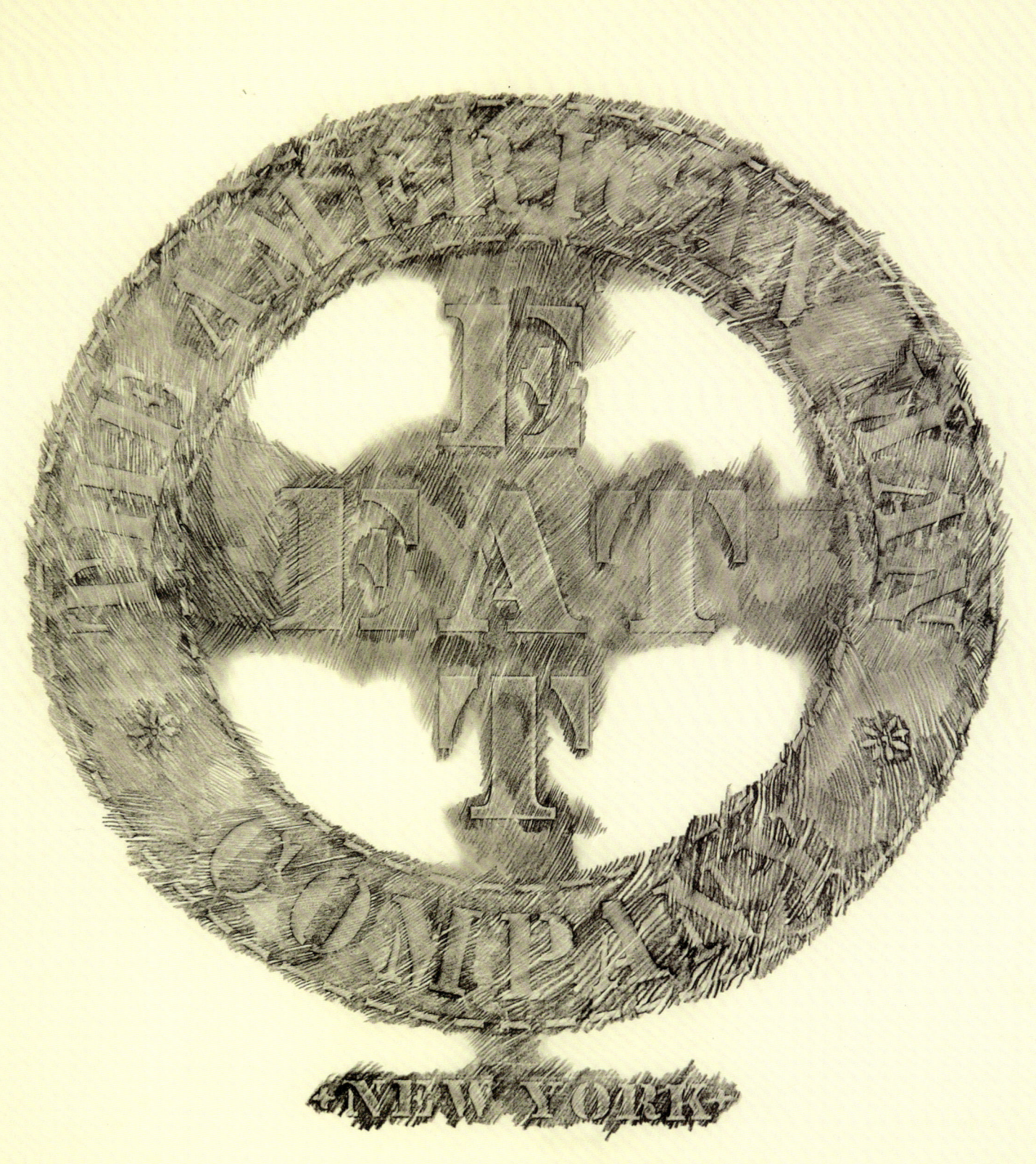

R Indiana '62

Jess

Long Beach, California
1923 – 2004
San Francisco, California

The Hang'd Man: Tarot XIII, 1959
magazine reproductions on
window shade in wooden frame,
with screen door
80 x 30 1/2 inches
Krannert Art Museum and
Kinkead Pavilion
University of Illinois, Urbana-
Champaign
Purchase John Needles
Chester Fund

Born in Long Beach, California, Jess [Collins] was initially a scientist who spent several years working on projects associated with the production of nuclear weapons. Horrified by the use of the atomic bomb in Hiroshima, he began a formal study of painting, although he soon overthrew that academic training to pursue a more individual course focused on the manipulation of found, preexisting images, a course influenced and supported by his close personal relationship with the poet and scholar Robert Duncan. Although Jess' work takes a number of forms, his "paste ups" dominate. These collages bring images taken from various sources together to suggest complex, underlying meanings.

In *The Hang'd Man: Tarot XIII* (1959), one of the largest and among the most remarkable "paste ups" Jess produced, the found illustrations are mounted on a window shade set within the frame of a screen door. The image of a flayed man hanging upside down extends the length of the work, which is otherwise occupied by a human landscape reminiscent of those found in the work of the fifteenth-century Dutch painter Hieronymus Bosch, consisting of figures and figural groupings of differing scales. While the title of Jess' piece refers to the tarot, the set of twenty-two pictorial cards used for purposes of divination, the artist seems to have taken poetic license with the traditional iconography of the deck, as the thirteenth card is generally Death, and not Jess' *Hang'd Man*. The Hanged Man, traditionally tarot card number twelve, is commonly depicted as a clothed figure with skin intact. The meaning of the piece, then, remains ambiguous and open to interpretation.

Suggested Reading:
Auping, Michael. *Jess, A Grand Collage, 1951-1993*. Exhibition catalogue. Buffalo, NY: Albright-Knox Art Gallery, 1993.

Plate 10

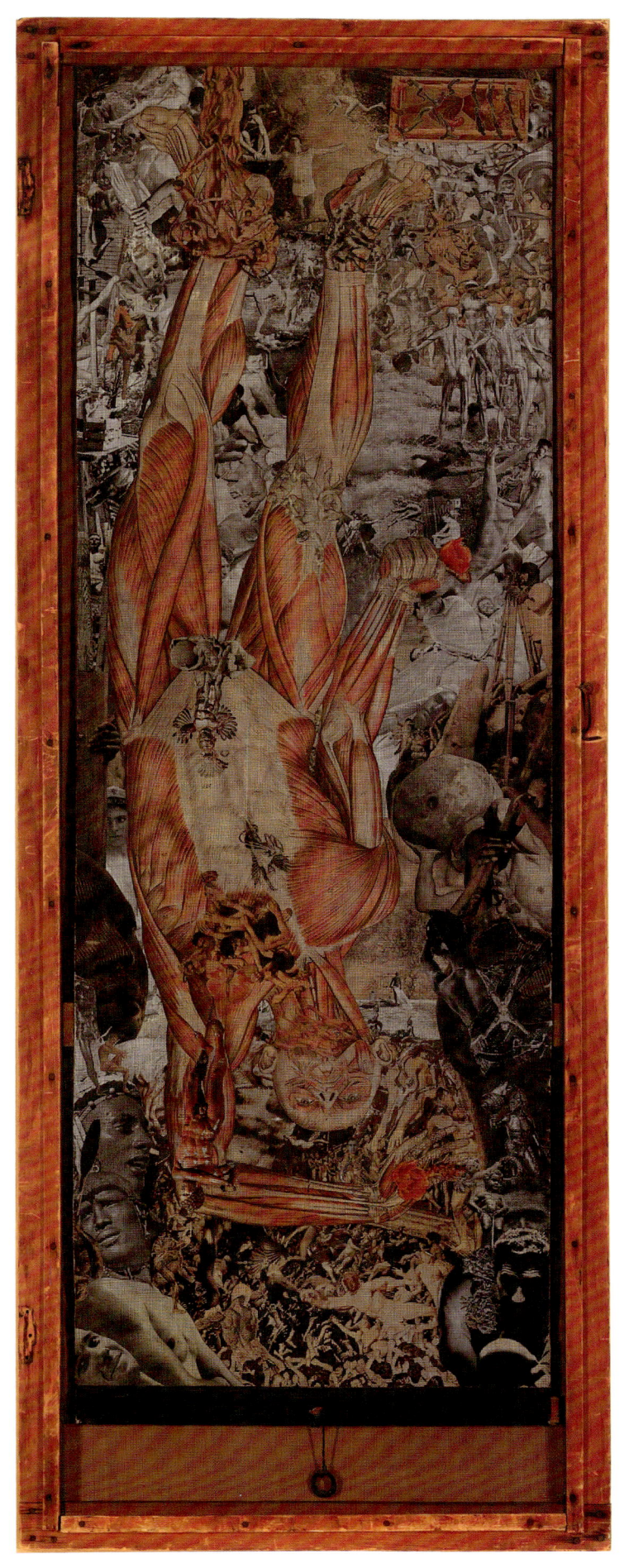

Jasper Johns

Born in Augusta, Georgia, 1930;
lives in Sharon, Connecticut and
St. Martin, U.S. Virgin Islands

Flashlight II, 1958
papier mâché and glass
3 x 8 3/4 x 4 inches
Estate of Robert Rauschenberg

Along with Robert Rauschenberg, Jasper Johns is generally regarded as being the major transition figure between Abstract Expressionism and Pop Art by way of Assemblage. In 1955, Johns began to produce paintings in which layers of newspaper collage were covered with encaustic, a wax-based medium. The subjects of these paintings, which were featured in Johns' first solo show at the Leo Castelli Gallery in 1958, were American flags, targets, numbers, and "things," as Johns said, "the mind already knows."

Also in 1958, Johns turned his attention to sculpture, producing a series of works based on the forms of commonplace light bulbs and flashlights. Inspired by Marcel Duchamp's Readymades, in which manufactured objects were designated works of art by their displacement into an art gallery or museum, Johns' *Flashlight II* departs from Duchamp's model in being handmade by the artist (although the glass front is a realistic detail). Painted dark gray and resting upon a craggy, slab-like base, the flashlight appears humble and ordinary, even impotent, in contrast to its more glorified treatment in Johns' previous version of the same motif in which an actual flashlight was suspended above a wooden base on two thin, metal rods, as if it were a treasured archeological find. Johns' flashlight series as a whole, which looked ahead to Warhol's canonization of the everyday object in his Campbell's soup can paintings and Brillo box sculptures, can be related to Johns' "Sketchbook Note" that reads:

> "Take an object
> Do something to it.
> Do something else to it.
> " " " " "

Suggested Reading:
Varnedoe, Kirk. *Jasper Johns: A Retrospective*. Exhibition catalogue. New York: Museum of Modern Art, 1996. Distributed by Harry N. Abrams.

Plate 11

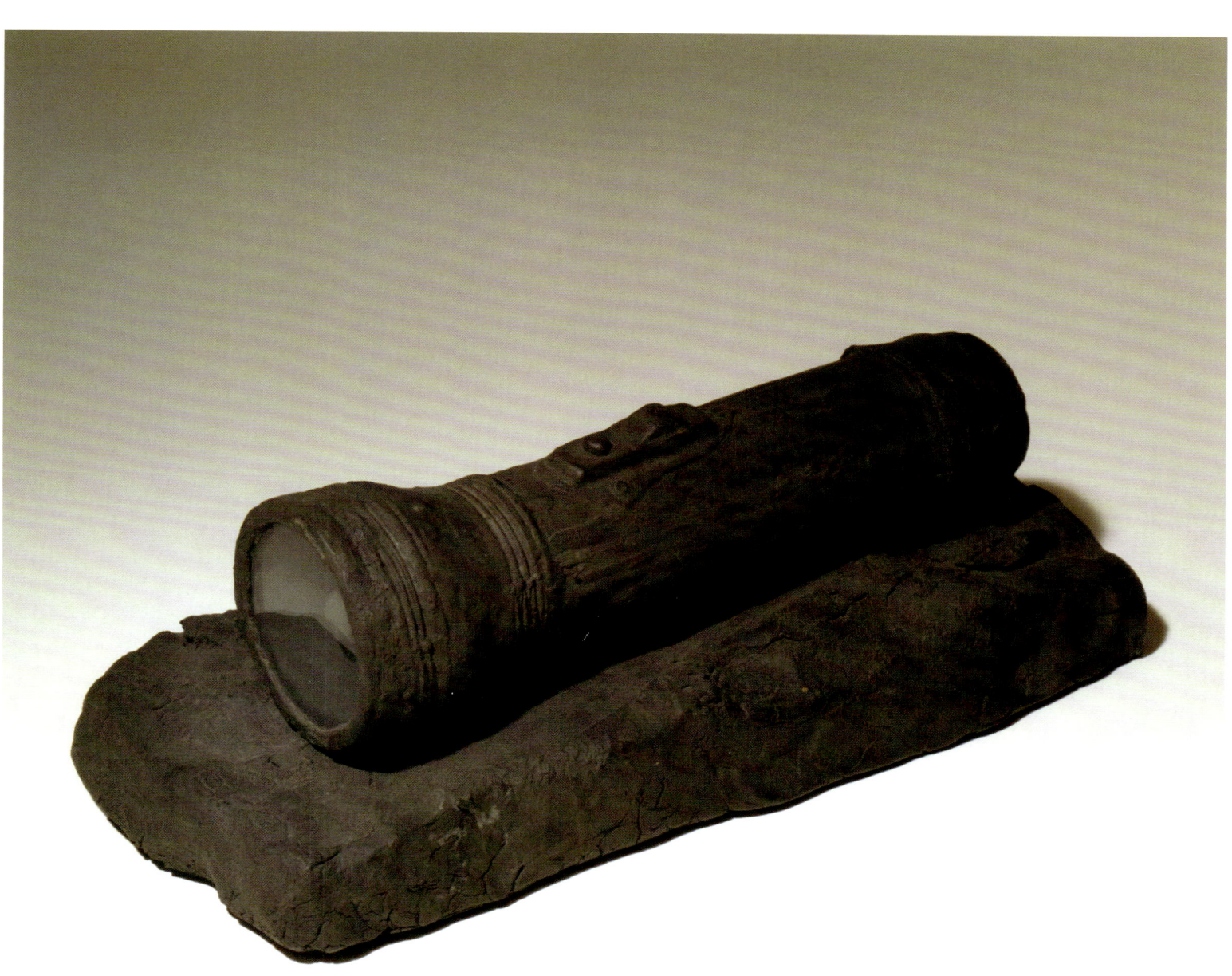

Ray Johnson
Detroit, Michigan
1927 – 1995
Long Island, New York

Movie Star with Horse, 1958
mixed-media collage
16 5/8 x 13 1/2 inches
Frances Beatty and Allen Adler

Untitled (James Dean in the Rain), c. 1955–58
mixed-media collage
15 1/2 x 11 3/4 inches
Estate of Ray Johnson, Richard L. Feigen & Co., New York

Ray Johnson attended Black Mountain College in Asheville, North Carolina, from 1945 to 1948, studying design, painting, and color with the Bauhaus master, Josef Albers. Under Albers' influence, Johnson worked for several years in a highly formal, abstract, and geometric manner. Moving to New York in 1948, Johnson shared an apartment with the sculptor Richard Lippold and their neighbors were Merce Cunningham and John Cage. Gradually, Cage's influence on Johnson supplanted that of Albers and, by 1955, Johnson was creating collages made up of both plain papers and images derived from newspapers and magazines. Johnson called his works "moticos," an anagram of the word "osmotic," which, according to Johnson, signified continual "change, like the news in the paper or the images on a movie screen." Johnson worked in a standardized format of 11 by 8 inches, the size of the shirt cardboards he used for his supports. While small in scale and made of discarded and ephemeral materials, each of Johnson's moticos is intricately worked and composed.

Movie Star with Horse (1958) presents a multilayered design made up of a starlet in a "cheesecake" pose, a horse, a pictogram, a telephone, and other images as well as a series of cut-out forms that suggest letters and writing but defy decoding. Delicate washes of paint used upon the surface have been modulated and striated with sandpaper, employed by the artist in lieu of a brush. Other works by Johnson feature known movie stars of the day, like Elvis Presley and James Dean, and labels from such commercial goods as Lucky Strike cigarettes, so that Johnson's work anticipated by several years the emergence of Pop Art. Johnson's reputation, however, has remained as modest as the scale of his works, largely because the artist tended to defy traditional art world exhibition and distribution systems, showing the work in his studio or under very controlled circumstances and distributing it through the United States Postal Service via a network of his own devising that he called "The New York Correspondence School." In the early sixties, Johnson's art, ideas, and defiance of art world protocol found a parallel in aspects of Fluxus Art.

Suggested Reading:
De Salvo, Donna and Catherine Gudis, eds. *Ray Johnson: Correspondence*. Exhibition catalogue. Columbus, OH: Wexner Center for the Arts, 1999.

Plate 12
Plate 13

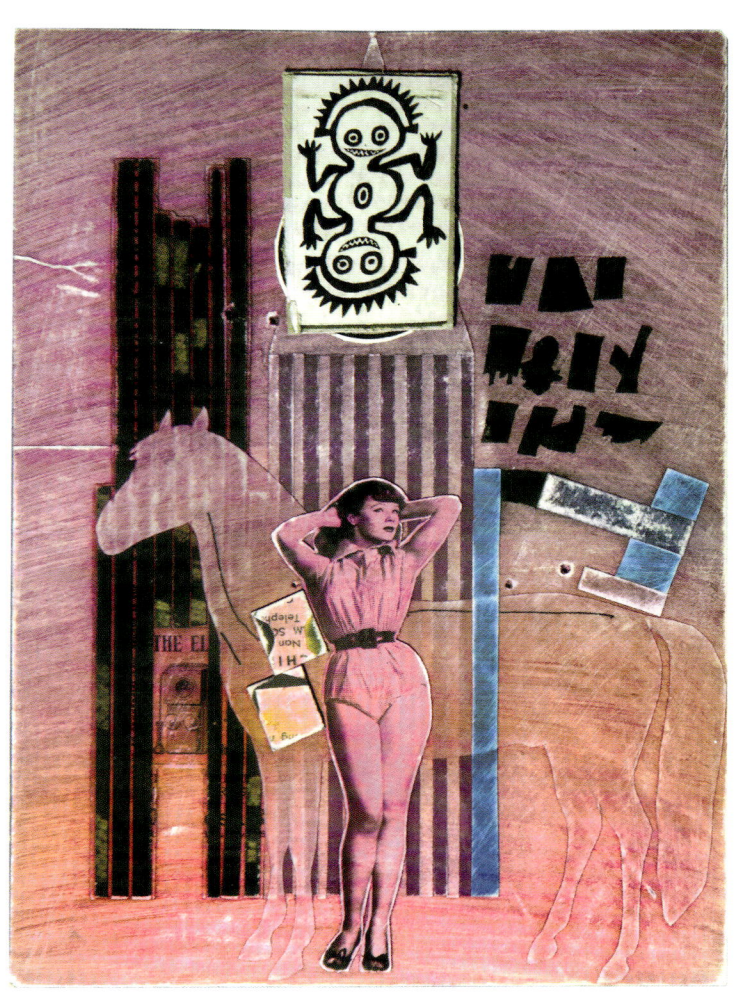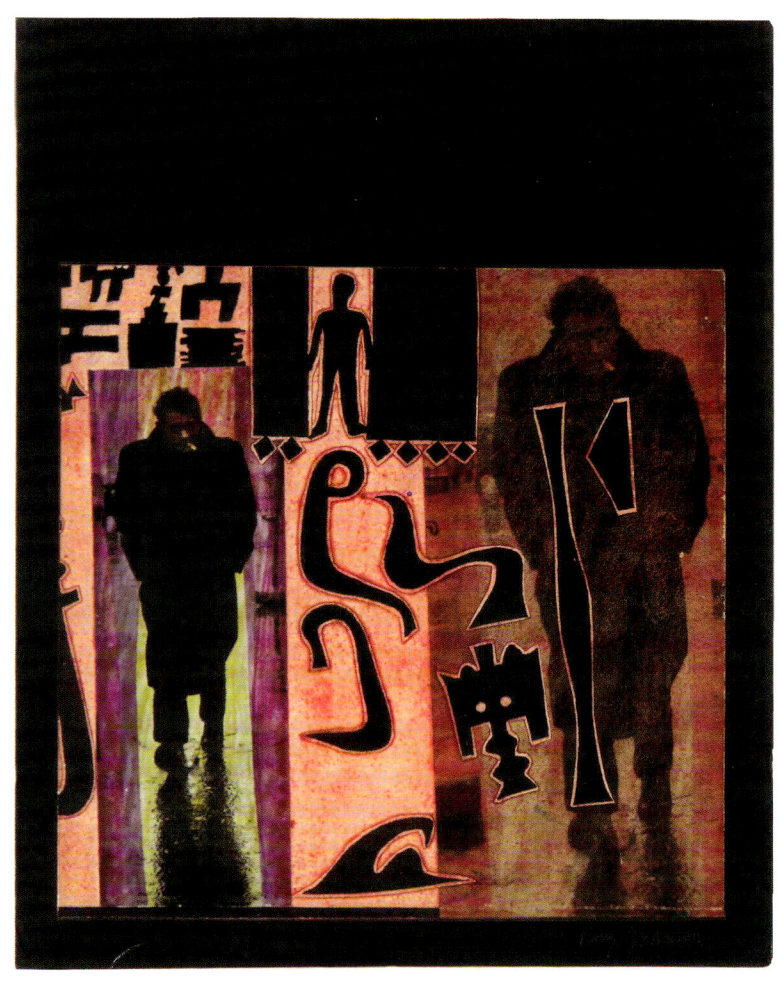

Allan Kaprow
Atlantic City, New Jersey
1927 – 2006
Encinitas, California

Untitled, 1959
stepladder, chicken wire,
newspaper, and tape
dimensions variable
approx. 77 x 108 x 64 inches
Realized in 2008 with permission
from the artist's estate, courtesy
of Hauser and Wirth, London

Allan Kaprow studied painting with Hans Hofmann, art history at Columbia University with Meyer Schapiro and, from 1957 to 1959, attended the class in experimental musical composition taught by the composer John Cage at the New School for Social Research in New York. The Zen- and Dada-inspired aesthetic of Cage motivated Kaprow, who had for some years been creating Assemblages consisting of found materials, literally to enlarge his concept to room-scale installations or "Environments" filled with everyday objects and to performances, which he called "Happenings," made up of commonplace events.

Untitled (1959), which consists of a mound of crumpled newspaper set over a chicken wire support, is something of a hybrid work, an "Environmental Assemblage," as it were, as it is atypically small and self-contained. During the late fifties/early sixties, Kaprow generally filled whole rooms or galleries with his concept and this untitled work, with its repetition of a singular unit, most recalls his large-scale Environment, *Yard* (1961), in which hundreds of automobile tires filled a gallery's courtyard (visitors were invited to climb through them at will). The scale limitations Kaprow imposed on *Untitled* were no doubt dictated by the fact that it was originally created for a group exhibition, *Below Zero*, held at the Reuben Gallery from December 18, 1959, to January 5, 1960, and had to share the space with the work of other artists, as it does in *Circa 1958*. Among the artists represented in both shows are Kaprow, George Brecht, Ray Johnson, Robert Rauschenberg, Claes Oldenburg, Jim Dine, Red Grooms, and George Segal, many of whom were directly affected by Kaprow's art, writing, and dynamic presence.

Suggested Reading:
Meyer-Hermann, Eva, Andrew Perchuk, and Stephanie Rosenthal, eds. *Allan Kaprow—Art as Life*. Los Angeles: Getty Research Institute, 2008.

Plate 14

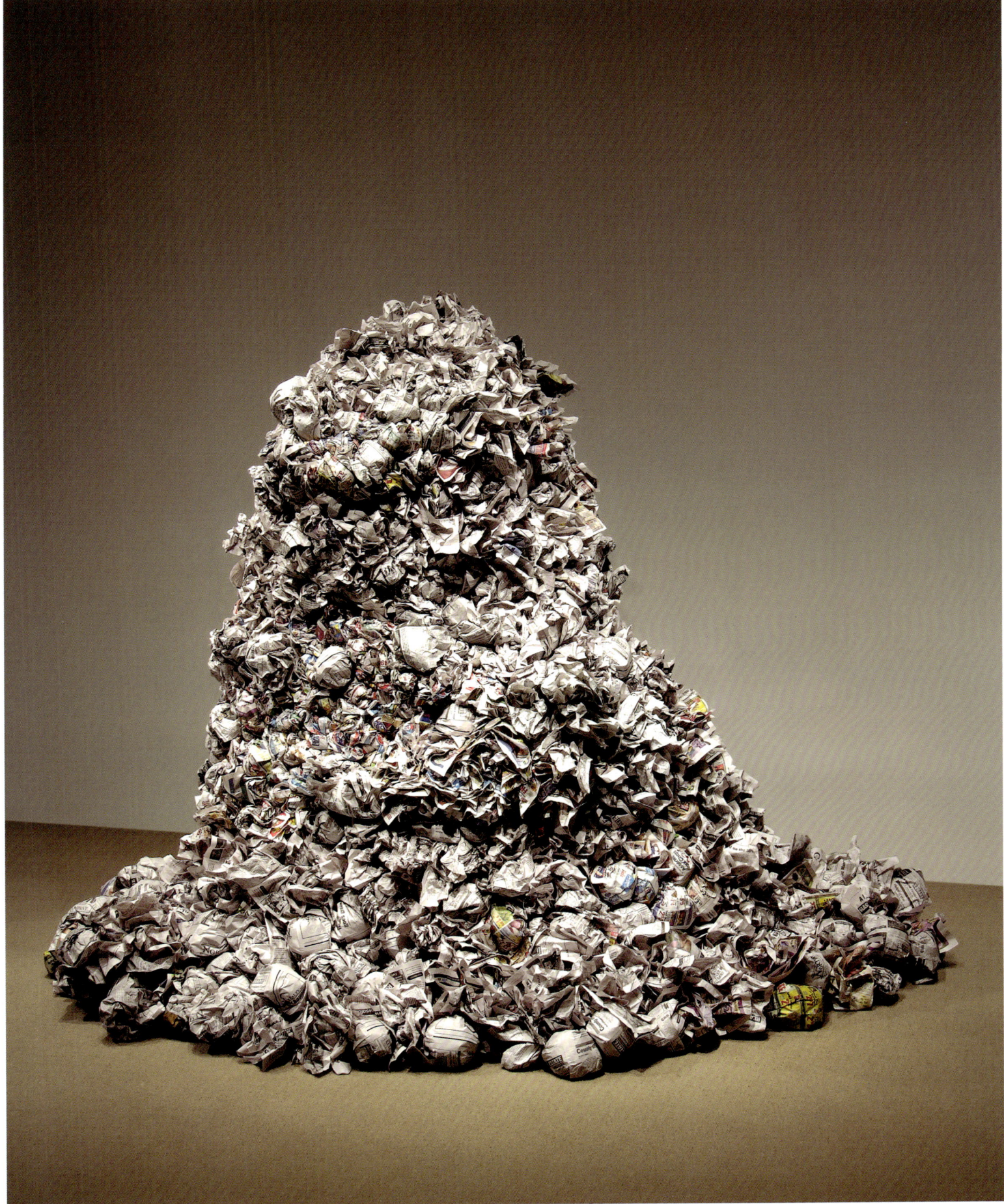

Ed Kienholz
Fairfield, Washington
1927 – 1994
Hope, Idaho

John Doe, 1959
free-standing assemblage: oil
paint on mannequin parts, child's
perambulator, toy, wood, metal,
plaster, and rubber
39 1/2 x 19 x 31 1/4 inches
The Menil Collection, Houston

A rancher's son who had never received any formal art training, Ed Kienholz arrived in Los Angeles in 1953 and decided to become an artist. By then, he had worked as a car salesman, a vacuum cleaner salesman, an attendant in a mental institution, and in a club in Las Vegas. Once the decision was made, he devoted himself to creating satirical and moralistic work that would reveal the tragic absurdities of the human condition. In the mid-fifties, he produced deliberately crude wooden reliefs, some of them painted with commercial paints using a kitchen broom, which he showed at the Ferus Gallery, a major center of avant-garde activity in California founded by Kienholz and Walter Hopps in 1957.

In 1959, Kienholz moved from wall-hung constructions to freestanding representational Assemblages made from objects and materials scavenged from the environment, as exemplified by what is widely held to be his first significant work of this type, *John Doe* (1959). It is an at once poignant and grotesque depiction of the "typical" American male, black resin and red paint dripping like blood from the head and armless torso of a male mannequin mounted on a child's stroller. Inserted into a hollowed-out circle in its chest is a Christian cross. The hypocrisy of this infantilized, purportedly religious figure is revealed when the viewer steps around the back of the piece to encounter his sexuality in what is literally his "other half." In 1961, Kienholz extended his work beyond Assemblage to full-scale Environments in which he pursued politically motivated themes.

Suggested Reading:
Kienholz: A Retrospecitve. Exhibition catalogue. New York: Whitney Museum of American Art. in association with Distributed Art Publishers, 1996.

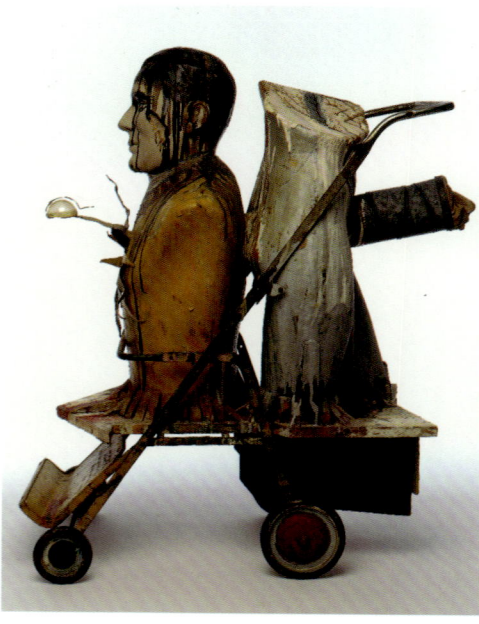

Plate 15 a, b

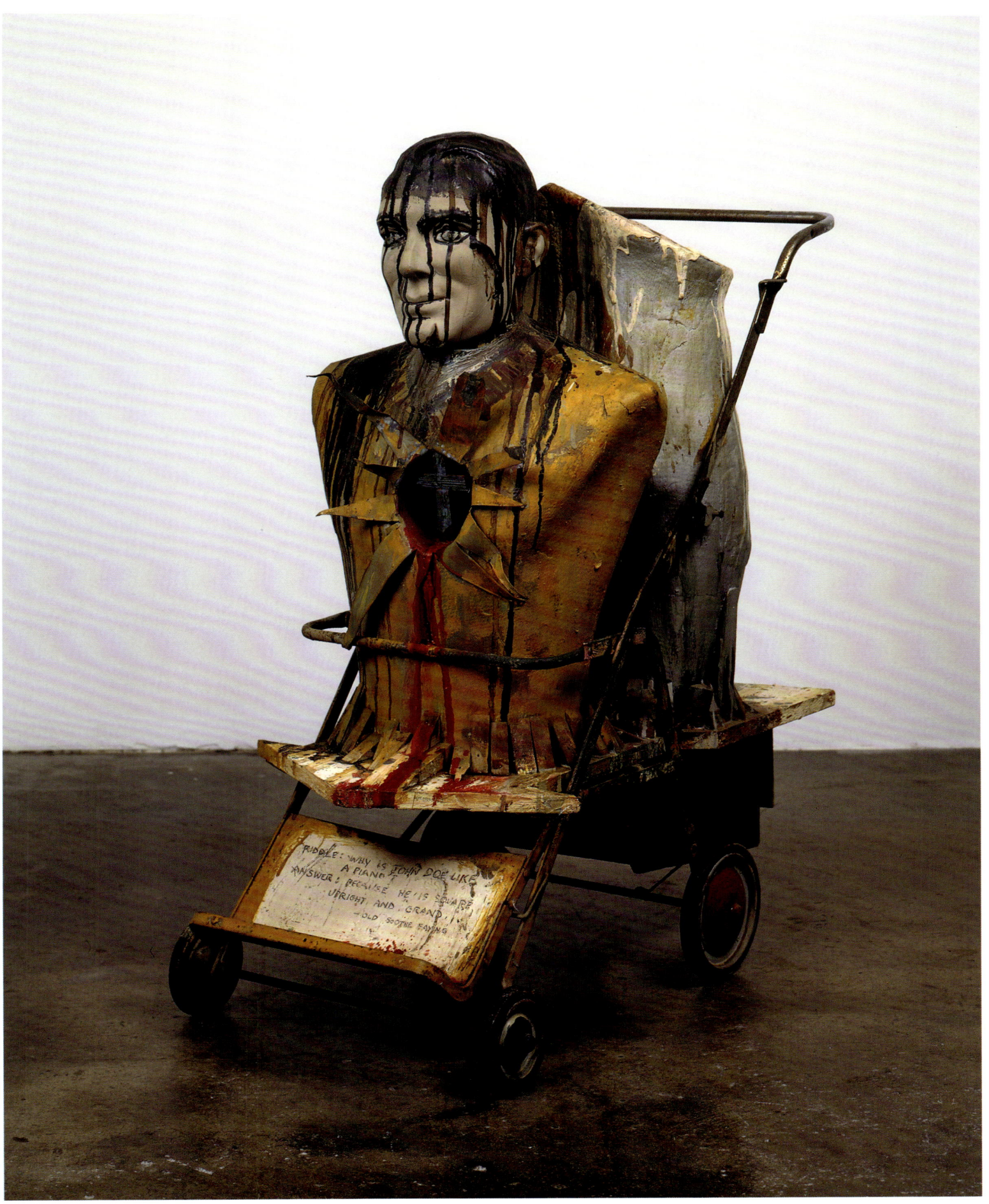

Roy Lichtenstein
New York City
1923 – 1997
New York City

The Bad Man, 1956
oil on canvas
22 5/8 x 18 5/8 inches
Mr. Eric B. Schnurer,
West Chester, Pennsylvania

After receiving his M.F.A. from Ohio State University where he studied with Hoyt L. Sherman and then taught for several years, Roy Lichtenstein moved to Cleveland in 1951, supporting himself by working a series of day jobs. During this time, he devoted himself to painting an extended series of works devoted to the theme of the American Indian and the Wild West. These paintings were based on preexisting sources—reproductions of paintings by George Catlin, Albert Bierstadt, and Karl Bodmer, as well as anonymous illustrations found in American history books. Lichtenstein translated these found nineteenth-century images into a Modernist idiom heavily influenced by Pablo Picasso, Joan Miró, Paul Klee, and others in such a way that they appeared as highly stylized, flatly patterned caricatures. While Jackson Pollock, Adolf Gottlieb, and other Abstract Expressionists had looked to Native American art for inspiration during the formative years of their careers as part of their search for images embodying spiritual power, Lichtenstein exploited images of "cowboys and Indians" as visual clichés, as a critique of the stereotypical images by which American culture defined itself, and in so doing forged an individual and unconventional path. *The Bad Man* (1956), which was among the American frontier paintings included in the artist's 1957 exhibition at the Joseph Heller Gallery, New York, is distinctly Picassoid in its childlike nature, outlined forms, and surface detail, although the subject of a masked outlaw with a gun, whose source is unknown, certainly never appeared in the Spanish master's art.

In 1957, Lichtenstein began teaching at the State University of New York, Oswego, and abandoned American themes, working instead in a high color gestural style influenced by de Kooning and others. In 1960, he became an instructor at Douglass College of Rutgers University where he met Allan Kaprow, George Segal, George Brecht, Lucas Samaras, and others and a year later produced *Look Mickey*, a painting featuring Mickey Mouse and Donald Duck and his first work in which a comic book source was rendered in a congruent comic book style. While such works were to make Lichtenstein a leading figure in Pop Art, his flatly rendered, cartoonish painting *The Bad Man* stands as a precursor, demonstrating Lichtenstein's predilection for dealing with stereotypical American images.

Suggested Reading:
Stavitsky, Gail and Twig Johnson. *Roy Lichtenstein: American Indian Encounters*. Exhibition catalogue. Montclair, NJ: Montclair Art Museum, 2005.

Plate 16

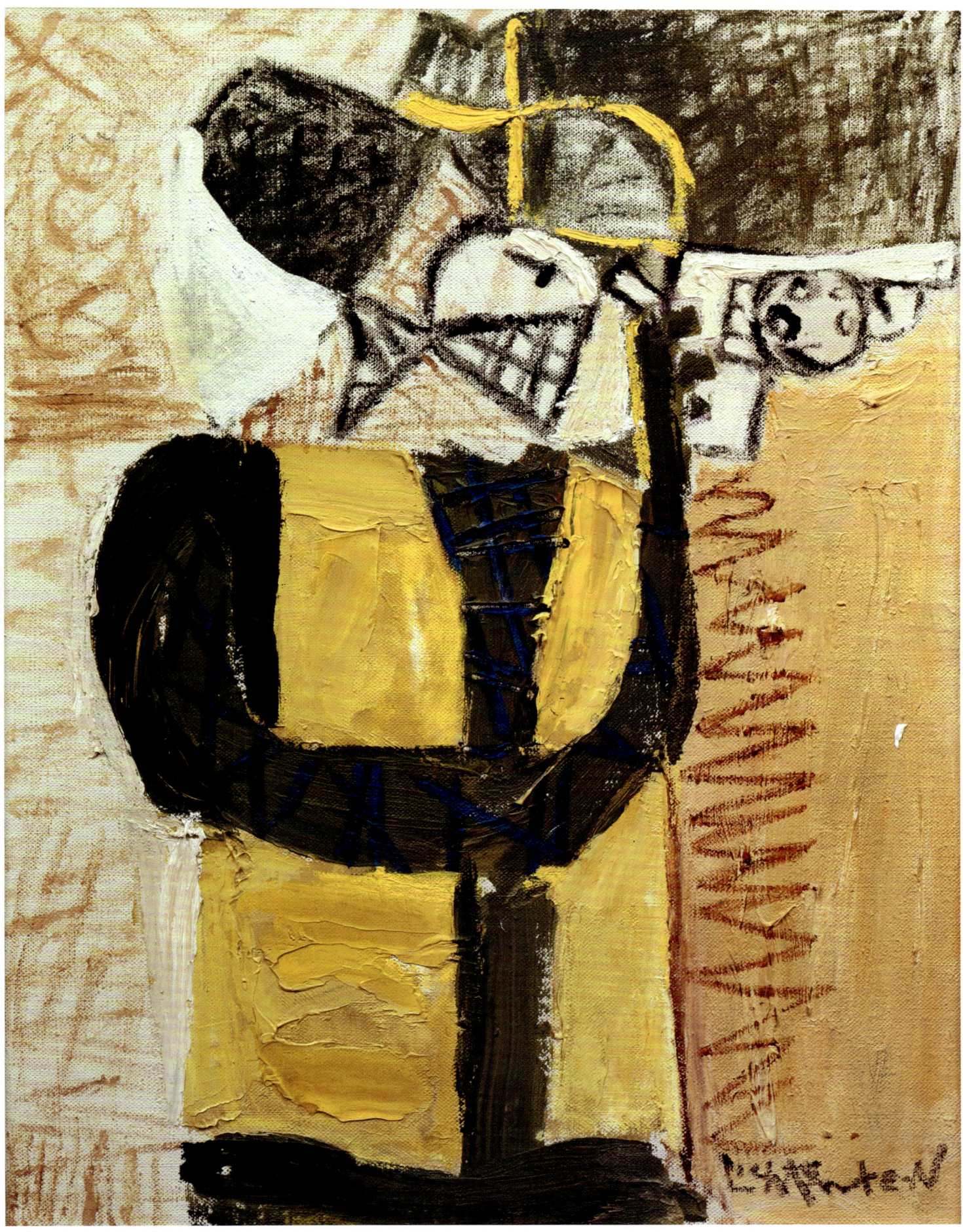

Robert Mallary
Toledo, Ohio
1917 – 1997
Northhampton, Massachusetts

Untitled, undated
mixed-media resin
91 x 45 1/2 x 6 3/4 inches
Private Collection, courtesy Allan
Stone Gallery, New York

In 1959, Robert Mallary moved to New York from New Mexico, where he had been teaching art at the state university, and quickly became a leading figure in Assemblage Art. His work was included in the *Sixteen Americans* exhibition at MoMA in 1959 and in the *Art of Assemblage* show at the same museum in 1961. Mallary produced intensely physical wall reliefs that translated the painted gestures of such Abstract Expressionists as Willem de Kooning and Franz Kline into found materials in actual space. *Untitled*, whose surface resembles petrified wood, is at once abstract and allusive, its shape suggesting a human profile or bird. At the same time, the form appears unstable, its dangling components seeming to threaten to break away from the whole, although it adheres through the use of polyester resin. In 1938, Mallary had begun to experiment with new plastics under the inspiration of the Mexican muralist, David Alfaro Siqueros, and a decade later became preoccupied with the artistic possibilities offered by polyester resin. He abandoned the use of the resin in 1964 due to severe liver problems caused by its toxicity and became one of the first artists to write about its hazards. In the late sixties, Mallary pioneered computer-generated art.

Suggested Reading:
Robert Mallary's official website, "Robert Mallary," http://www.RobertMallary.com.

Plate 17

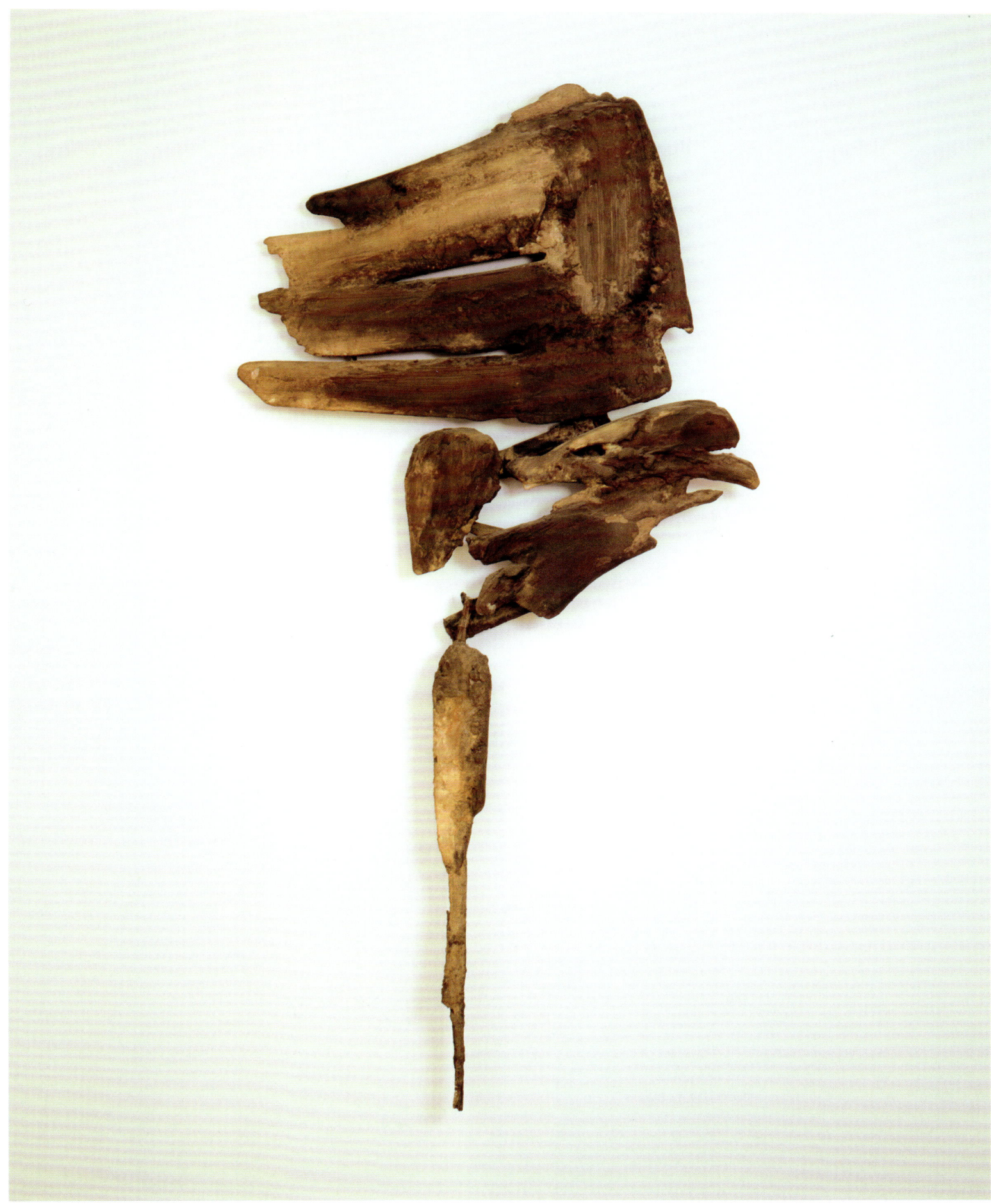

Marisol
Born in Paris, 1930; lives in
New York City

The Large Family Group, 1957
painted wood
37 x 38 x 6 1/2 inches
The Corcoran Gallery of Art,
Washington, DC, Gift of Mr. and
Mrs. C. M. Lewis

Born in Paris to Venezuelan parents, Marisol Escobar studied briefly at the École des Beaux-Arts, Paris, and at the Art Students League in New York, before spending the years 1951-54 at Hans Hofmann's school, during which time she shifted her focus from painting to sculpture. Her sculptures of the mid-fifties were included in the Stable Gallery Annual exhibitions and at the Leo Castelli Gallery in 1957, in her first solo show. These works consisted of tiny, animated clay, bronze, and wood figurines influenced by Pre-Columbian and South American folk art that were set in compartmentalized, glass-fronted boxes.

Also included in the Leo Castelli show was the extraordinary, forward-looking piece, *The Large Family Group* (1957). Apparently inspired by a coffee grinder in the shape of a man, Marisol carved a cluster of five figures, lined up as for a photographic portrait, into a series of weathered wooden boards. Crudely carved, painted, and assembled to simulate naïve or folk art styles, this work anticipated the extended series of freestanding carved and often clothed wooden figures that became her point of focus in 1960. It was with these works that she became a prominent figure (and one of the only female artists) associated with Pop Art.

Suggested Reading:
Grove, Nancy. *Magical Mixtures: Marisol Portrait Sculpture*. Exhibition catalogue. Washington, DC: National Portrait Gallery; Smithsonian Institution Press, 1991.

Plate 18

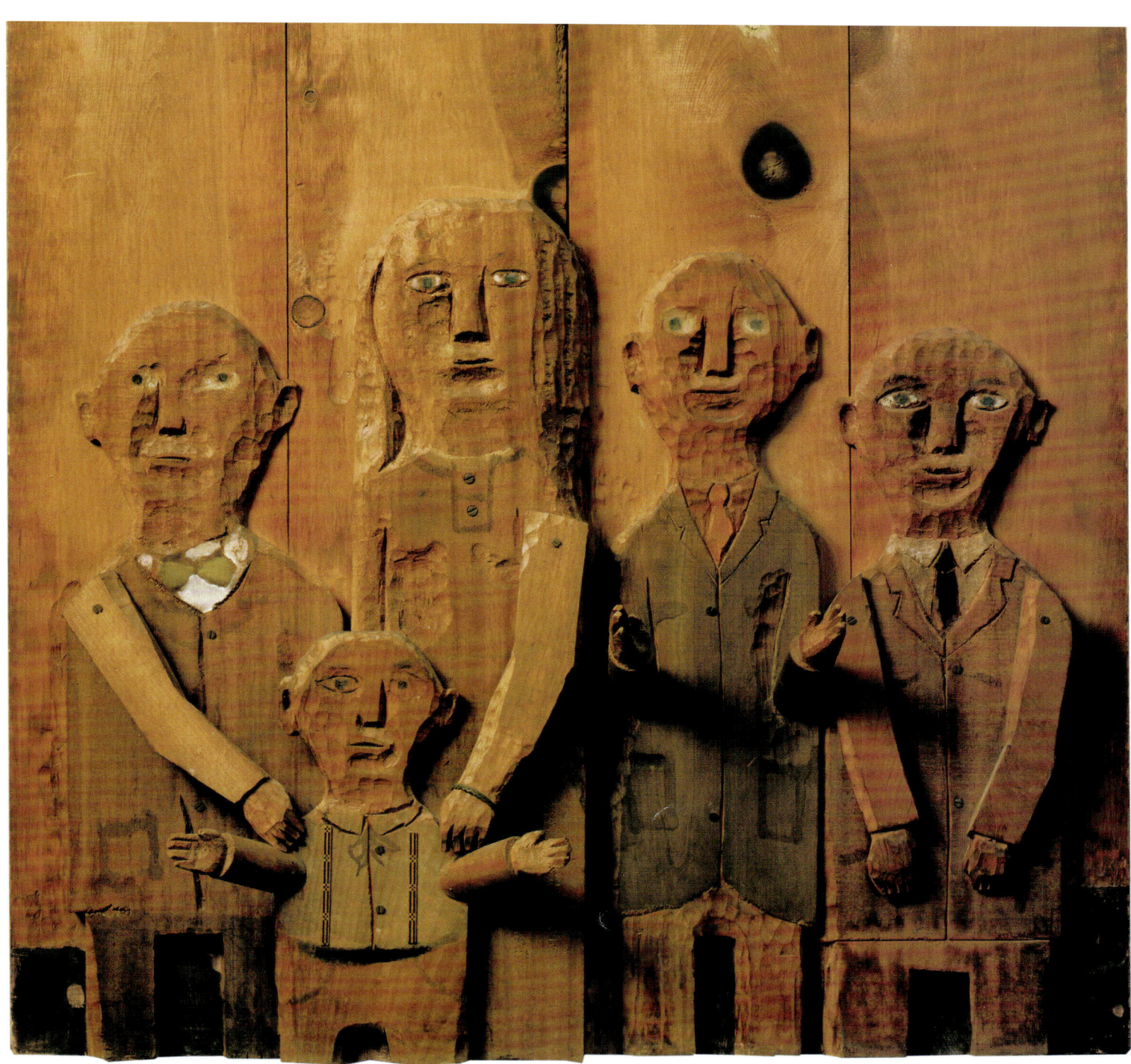

Robert Morris

Born in Kansas City, Missouri, 1931; lives in New York City and Gardner, New York

Box with the Sound of Its Own Making, 1961
(recreated by the artist in 1993)
walnut box, speaker, audio recording
9 1/2 x 9 1/2 x 9 1/2 inches
Collection of the artist

In 1961, Robert Morris moved to New York from San Francisco, where, although schooled in the visual arts, he had spent much time involved with experimental dance and improvisational theatre. One of the first art objects he executed after his arrival in New York was *Box with the Sound of Its Own Making* (1961), which has since been recreated. It is a nine-inch square wooden box that contains a three-hour tape recording of its actual construction, sounds of hammering and nailing punctuated by quieter periods of measuring and fitting. This concept- and process-oriented object was influenced, as was much of Morris' early work, by the art and thought of Marcel Duchamp, particularly such works as his 1916 sculpture *With a Hidden Noise*, a small Assemblage into which an unidentified object was inserted, so that it rattles when shaken. Tellingly, the first person Morris invited to view his sculpture was John Cage, who sat and listened to the piece for its three-hour duration, as he appreciated its theatrical nature and the fact that, like the art he advocated, it was composed of the stuff of life. By 1962, Morris was creating plywood sculptures, most of them painted gray and in box form, which he set in various situations within the space of a gallery. In these pieces, which made him a leading figure in Minimal Art, Morris took the performative or theatrical aspect away from the art object, as found in *Box with the Sound of Its Own Making*, and made it a function of the viewer's physical interaction with the work.

Suggested Reading:
Robert Morris: The Mind-Body Problem. Exhibition catalogue. New York: Solomon R. Guggenheim Museum, 1994.

Plate 19

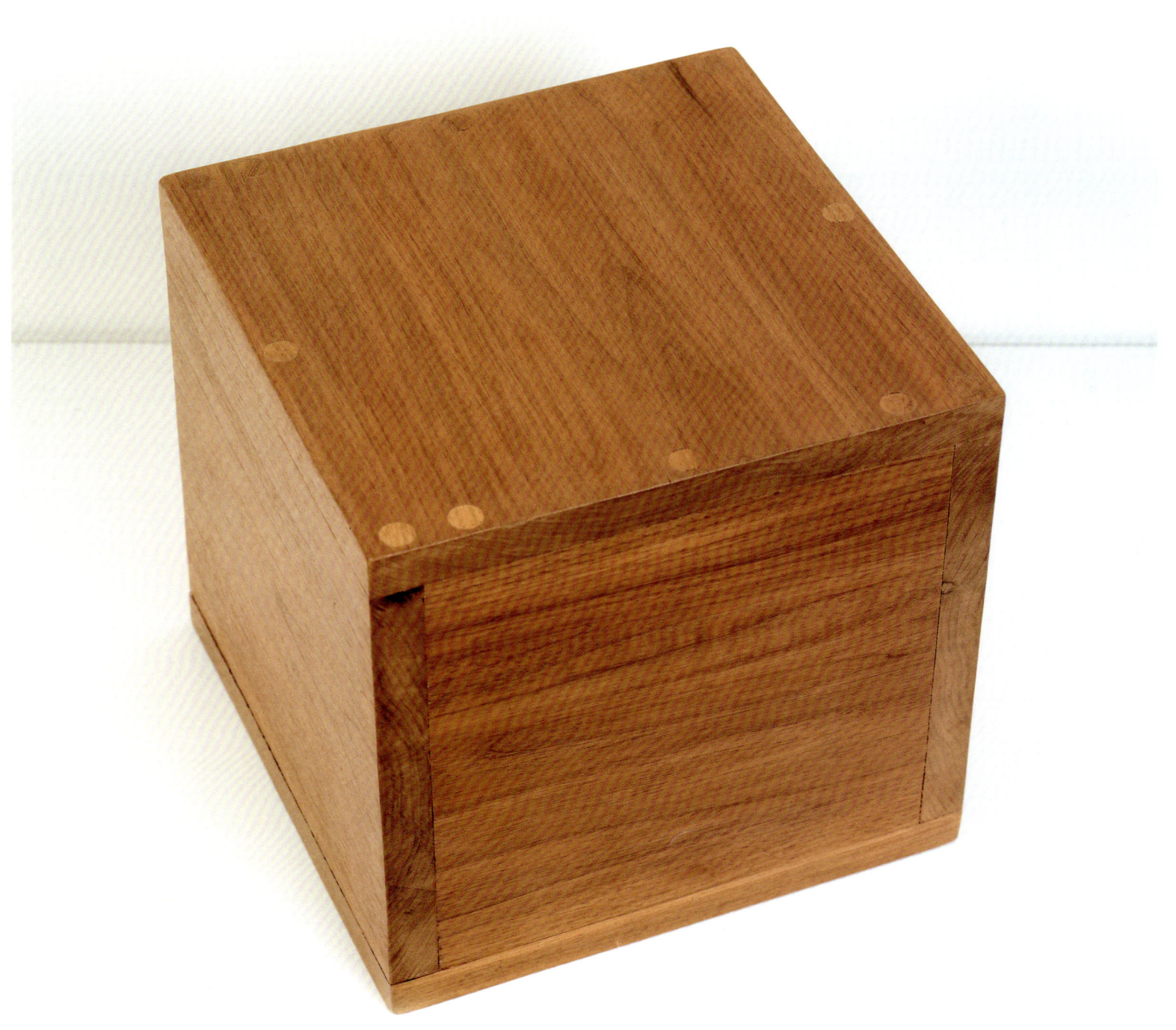

Louise Nevelson
Kiev, Russia
1899 – 1988
New York City

Distant Cathedral, 1955
wood painted black
47 x 24 x 18 inches
Courtesy PaceWildenstein

Born in Kiev, Russia in 1899, Nevelson was raised in Rockland, Maine, where her father owned a lumberyard. Although she created sculptures using a wide range of materials during the early years of her career, in her exhibition *Ancient Games, Ancient Places*, held at the Grand Central Moderns Gallery, New York, in 1955, she showed a number of tabletop-scale assemblages consisting of black-painted, found wooden elements, as exemplified by *Distant Cathedral* (1955). From this point on, Nevelson made exclusive use of discarded wooden furniture parts and scraps in her work, making her a pioneering figure in "junk sculpture" or Assemblage. Her work in the mid-fifties was inspired by travels to archeological sites in Mexico and Central America; there, she saw architecture and sculpture infused with spirit and magic, which she sought to capture in her own work, as the upward-reaching "Gothic" forms and title of *Distant Cathedral* implies. In 1958, she extended this concept in her first room-scale Environment, *Moon Garden + One*, in which stacked wooden boxes filled with found wood relief groupings lined the walls and stood in the center of the room. Nevelson exploited the mystery and spiritual intensity of black in her work until the *Sixteen Americans* exhibition of 1959, when she showed her first white-painted Environment.

Suggested Reading:
Rapaport, Brooke Kamin, ed. *The Sculpture of Louise Nevelson: Constructing a Legend*. Exhibition catalogue. New York: The Jewish Museum; New Haven: Yale University Press, 2007.

Plate 20

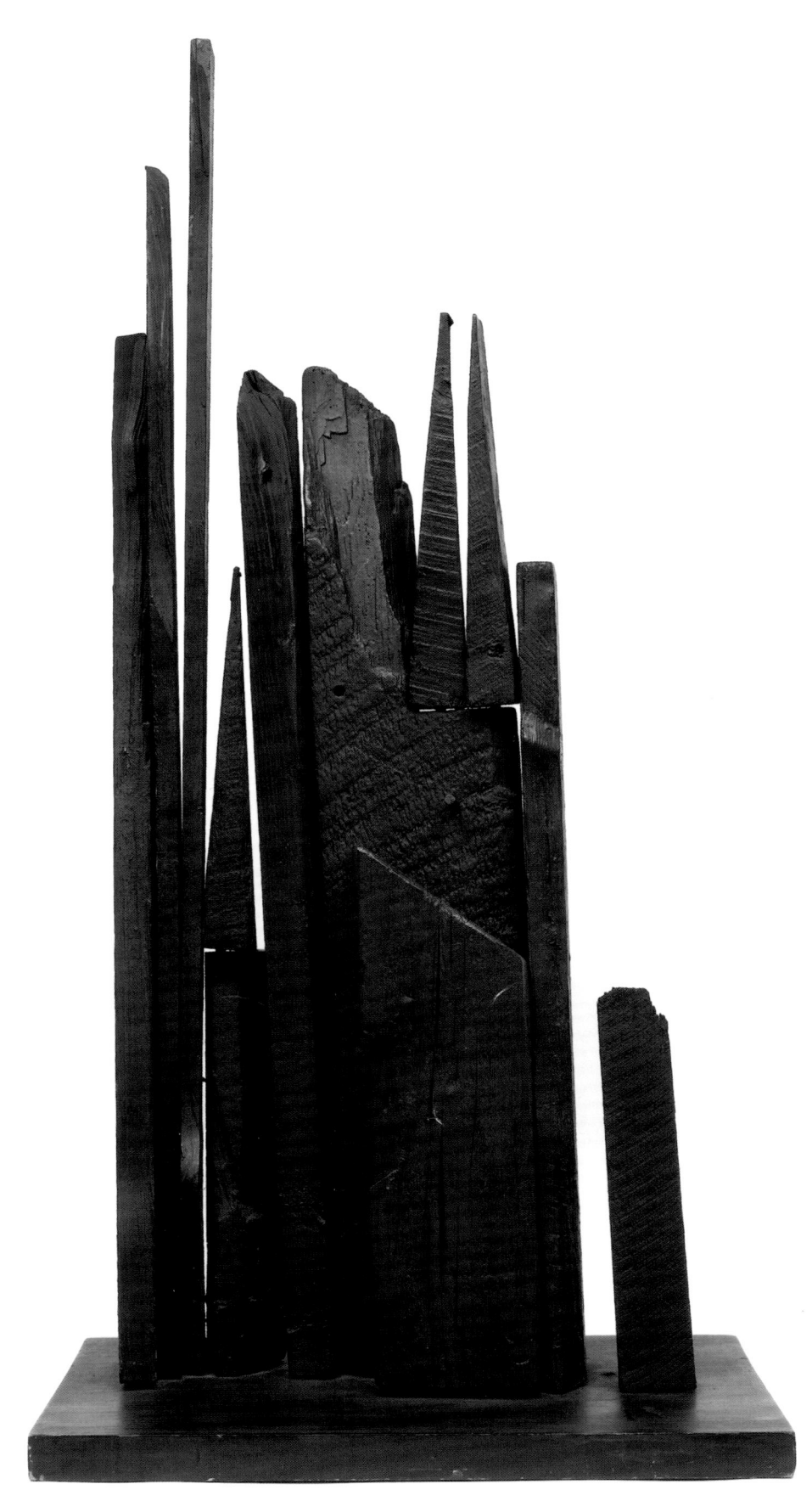

Claes Oldenburg
Born in Stockholm, Sweden,
1929; lives in New York City

(left top)
The Old Dump Flag, 1960
wood
8 3/4 x 10 3/4 inches
Claes Oldenburg
and Coosje van Bruggen

(left bottom)
Heel Flag, 1960
heel, nails, wood, rope
7 3/4 x 9 1/2 x 1 1/2 in box 13
1/4 x 14 1/2 x 1 3/4 inches
Claes Oldenburg
and Coosje van Bruggen

(right)
Left-Handed Flag, 1960
wood and nails
17 1/2 x 12 x 1 7/8 inches
Claes Oldenburg
and Coosje van Bruggen

Born in Stockholm, the son of a diplomat, Claes Oldenburg studied literature and art history at Yale University in New Haven, before conducting formal art studies at the Art Institute of Chicago from 1950-54. He moved to New York in 1956 and soon became acquainted with Allan Kaprow, Jim Dine, Red Grooms, and others who were moving their art from Assemblages to Environments and Happenings.

Oldenburg's gritty installation of crudely assembled forms, *The Street*, was presented at the Judson Gallery from February to March 1960 and served as the setting for his first Happening, *Snapshots from the City*, an expressionistic performance piece that focused on the hardships of slum life. During the summer of 1960, Oldenburg worked as a dishwasher in Provincetown, Massachusetts, on Cape Cod, and the relaxed atmosphere of the beach town brought about a change of orientation in his art. Collecting driftwood and other debris, he created a series of "Provincetown flags," sensitive, weather-beaten reliefs based on the design of the American flag, which owes less to the precedent offered by the work of Jasper Johns than to the collages of the early American Modernist Arthur Dove as well as to American folk art. These pieces, some of which were exhibited in Provincetown galleries that summer, also owed their inspiration to picture postcards and souvenir items ubiquitous in the Cape that sought to commercialize on American history and patriotic feeling. Upon his return to New York in the fall, Oldenburg began to create upbeat plaster reliefs and freestanding sculptures painted with shiny enamel paint of flags, clothing, and food items, which he showed in *The Store* in 1961 (page 9, fig. 7), an actual storefront in which art representing consumer items was offered as commodity.

Suggested Reading:
Claes Oldenburg: An Anthology. Exhibition catalogue. New York: Solomon R. Guggenheim Museum, 1995.

Rose, Barbara. *Claes Oldenburg*. Exhibition catalogue. New York: Museum of Modern Art, 1970. Greenwich, Connecticut. Distributed by New York Graphic Society.

Plate 21
Plate 22
Plate 23

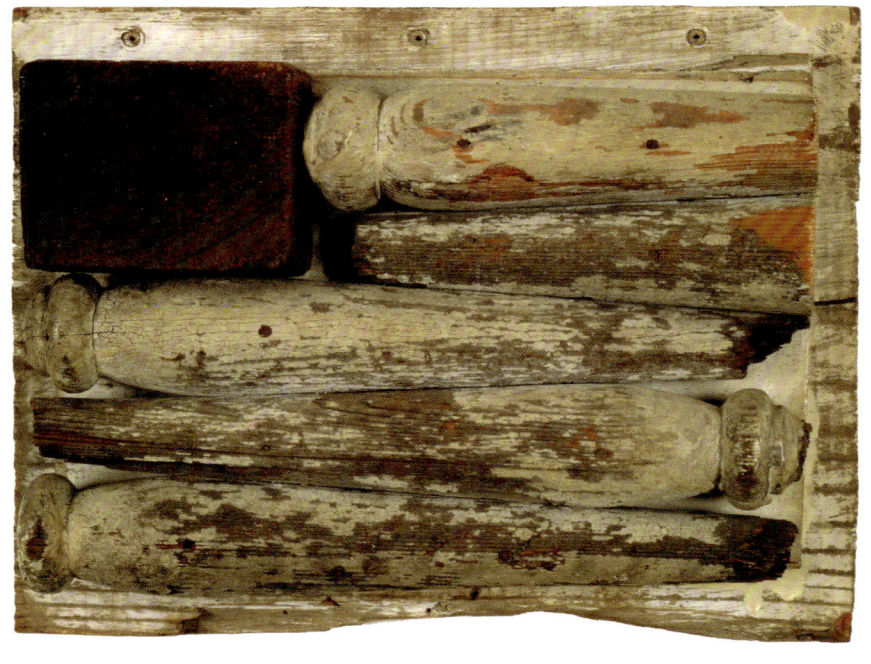

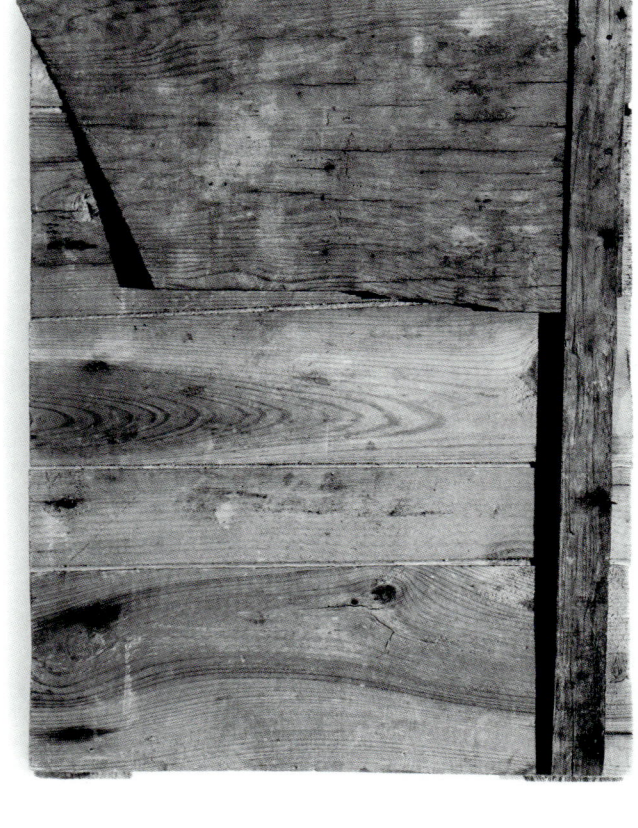

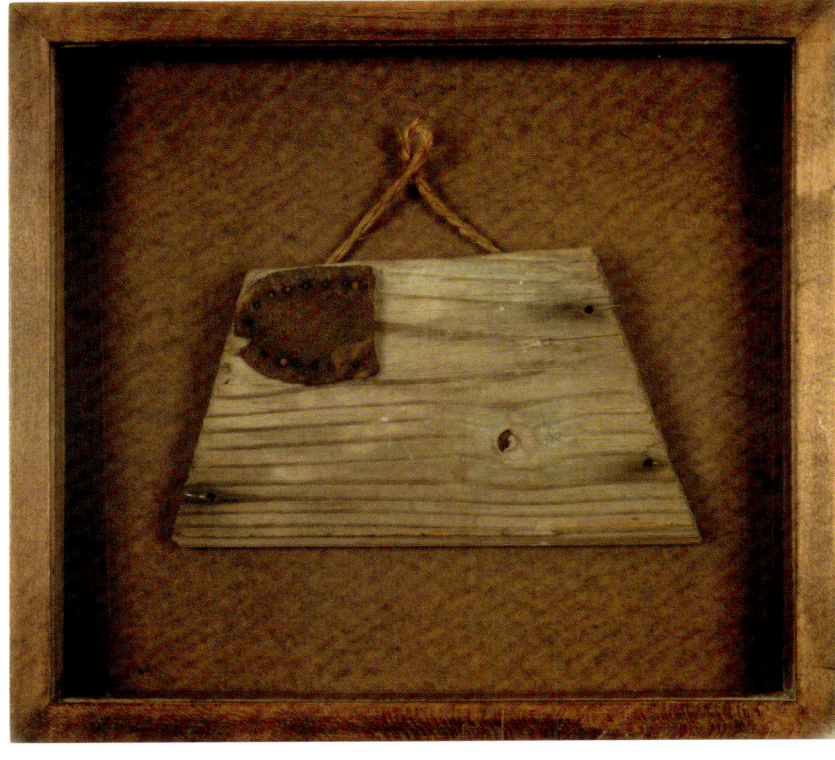

Yoko Ono
Born in Tokyo, Japan 1933; lives
in Colorado

Painting to Hammer a Nail,
1961/1966
painted wood panel, nails,
container for the nails, painted
wood-handled hammer, chain,
and a white painted chair
approx. 13 3/4 x 10 1/2 x 4 1/2
inches
version illustrated:
Collection of the artist
Realized in 2008 with permission
from the artist

A multimedia artist, composer, and musician, Yoko Ono was born into a prominent Japanese banking family and spent her childhood living in both America and Japan. During the late fifties, she became involved with the avant-garde art and music communities in New York and from December 1960 through June 1961 she hosted a series of performances in her downtown loft that included work by LaMonte Young, Jackson Mac Low, Robert Morris, and herself, all of whom were soon to be involved with the Dada- and John Cage-inspired Fluxus movement consisting of everyday objects and events presented with the utmost economy (in contrast to the excesses of Assemblage and Happenings). Also in 1961 was a solo exhibition of her concept-based "Instruction Paintings" and calligraphic drawing at Fluxus founder George Maciunas' AG Gallery, New York, and a concert of her musical work at Carnegie Hall. *Painting to Hammer a Nail* (1961/1996), recreated for this exhibition, is an "Instruction Painting" dating to 1961. It is a manifestation of the following concept, later published in her book *Grapefruit* (1964), which was a compilation of her instructions and scores.

Painting to Hammer a Nail

Hammer a nail into a mirror, a piece of glass, a canvas, wood or metal every morning. Also, pick up a hair that came off when you combed in the morning and tie it around the hammered nail. The painting ends when the surface is covered with nails.

y.o.
1961 winter

Although the addition of a hair is called for, this is generally not included as part of the piece. Ono, however, explained the importance of the hair as follows: "Japanese temples have a place for you to tie wish knots, in the case of this painting the wish knot is tied with your hair."*

For *Circa 1958*, Ono approved a construction that included mirror foil, wood, nails, and other materials. This variation appeared in the exhibition only and is not illustrated in this catalogue.

Suggested Reading:
*Monroe, Alexandra and Jon Hendricks. *Yes Yoko Ono*. Exhibition catalogue. New York: Japan Society; Harry N. Abrams, Inc., 2001.

Plate 24

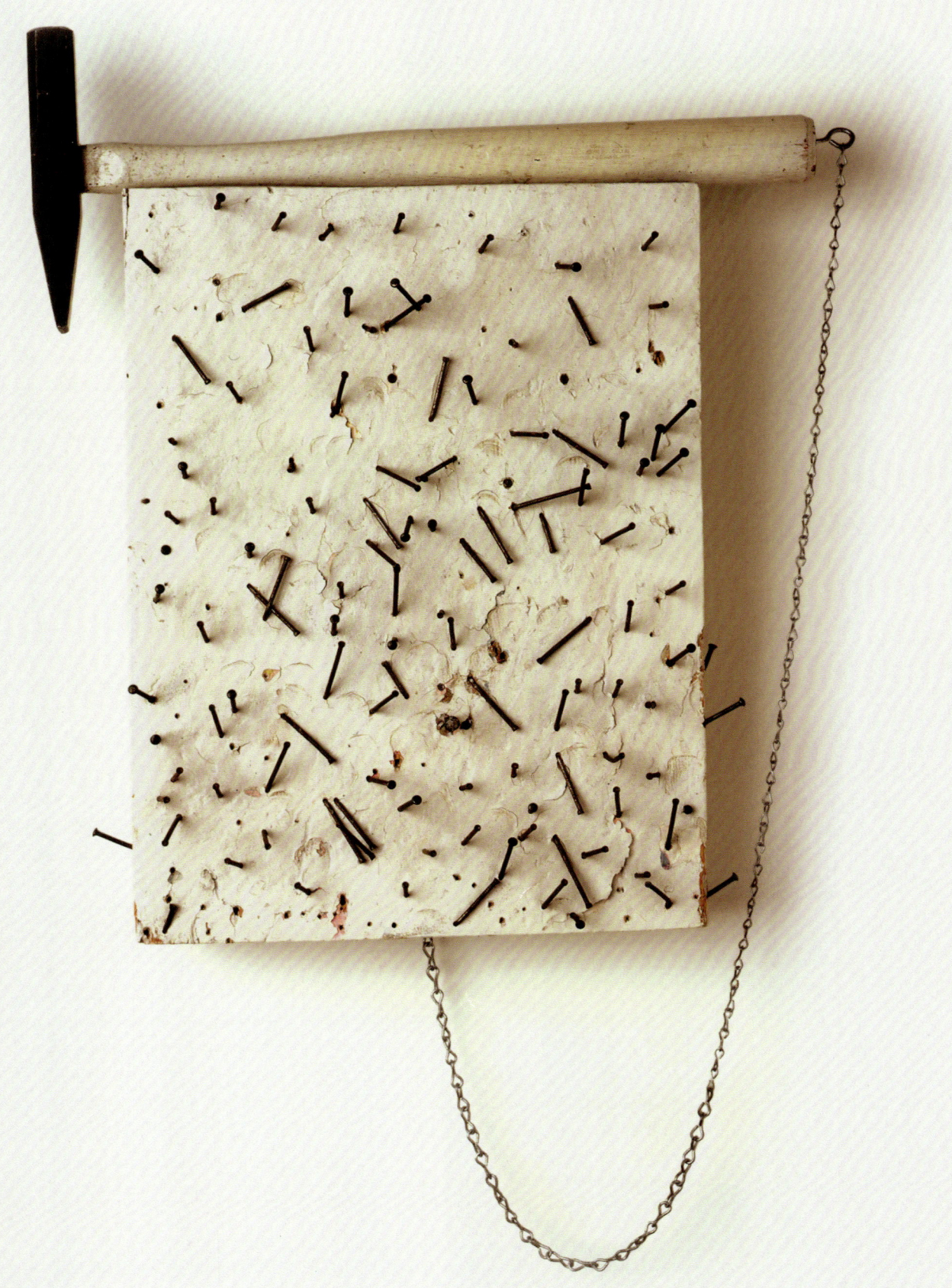

Robert Rauschenberg
Port Arthur, Texas
1925 – 2008
Captiva Island, Florida

Painting with Grey Wing, 1959
Combine: oil, printed reproductions, unpainted paint by number board, typed print on paper, photographs, fabric, stuffed bird wing, and dime on canvas
31 3/4 x 21 1/2 x 2 1/2 inches
The Museum of Contemporary Art, Los Angeles
The Panza Collection

Slow Fall, 1961
Combine: oil, metal, fabric, newspaper, nineteenth-century nail on board with crushed can, string, cola can, lead weight, nail, and milk carton
56 1/2 x 21 x 12 inches
The Museum of Contemporary Art, Los Angeles
The Panza Collection

A leading figure in Assemblage Art, Robert Rauschenberg is widely recognized as having effected the transition between Abstract Expressionism and Pop Art through his "Combines" of 1954-62. These were an extended series of works (so-called because they "combined" aspects of painting and sculpture) in which all manner of objects and materials of the real world were introduced into the context of painting. As is ably demonstrated in the small but extraordinary *Painting with Grey Wing* (1959), the Combines did not offer random accumulations of the stuff of life, but brilliantly orchestrated assemblies of interlocking thoughts, associations, and formal ideas which extend in myriad, unfathomable directions. The grey wing of the title, which recalls numerous previous works by Rauschenberg that incorporate stuffed birds and fowl in their entirety, is lanced to the surface with rope, whose shape and color are echoed to the right and below in thin drips of orange paint. The bound wing seems to bear a relation to the image of a woman in a writhing posture seen in a photograph below, although it is in actuality a photograph of Rauschenberg's one-time wife, the artist Susan Weil, pregnant with their son, leaning against a tree. Her striped dress and posture are cat-like and to her left is an uncolored, paint-by-numbers page featuring the image of tigers. To her right is a reproduction of a fragment of a Francisco de Goya etching showing a man in flight with a pair of strapped-on wings, which, together with the old Mercury dime attached to the canvas above, point to the theme of flight and the pinioned wing. *Painting with Grey Wing* is replete with other objects, images, and painterly touches and details, the work serving as an invitation for viewers to participate in the work with their eyes and minds.

During the 1960-61 period, significant changes occurred in the nature, form, and content of the Combines, among the most notable being the artist's move toward painterly painting (looking directly back to Abstract Expressionist handling) on the one hand and toward sculpture on the other. In *Slow Fall* (1961), in which a large, crumpled piece of metal is suspended in front of a gesturally painted wooden support, these factors go hand in hand. Also typical of Rauschenberg's later Combines is that fact that flat elements of collage, like pasted papers and photographic images, have disappeared from this work in favor of tangible objects, such as the half-pint milk carton and tin can hanging from a string. Physical values, such as movement and gravitational force, were now of greater interest to the artist than the specificity of content (the concern with reading and meaning) seen in *Painting with Grey Wing*. Allusive content here, however, continues to play a part as the crumpled metal seems to represent a waterfall or cascade, an interpretation reinforced by the title as well as by the frothy blue strokes of paint on the wall-mounted support.

Suggested Reading:
Feinstein, Roni. "Random Order: The First Fifteen Years of Robert Rauschenberg's Art, 1949-1964." PhD diss. New York University, 1990.

Schimmel, Paul. *Robert Rauschenberg Combines*. Exhibition catalogue. Los Angeles: The Museum of Contemporary Art, 2005.

Plate 25
Plate 26

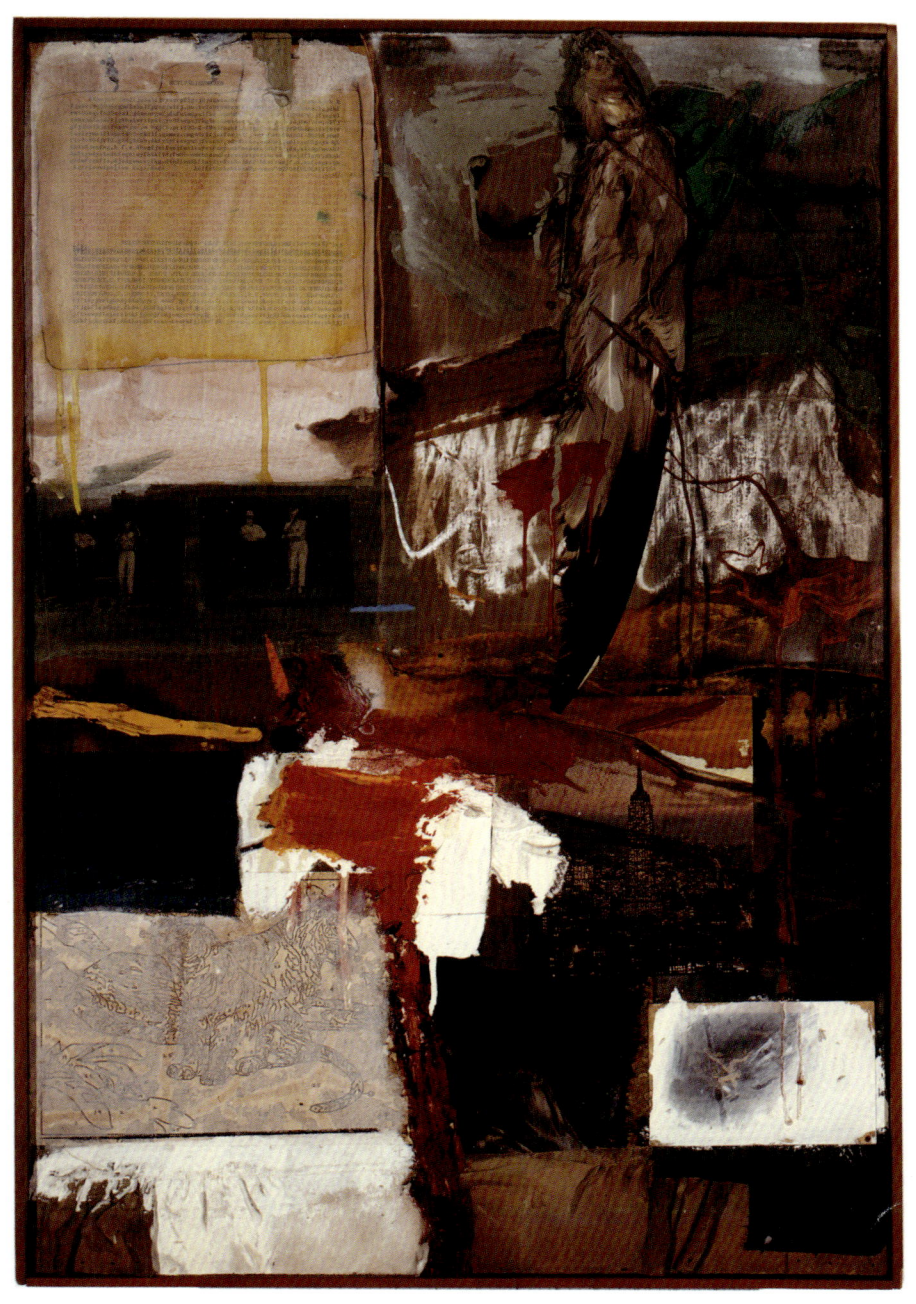
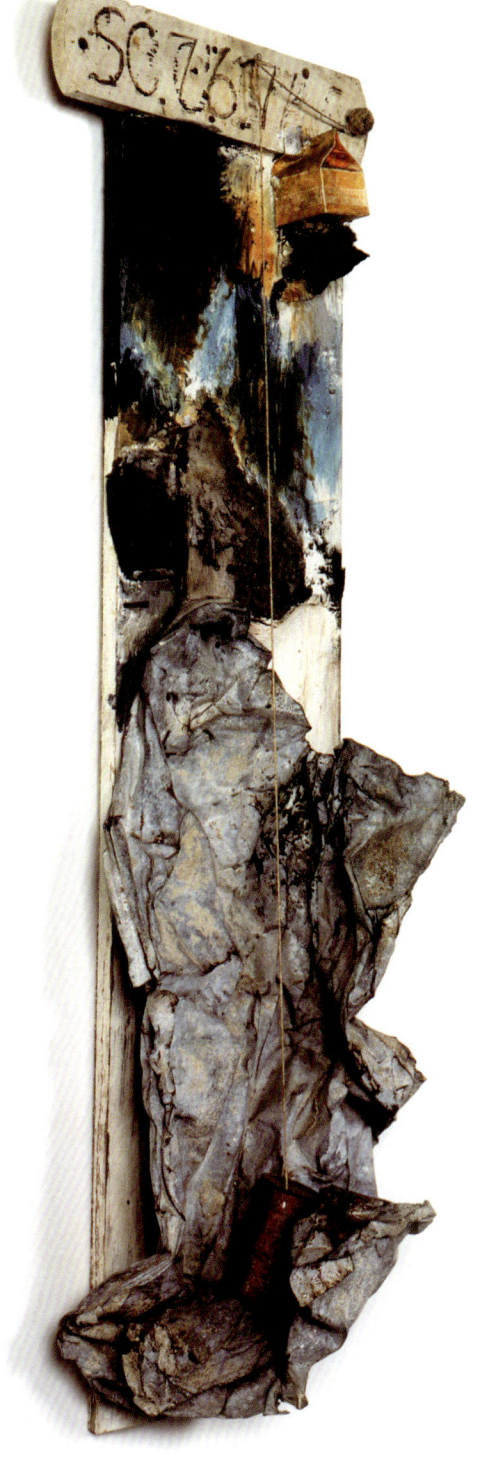

James Rosenquist
Born in Grand Forks, North
Dakota, 1933; lives in Aripeka,
Florida, and New York City

Coenties Slip Studio, 1961
oil on shaped canvas
34 x 43 inches
Collection of the artist

In the early 1960s, influenced by his experience painting commercial billboards, James Rosenquist developed a style of painting in which images drawn from mass media sources, rendered as fragments and on colossal scale, are brought together on large canvases. His use of commercial techniques to render popular images made him a leading figure in Pop Art. Unlike most Pop artists, who tended to focus on single images, Rosenquist, like Rauschenberg before him, exploited the formal and thematic relationships between several images that were complexly juxtaposed so as to generate plays of space, scale, color (and non-color), and form. As the artist has indicated, these pictures "tell stories," although determining the nature of these "stories" is the job of the viewer, whose observations and associations bring meaning to the work.

The early painting, *Coenties Slip Studio* (1961), departs from the artist's usual practice of using found sources in that it offers a personal image—a view reflected in the enlarged spoon of the interior of his studio in the famed artist's neighborhood in lower Manhattan. A fork is positioned above, and to its left is an image fragment that has hitherto defied interpretation, although the artist recently revealed it to be "snow-covered cars."* Attached to the canvas to the right is a representation of a length of a woman's hair painted on a canvas formed to correspond to the fall of the hair, which is one of the first instances of a shaped canvas in Rosenquist's art. The hair is painted black, white, and shades of gray, as is the image of the cars, so that the work is bracketed by *grisaille*; in the center, the spoon, a fork, and a "sunny side up" egg offer a subtle play on the primary colors (the spoon being reddish in tone and the fork a muted blue). The hair insinuates a woman's presence into the space of the studio. It is left to the viewer to speculate on her role.

Suggested Reading:
Hopps, Walter and Sarah Bancroft. *James Rosenquist: A Retrospective*. Exhibition catalogue. New York: Guggenheim Museum Publications, 2003.

*Telephone conversation with Roni Feinstein and Michael Findlay, director, Acquavella Gallery, New York, February 2008.

Plate 27

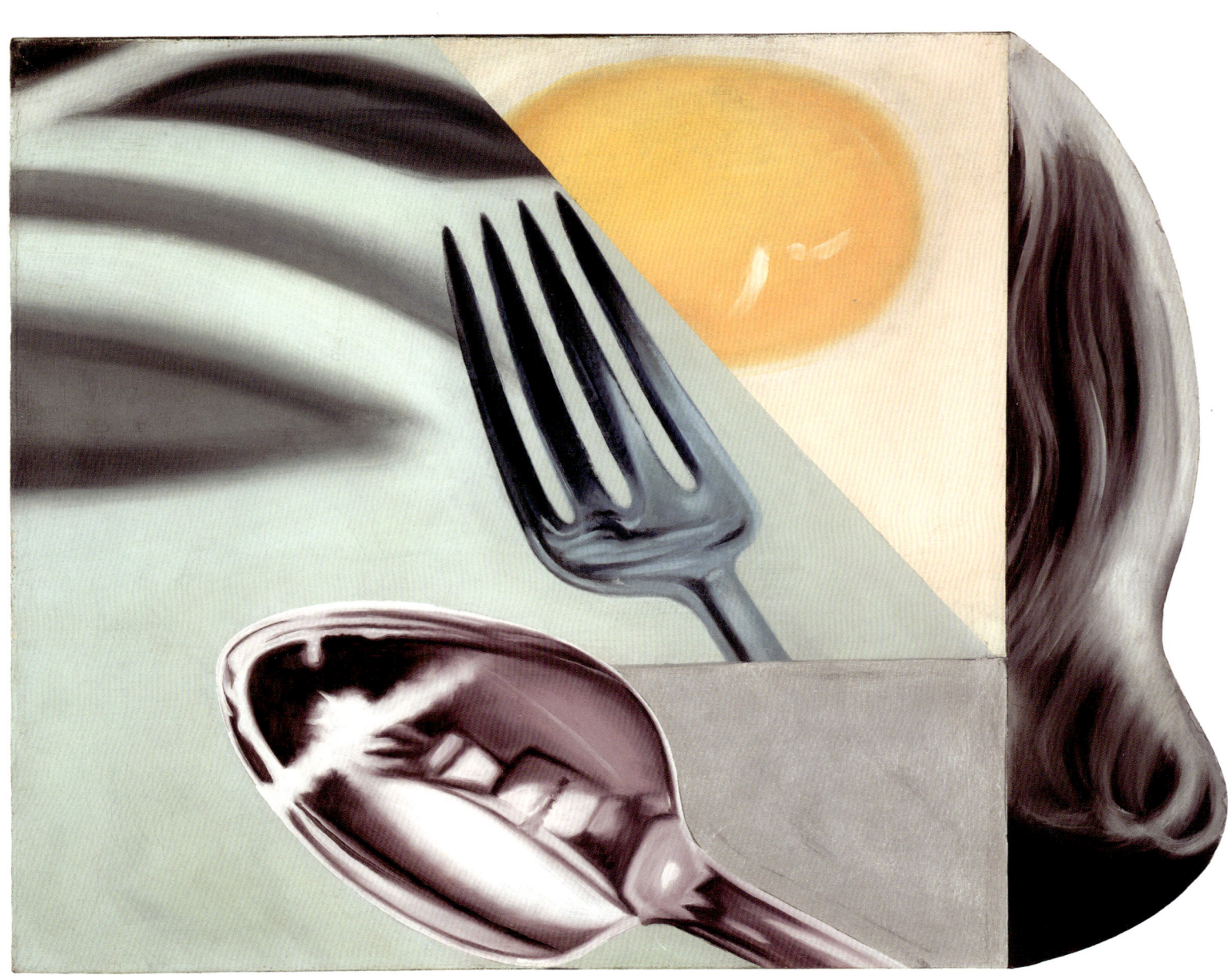

Ed Ruscha
Born in Omaha, Nebraska, 1937;
lives in Los Angeles, California

E. Ruscha, 1959
oil on canvas
45 1/4 x 45 1/4 inches
Courtesy of Ed Ruscha

Ed Ruscha once told an interviewer, "When I first became attracted to the idea of being an artist, painting was the last method, it was an almost obsolete, archaic form of communication . . . . I felt newspapers, magazines, books, words, to be more meaningful than what some damn oil painter was doing."*

Ruscha went on to become a painter who revitalized this "archaic form of communication" by creating an art focused on words. After completing high school in Oklahoma City, Ruscha moved to Los Angeles, where he attended the Chouinard Art Institute from 1956-1960 (now California Institute of Arts), with the intention of becoming a commercial artist. Exposure to the art of Jasper Johns and Robert Rauschenberg caused him to shift directions and to rethink the Abstract Expressionist painting with which he was then involved. *E. Ruscha* (1959), one of his first paintings to focus on language, was a student work. It takes as its subject the artist's name, which is rendered in large capital letters split onto two differently scaled lines, a painted arrow indicating the directional flow. In light of its prosaic subject matter, the whole embraces irony and low-key humor in the manner in which it is lusciously and expressionistically brushed, the letters of the artist's name silhouetted against an open airy space, recalling the famous Hollywood sign found in Ruscha's adopted city. Ruscha, who had his first solo show at the Ferus Gallery, Los Angeles, in 1963, was included the year before in *New Paintings of Common Objects*, organized by Walter Hopps for the Pasadena Museum, the first museum exhibition devoted to what was soon to be labeled "Pop Art."

Suggested Reading:
Marshall, Richard. *Ed Ruscha*. London, New York: Phaidon, 2003.

*Ruscha quoted in Paul J. Kalrstrom, *Interview with Edward Ruscha*, California Oral History Project, Archives of American Art, Smithsonian Institution, Washington, DC, 1980-81.

Plate 28

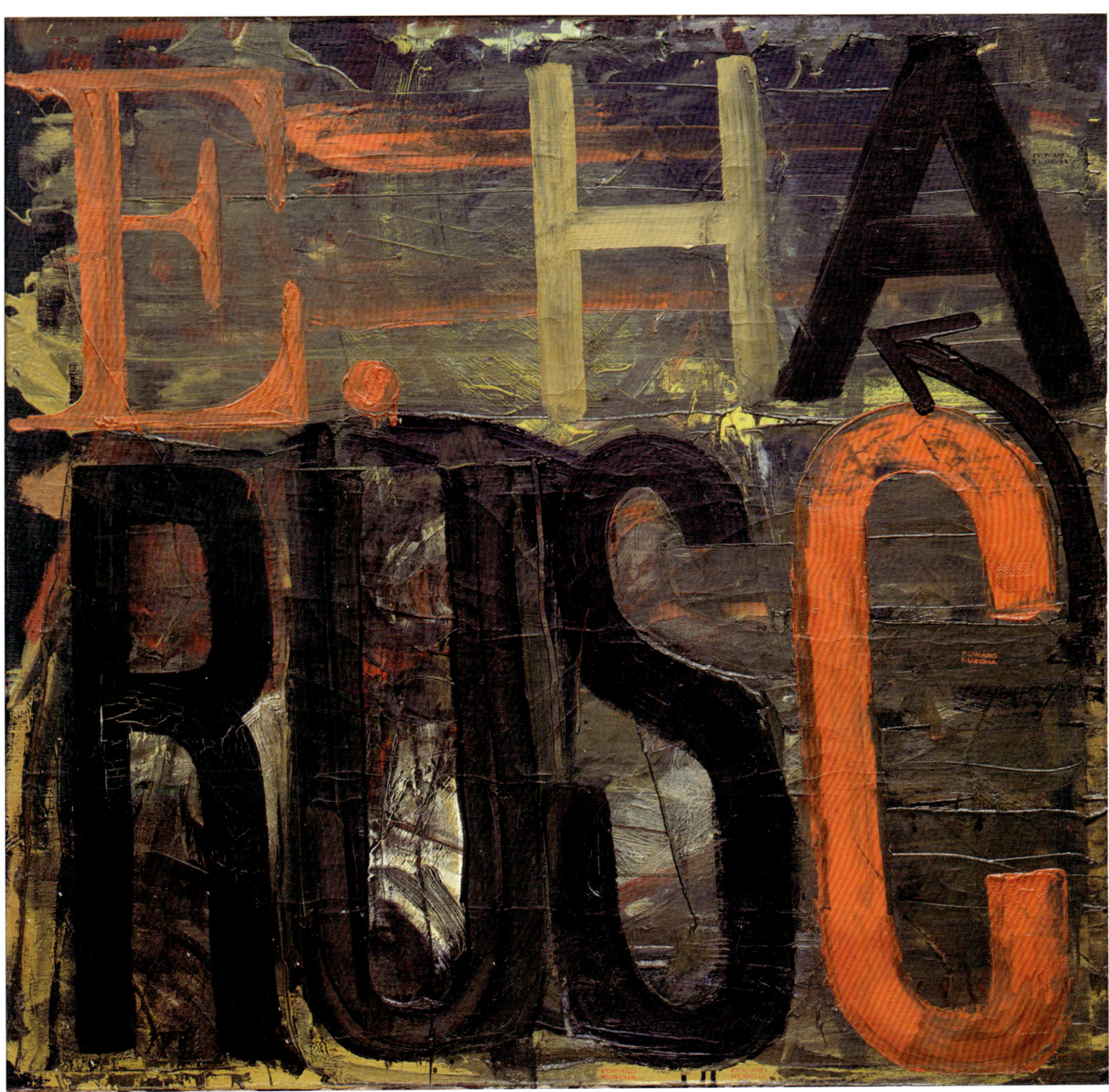

Lucas Samaras

Born in Kastoria, Macedonia, Greece, 1936; lives in New York City

Pin Box, 1963
construction with box, pins, glass, jar, and wool
12 x 19 x 10 inches
The Robert B. Mayer Family Collection, Chicago

Raised in West New York, New Jersey, Lucas Samaras attended Rutgers University on a scholarship from 1955-59. During this time Allan Kaprow, an enthusiastic supporter of his work, was the acting head of the art department. Although Samaras worked predominantly in pastel at this time, he experimented with a wide range of materials and also pursued an interest in acting, which served him well in 1959 when he moved to New York to study art history at Columbia University and became a performer in Happenings staged by Kaprow, Oldenburg, Dine, Grooms, and others at the Reuben Gallery. Samaras exhibited pastels and his last paintings at the Reuben Gallery in 1959 and in 1960 exhibited one of his new, assembled box sculptures in *New Form-New Media II* at the Martha Jackson Gallery.

Samaras had begun to make box sculptures during the summer of 1960, in the earliest of which plaster, crêpe paper, and other materials were used to create faces that were framed by the rectangular edges of the box. Soon, however, the figurative dimension disappeared and the extended series of boxes, which numbered over 135, were filled with dense accumulations of found objects, most especially pins, razor blades, pieces of glass, yarn, and jewels to simultaneously attract and repel the viewer's imagined touch. The remarkable *Pin Box* (1963) is a shallow box with an open-frame top whose edges are entirely trimmed with meticulously aligned straight pins. The interior is encrusted with straight pins oriented in every direction, which rise to form a mound on the right side of the box. This mound is offset to the left by a shallow, frosted jar, whose lid lifts to reveal a "nest of eggs" (balls formed of different materials like yarn, tin foil, paper, and silver metal) set on a bed of pins. Such works by Samaras differed from the Assemblages of his colleagues in that they were focused on particular types of objects and were highly fetishistic in nature, focused on an iconography of violence, eroticism, and the physical self, which have been enduring themes in Samaras' theatrical, experience-oriented art.

Suggested Reading:
Levin, Kim. *Lucas Samaras*. New York: Harry N. Abrams, Inc., 1975.

Plate 29

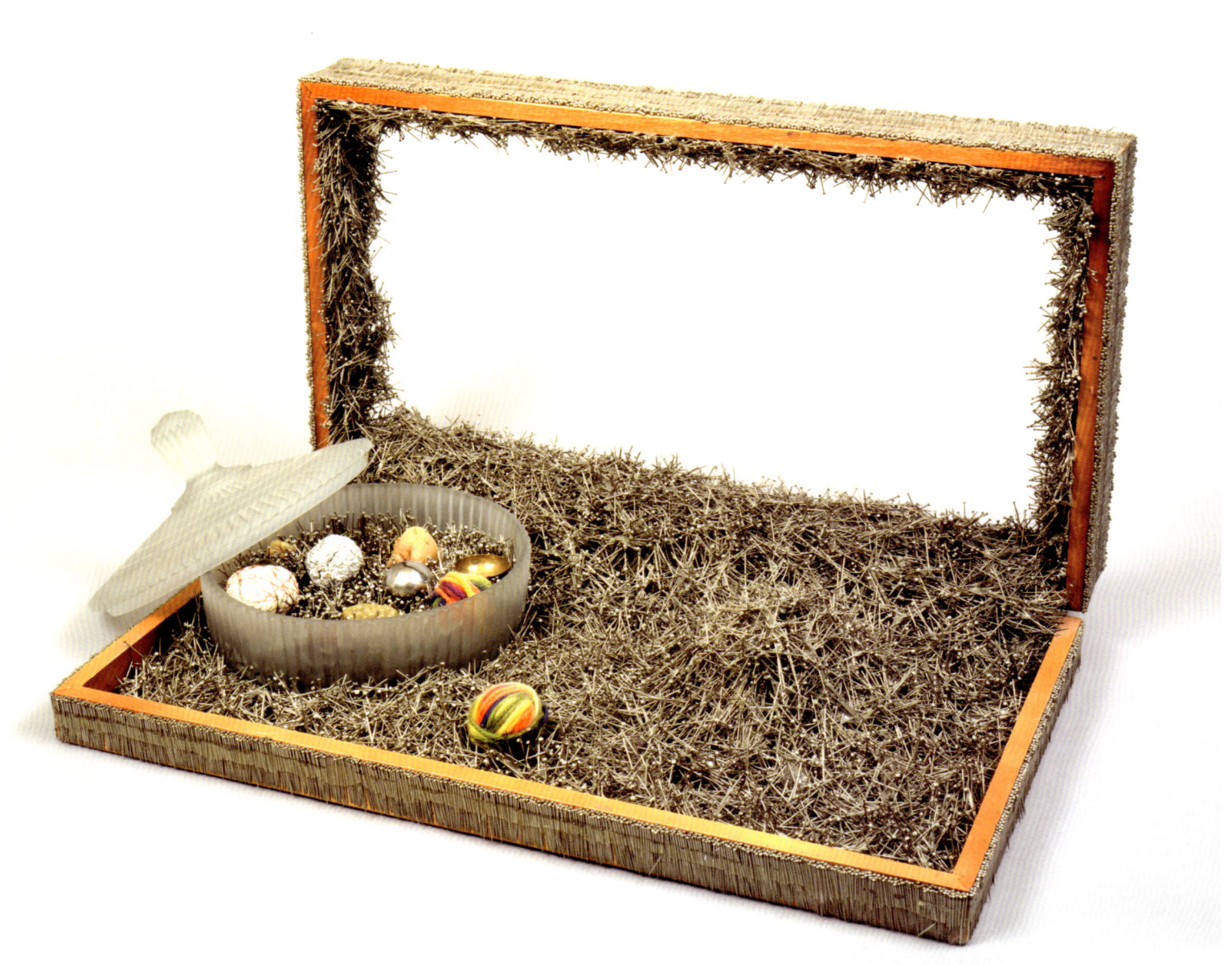

George Segal
New York City
1924 – 2000
Trenton, New Jersey

The Legend of Lot, 1958
plaster, wood, chicken wire,
wood base, and oil on canvas
Overall: 74 x 96 x 66 inches;
Painting: 72 x 96 inches;
Figure: 72 inches high
Courtesy of the George and
Helen Segal Foundation, Inc.
and Carroll Janis, Inc.

As an art education student at New York University in the late forties, George Segal frequented the Eighth Street Club and grew to admire the Abstract Expressionists who spoke about "exteriorizing inner realities" and whose art had muscularity, passion, and philosophical depth. Segal's own painting through the course of the fifties was executed in a figurative expressionist mode devoted largely to the female nude. To support himself and his family, Segal operated a chicken farm in New Brunswick, New Jersey, and in 1953 met Allan Kaprow, who was teaching at Rutgers University and had a house nearby. Kaprow introduced Segal to the cooperative Hansa Gallery, where Segal subsequently had yearly one-man shows, from 1956 to 1959. In the fourth and last of these, Segal exhibited his first works incorporating sculptural elements, among them *The Legend of Lot* (1958), based on the sorrowful Old Testament tale.

This work features a large painted canvas with loosely brushed and drawn life-sized figures in front of which stands the tormented and ravaged Lot, his schematically drawn counterpart seen on the painting behind him at the left. The sculpted figure was modeled in plaster over a wood and chicken wire armature. Segal's decision to move his work into literal space grew both out of a point of crisis he had reached in his painting regarding the handling of space—should it preserve flatness or portray illusionistic depth?—and out of his awareness of the Environments and Happenings of his contemporaries, one of Kaprow's first Happenings having taken place at Segal's chicken farm in the summer of that same year. Over the course of the next few years, Segal exhibited either paintings or rough plaster sculptures (the two forms no longer conjoined), until his breakthrough came in July 1961 with his discovery of the direct casting method. From this point, Segal cast human figures from life using plaster-soaked bandages. He set the figures in environmental tableaux that evoked contemporary experience, which caused his work to be associated with Pop Art, while continuing to explore their humanity and "inner realities."

Suggested Reading:
van der Marck, Jan. *George Segal*. New York: Harry N. Abrams, 1975.

Plate 30

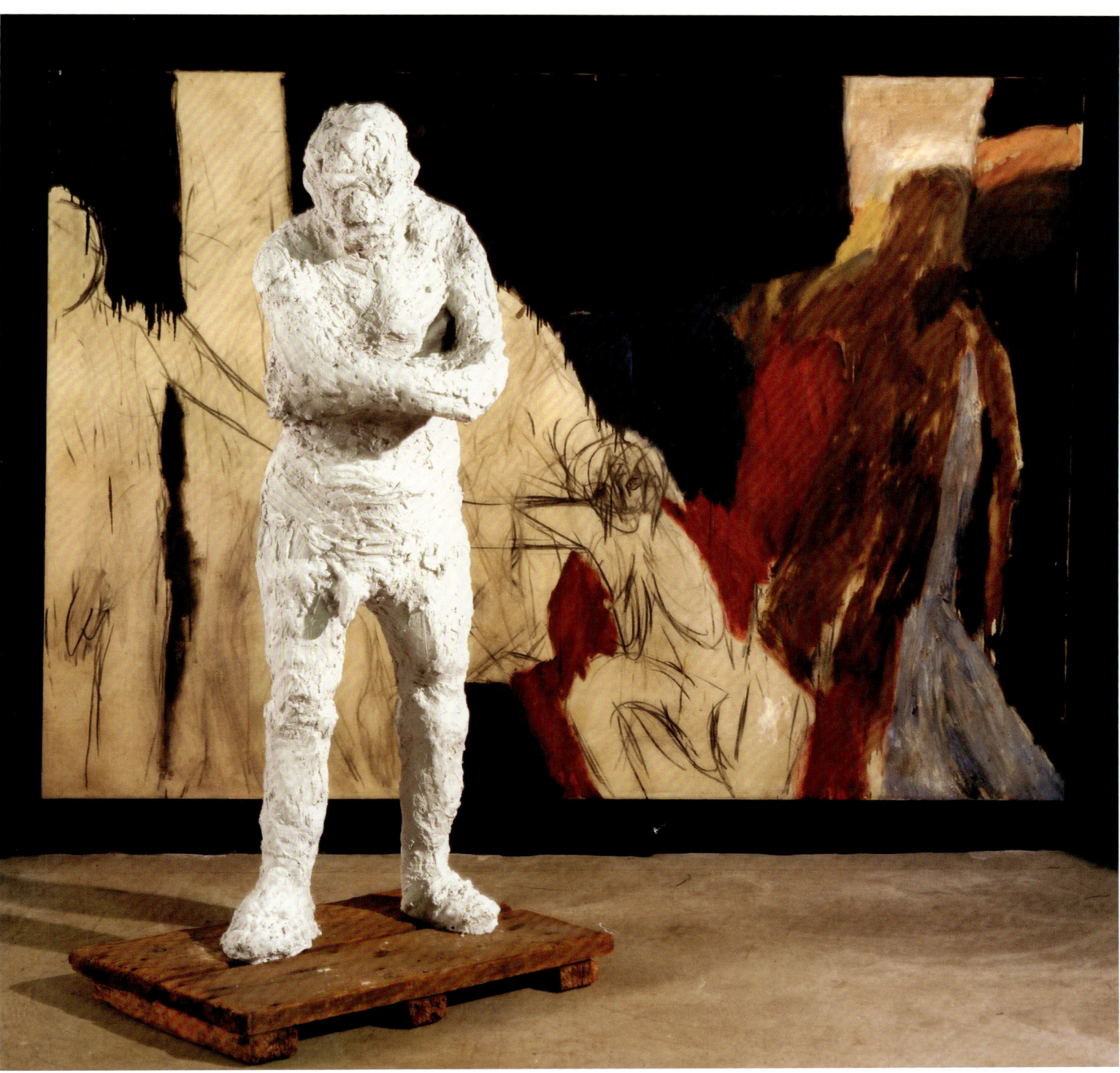

Richard Stankiewicz
Philadelphia, Pennsylvania
1922 – 1983
Worthington, Massachusetts

Railroad Urchin (1959-20), 1959
steel
51 x 41 x 20 inches
Zabriskie Gallery

Richard Stankiewicz studied with Hans Hofmann in New York in the late 1940s and with Fernand Leger and Ossip Zadkine in Paris (on the GI Bill) in the early fifties. Upon his return to New York in 1952, he was among the Hansa Gallery's founding members. One year later, Stankiewicz began to create figurative sculptures by welding together rusted and corroded industrial materials. Leaving the identity of his materials intact, he simultaneously transformed them into works of high formal order, intelligence, and whimsy. Although his work found antecedents in Picasso's sculptures incorporating found objects as well as in the otherworldly personages of the Surrealists, his improvisational and often satiric use of castoff industrial materials in New York in the early 1950s made him a pioneering "junk sculptor."

Although the title *Railroad Urchin* (1959) suggests that this is a figurative work, as are a number of other works devoted to the urchin theme created by Stankiewicz in the 1950s, few elements here refer to specifics of anatomy or facial structure. It is instead an abstracted, totemic piece that has been variously interpreted as representing a "streetwise child" or "hobo," although most intriguing is the notion that it might be a surrogate self-portrait. The artist can be considered a "railroad orphan" because his father, who worked for the Pennsylvania Railroad, was killed by an oncoming train when the artist was a toddler. Growing up later in Detroit, Stankiewicz has recounted that he often played among discarded machinery in local railroad yards. The sculpture, which incorporates half a gas tank, a massive chain, metal rods, a pipe, and nails, features complex internal relationships. In its high degree of abstraction, it looks ahead to Stankiewicz's later work, which tends to be untitled and to focus not on figuration but on the dynamic interaction of component parts.

Suggested Reading:
Miracle in the Scrap Heap: The Sculpture of Richard Stankiewicz. Exhibition catalogue. Addison Gallery of American Art, Phillips Academy, Andover, MA: 2003. Distributed by University of Washington Press.

Plate 31

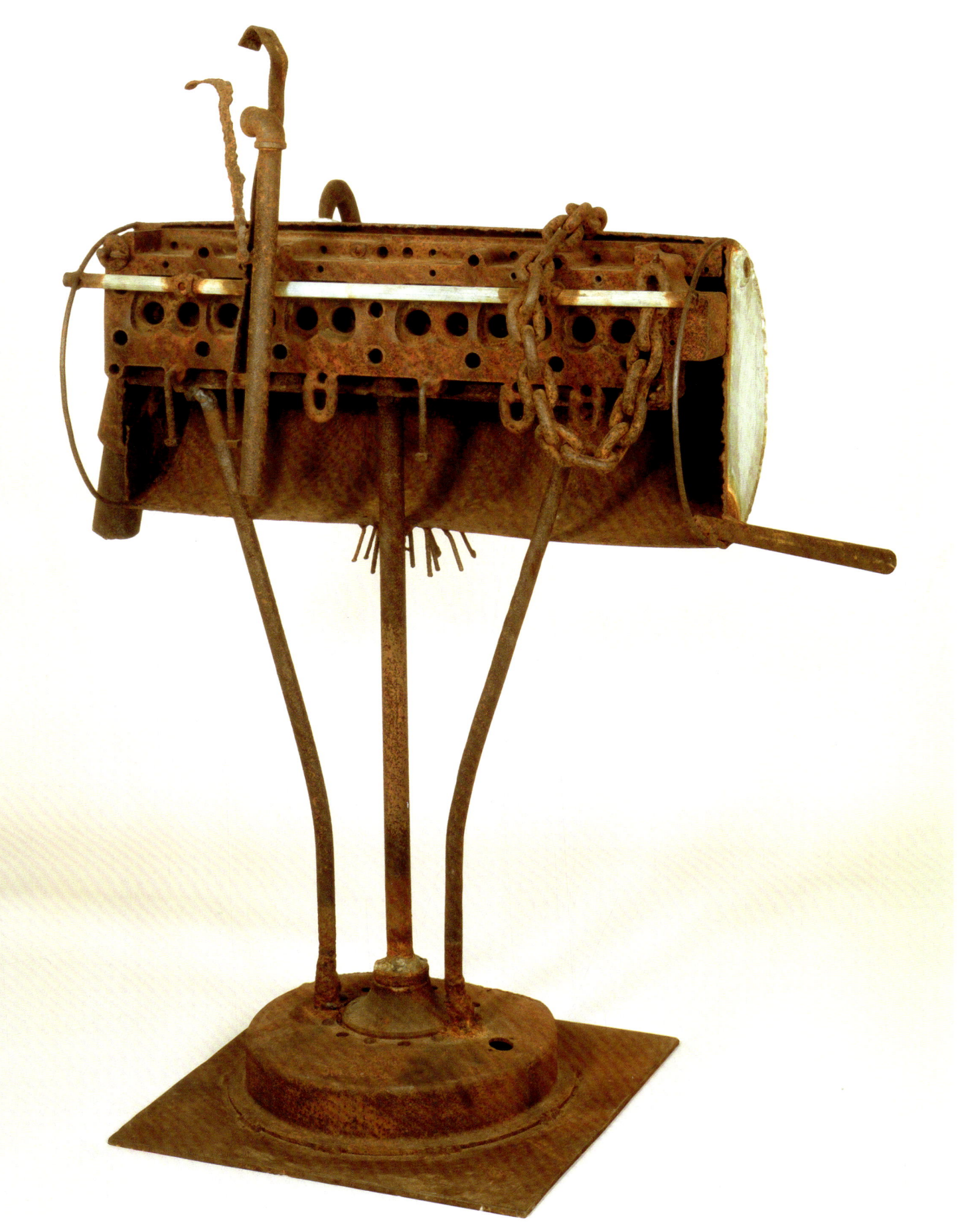

Lenore Tawney
Lorain, Ohio
1907 – 2007
New York City

Bound Man, 1957
wool, silk, linen, goat hair;
discontinuous weft brocade,
woven
91 x 36 inches
Museum of Arts & Design,
New York
Purchased by the American Craft
Council, 1958

In the late fifties, Lenore Tawney was a major force in redirecting the traditional craft of weaving to a new tendency that embraces both painting and sculpture and has come to be known as "fiber art." In the mid-forties, Tawney studied at Chicago's Bauhaus-oriented Institute of Design, where Alexander Archipenko acknowledged her talents as a sculptor. In 1954, she chose to pursue her interest in tapestry by studying with the distinguished Finnish weaver Martta Taipale at the Penland School of Crafts in North Carolina. Dedicating herself to fiber work, Tawney moved to New York in 1957, settling in Coenties Slip, where Jack Youngerman was her landlord and Agnes Martin became her close friend, the two influencing one another's work, Tawney's agile thread has often been compared to the elusive pencil lines seen in many of Martin's works. By inventing the means to weave free from the boundaries of the loom, Tawney created fiber pieces that hang freely in space and are of a scale and presence equivalent to those of the advanced painting of the time. *Bound Man* (1957) is one of Tawney's few works to feature a representational motif—a bound figure—most of her work being abstract in nature. Here, however, content and form (the binding of the figure through the use of heavy threads) are brilliantly merged. Areas of transparency contrast with more solidly woven sections, allowing light to pass through and act as a visual and symbolic force. While unusual among her fiber pieces, this poetic, emotionally evocative, figurative work anticipated the collages and Assemblages she began to produce in the mid-sixties.

Suggested Reading:
Mangan, Kathleen Nugent, ed. *Lenore Tawney: A Retrospective*. Exhibition catalogue. New York: American Craft Museum, 1990.

Plate 32

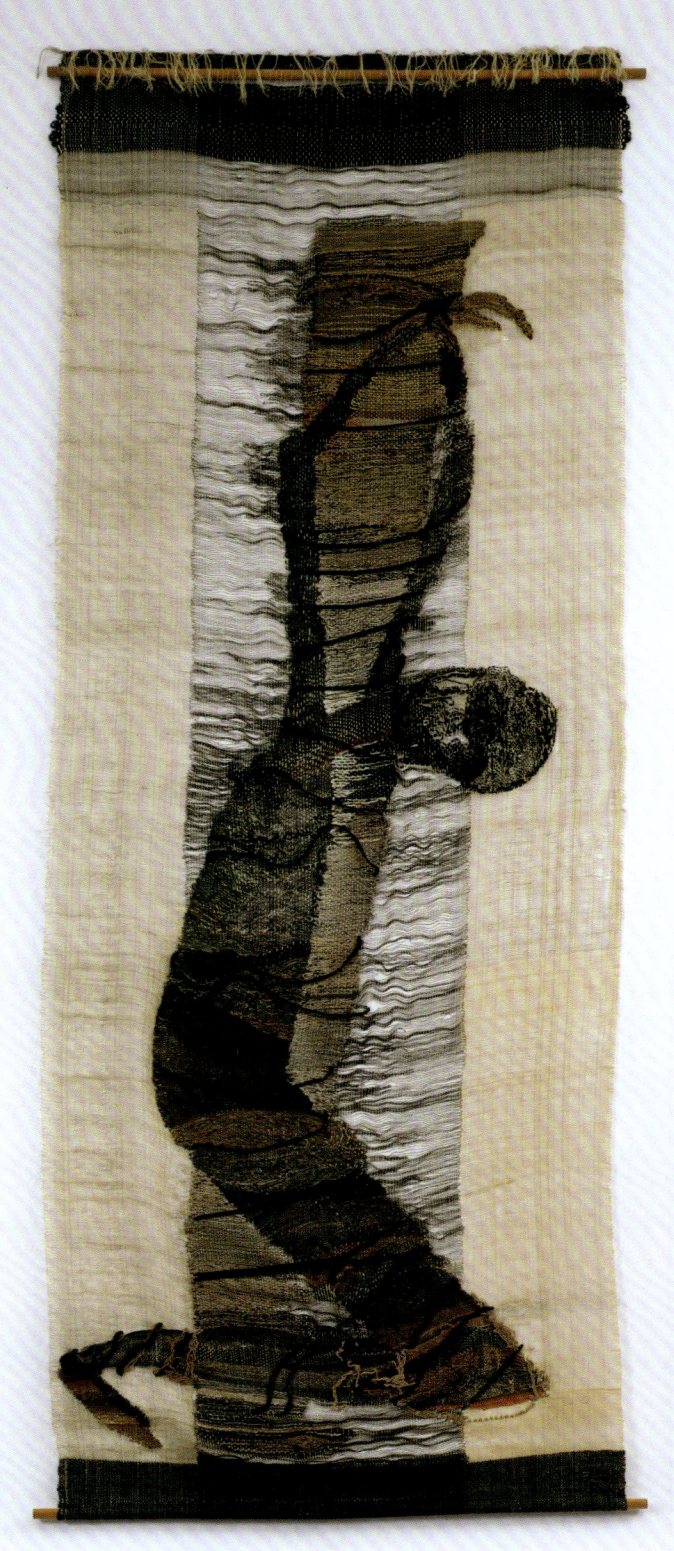

Tom Wesselmann
Cincinnati, Ohio
1931 – 2004
New York City

Portrait Collage #7, 1959
mixed media and collage
on board
8 x 10 inches
The Estate of Tom Wesselmann

Portrait Collage #16, 1960
mixed media and collage
on board
8 1/2 x 11 1/2 inches
The Estate of Tom Wesselmann

A leading figure in Pop Art in the 1960s, Tom Wesselmann is perhaps best known for the large scale, brightly colored works of his "Great American Nude" series begun in 1961 in which flatly painted, reclining female nudes occupy interiors replete with consumer products, fine art reproductions, and such actual objects as shower curtains, radios, and plastic fruit. These mixed media works had their source in Wesselmann's earlier art.

Wesselmann came to New York from Cincinnati in 1956 and, as an art student, was greatly influenced by the painting style of Willem de Kooning. He then began to translate de Kooning's style into collages consisting of random assortments of plain and printed papers. Wesselmann then turned his attention to intimately scaled collages representing imaginary portrait figures in tightly patterned domestic interiors. In creating these "portrait collages," Wesselmann looked not to current New York School practices, but back to such modern masters as Edouard Vuillard and Henri Matisse. That Wesselmann was keenly aware of historical precedent is evidenced by the profusion of Old Master portraits amusingly serving as wall decoration in the domestic interiors shown in his collages. Although spatial illusionism was to disappear from his later work, at this point he was still exploring its effects, as seen in the layering of forms, shadows, and the image of the vase set into the picture space in *Portrait Collage #16* (1960). A few "portrait collages" were included in his first professional exhibition, a two-person show held at the Judson Gallery in 1959. Two years later, the first works of his extended "Great American Nude" series were exhibited at the Tanager Gallery in his first solo show and his career as a Pop artist was launched.

Suggested Reading:
Glenn, Constance. *Tom Wesselmann, the Early Years: Collages, 1959-1962*. Exhibition catalogue. Long Beach: Art Galleries, California State University, 1974

Plate 34
Plate 35

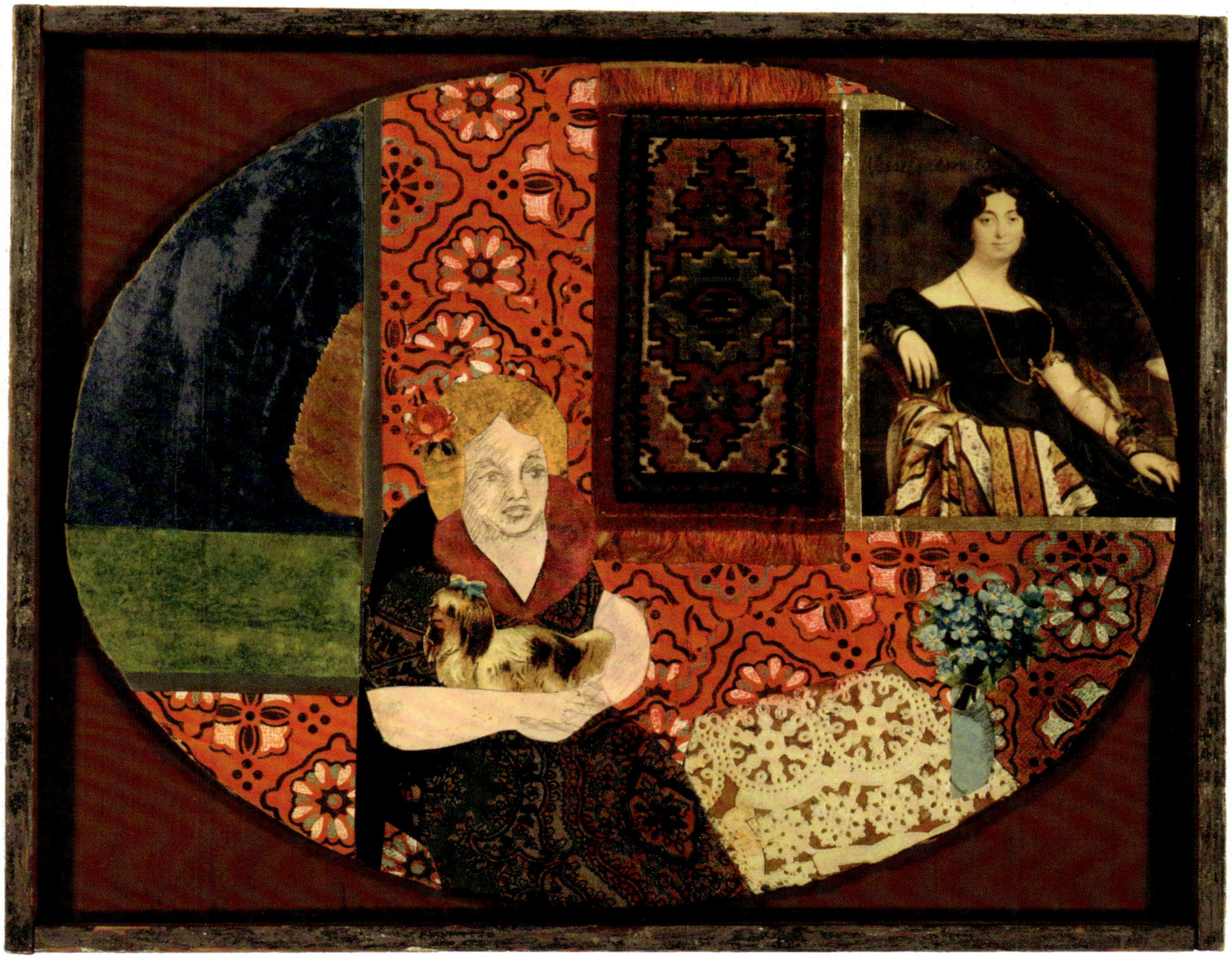

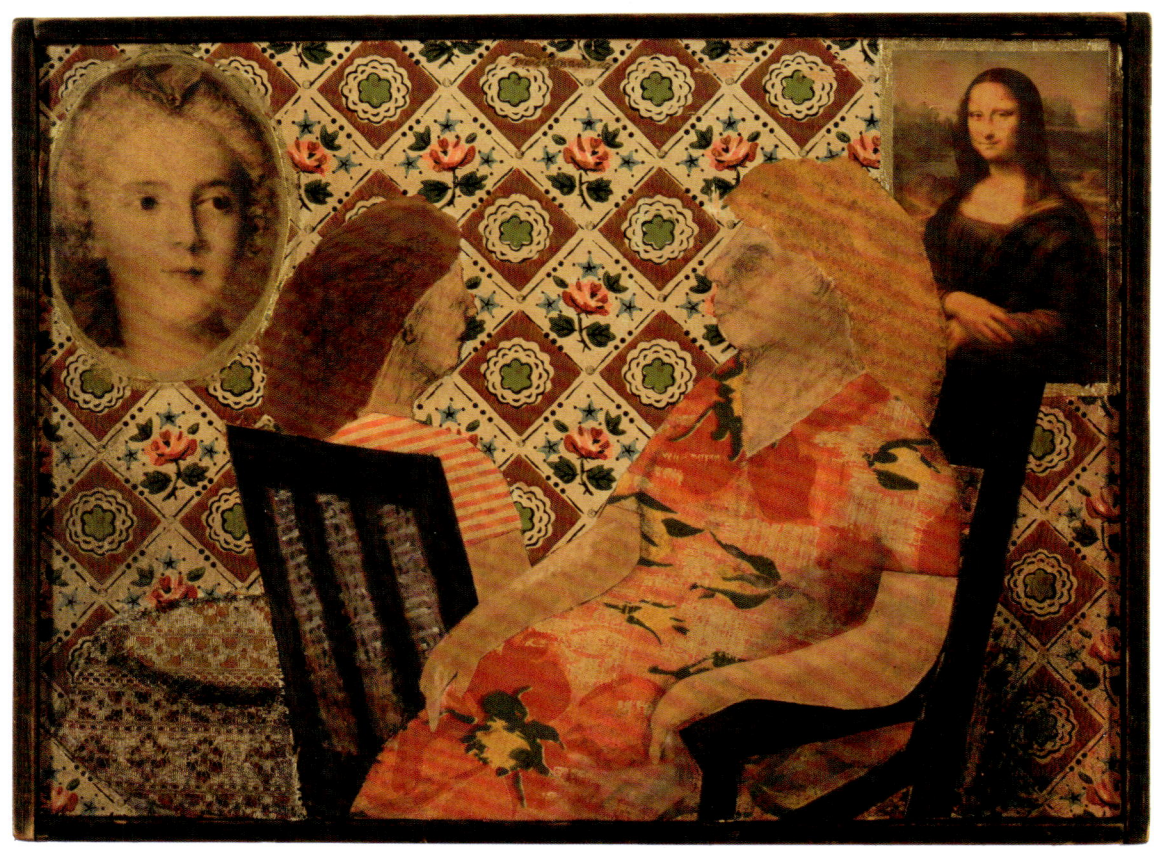

POST-PAINTERLY ABSTRACTION INTO MINIMALISM

. . . I always get into arguments with people who want to retain the old values in painting—the humanistic values that they always find on the canvas. If you pin them down, they always end up asserting that there is something there besides the paint on the canvas. My painting is based on the fact that only what can be seen there is there. It really is an object . . . . All I want anyone to get out of my paintings, and all I ever get out of them, is the fact that you can see the whole idea without any confusion . . . What you see is what you see."

Frank Stella

from
"Questions to Stella and Judd"
Bruce Glaser
ARTnews (September 1966)

Richard Anuszkiewicz
Born in Erie, Pennsylvania, 1930;
lives in Englewood, New Jersey

Circle Unretained, 1957
oil on canvas
36 x 32 inches
Collection of the artist, courtesy
Jacobson Howard Gallery

While the term "Op Art" was not coined until 1964 and the exhibition that christened the tendency was not held until 1965 (*The Responsive Eye*, curated by William C. Seitz at The Museum of Modern Art), nevertheless, art that dealt with the optical vibrations caused by strongly contrasting colors used in patterned arrangements appeared in the art of Richard Anuszkiewicz by 1957, as *Circle Unretained* reveals. The artist, then a resident of Coenties Slip in lower Manhattan, had studied at Yale University School of Art with Josef Albers, the Bauhaus master and former Black Mountain College art professor. Albers' theories on the interaction of colors had profound impact upon Anuszkiewicz's art and thought. In addition to Albers, Anuszkiewicz was influenced by the art of Paul Klee and by scientific principles of perceptual psychology then gaining currency in academic circles. An asymmetrical, highly calculated organization of circles and radiant lines gives form to the dynamic, pulsating *Circle Unretained*. As in the artist's other work, sensation takes precedence over expression.

Suggested Reading:
Lunde, Karl. *Anuszkiewicz*. New York: Harry N. Abrams, Inc., 1977.

Plate 36

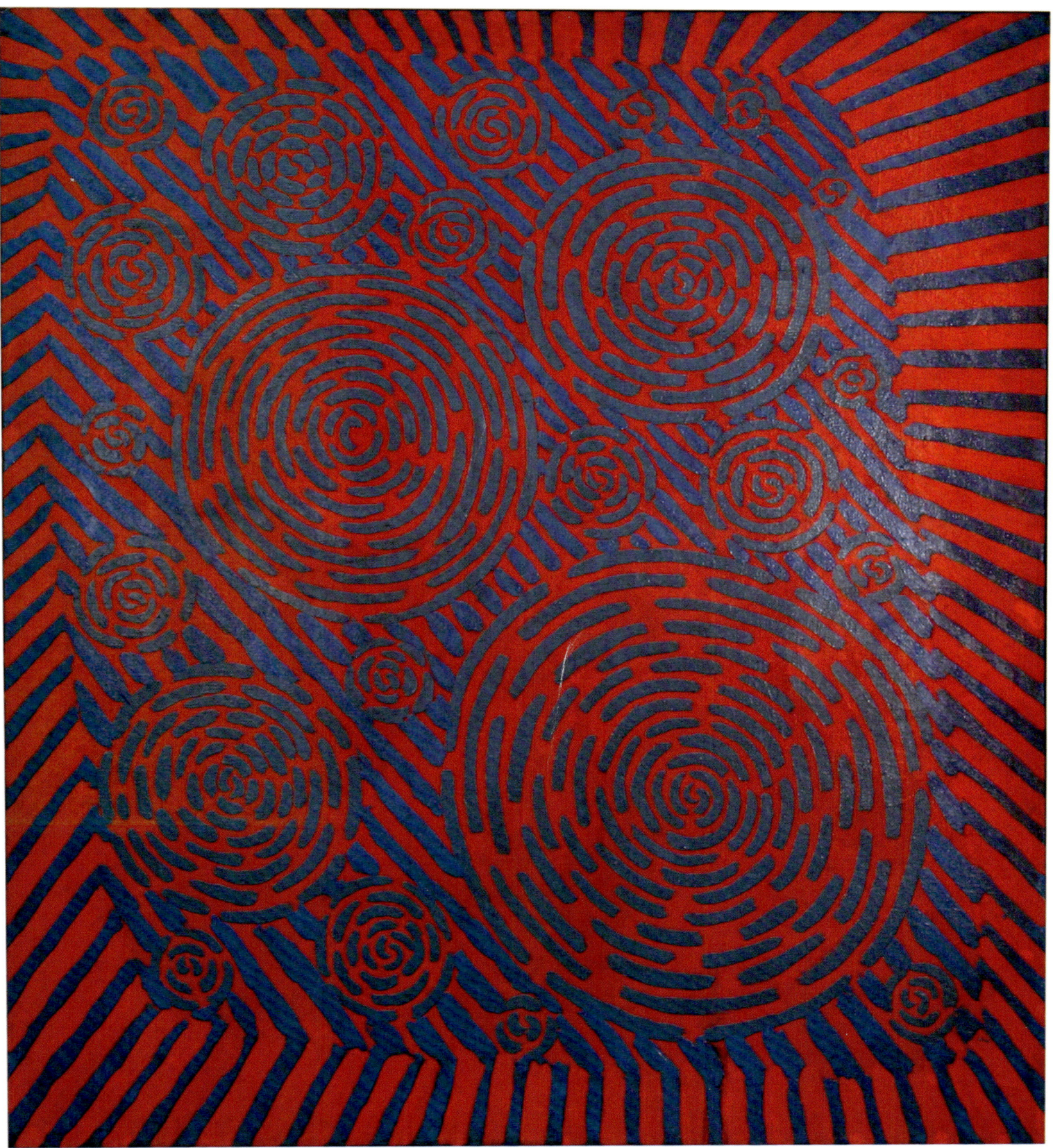

Darby Bannard

Born in New Haven,
Connecticut, 1934; lives in
Miami, Florida

Greenstone, 1960
alkyd resin on canvas
67 x 61 inches
Collection of the artist, courtesy
Jacobson Howard Gallery

In the late fifties, Darby Bannard was a close friend of the artist Frank Stella and the art critic Michael Fried at Princeton University, where they read with considerable interest the writings of Clement Greenberg extolling the virtues of flatness, impersonal execution, and other Formalist ideals. In 1959, Bannard began to produce an extended series of paintings in which a large flat shape of a single hue was set upon the surface of an otherwise bare canvas, as seen in *Greenstone* (1960). Here, a circle in a smoky shade of green floats just above center in the rectangular field. This poetic work looks back to the hovering rectangles in the Abstract Expressionist canvases of Mark Rothko, while anticipating the economy of means in Minimalist art.

Suggested Reading:
Cone, Jane Harrison. *Walter Darby Bannard*. Exhibition catalogue. Baltimore, MD: Baltimore Museum of Art, 1973.

Darby Bannard's official website, "Darby Bannard," www.bannard.com.

Plate 37

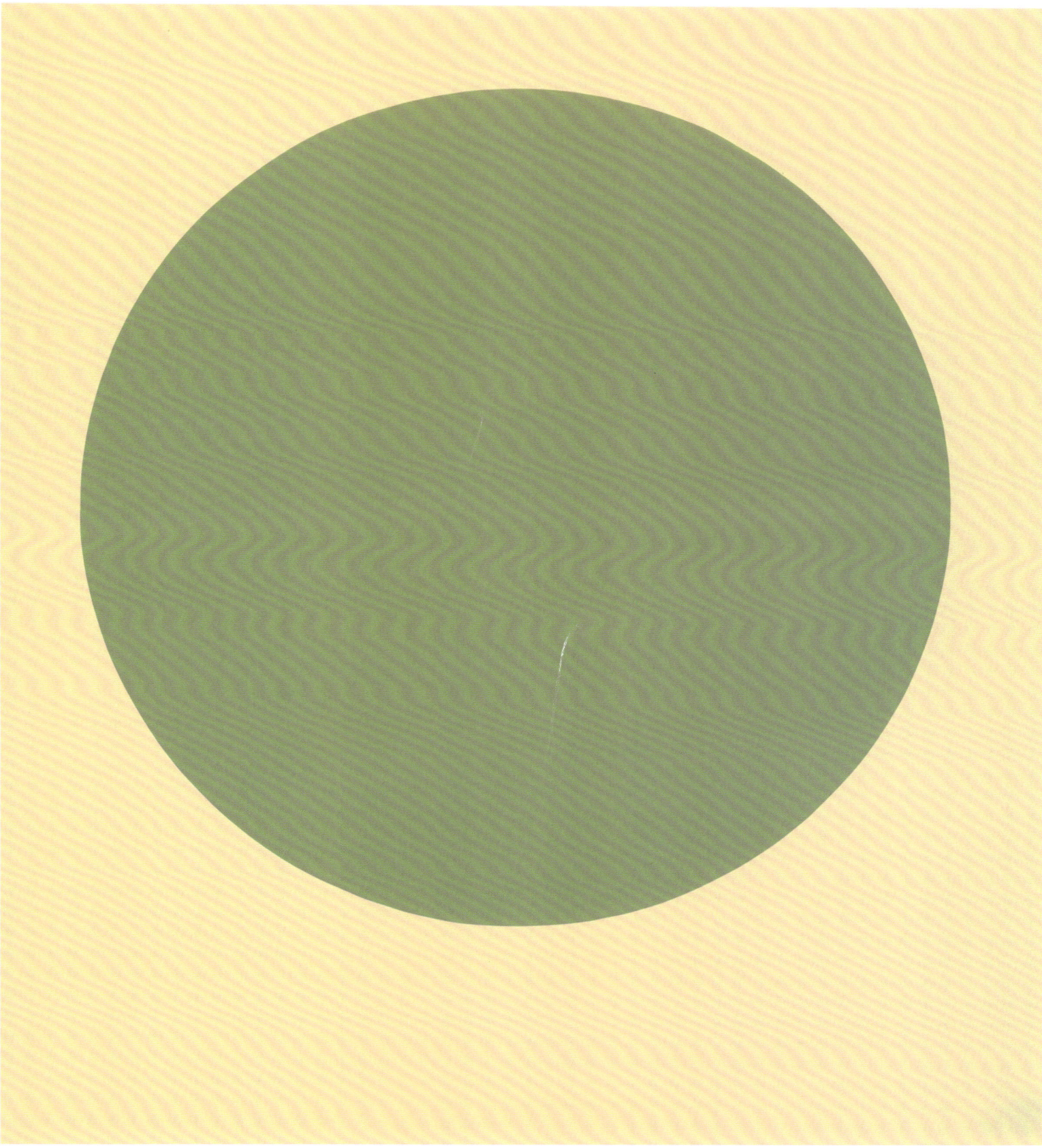

Larry Bell

Born in Chicago, Illinois, 1939;
lives in Taos, New Mexico, and
Venice, California

Untitled, 1961
mirror, wood, paint
12 x 12 x 5 inches
Collection of the artist

Working in a picture framing shop to earn money while he attended the Chouinard Art Institute in the late fifties, Larry Bell began to produce box constructions incorporating leftover off-cuts of glass. Initially, his interest resided in exploiting an interior shape—a parallelogram or cubic diagram—as seen in the center of his white-framed shadow box, *Untitled* (1961), which was included in his first solo show at the Ferus Gallery in 1962. The volume of the box construction itself, however, soon became his prime concern, along with continuing to explore the reflected and transmitted light of the mirrored and transparent glass surfaces. By the mid-sixties, Bell was producing pure glass cubes of highly refined finish that interacted, through their transparency and reflective properties, with their environment. These works were associated both with Minimal Art and California "Light and Space Art," a West Coast phenomenon made up of artists primarily concerned with the visual perception of light, space, reflections, shadows, and so on, which they sought to explore using minimal and sometimes even immaterial means.

Suggested Reading:
Zones of Experience: The Art of Larry Bell. Exhibition catalogue. Albuquerque, NM: Albuquerque Museum, 1997.

Plate 38

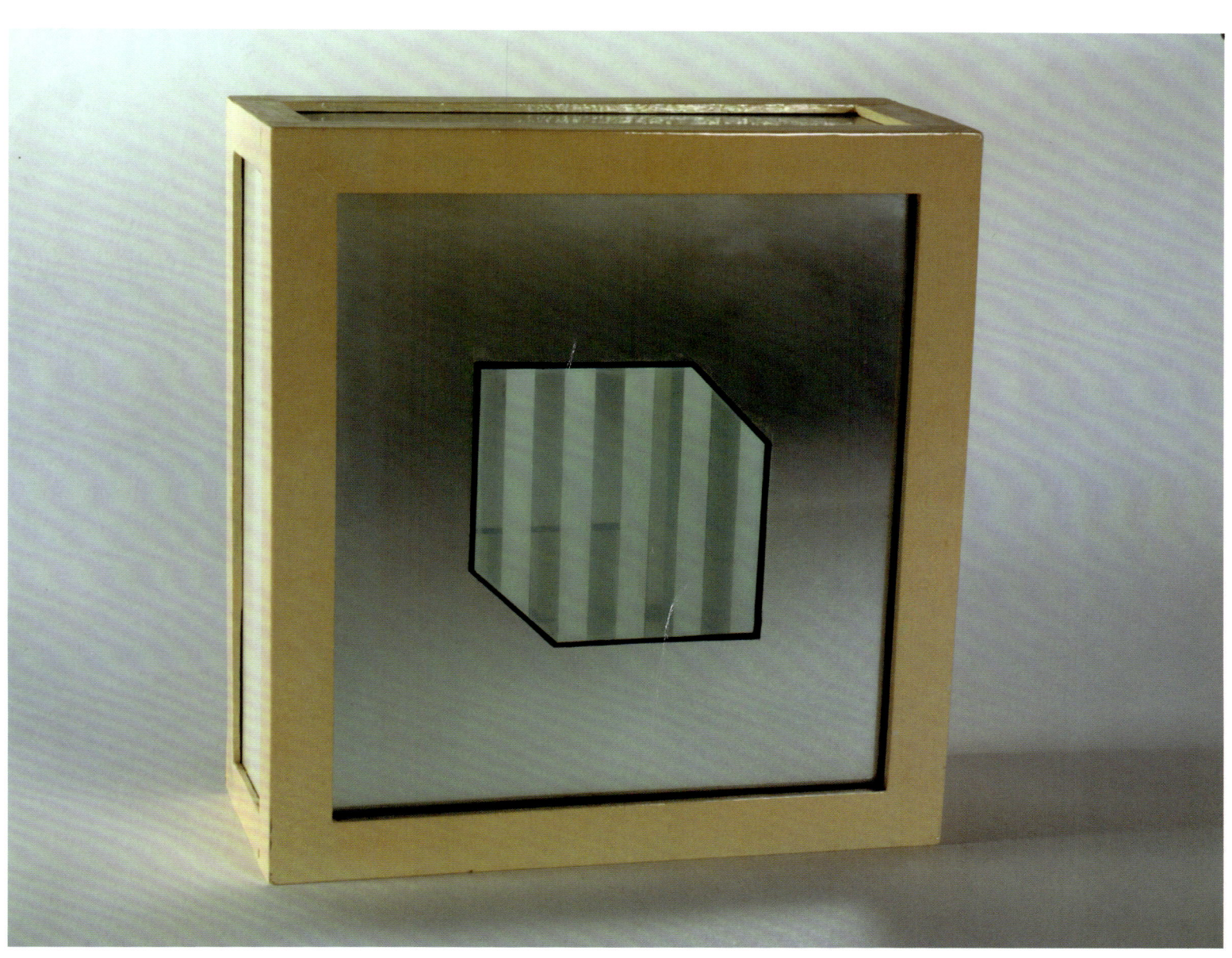

Billy Al Bengston

Born in Dodge City, Kansas, 1934; lives in Los Angeles, California and Victoria, British Columbia, Canada

Sophia, 1960
oil on canvas
21 x 21 inches
Courtesy of Samuel Freeman

In the mid-fifties, Billy Al Bengston devoted himself to ceramics, studying with Peter Voulkos at the Los Angeles County Art Institute (now the Otis Art Institute), where Voulkos had revolutionized the field of ceramics by leading it away from its traditional functional role and into a dynamic sculptural realm influenced by the gestural expressionism of the New York School painters. Kenny Price, who was to further extend the possibilities of ceramicists in California, became Bengston's close friend. In 1956, however, Bengston abandoned ceramics in order to devote himself to producing lively, gestural abstractions that were included in his first solo exhibition at the Ferus Gallery in 1958. Later that year, inspired by Jasper Johns' "Flag" and "Target" paintings, he began to center a few basic forms—a cross, an iris, and soon a stacked chevron—upon a square-format canvas.

In *Sophia* (1960), an optically vibrating heart is rendered in a clean-edged, non-painterly style, the heart or "valentine," which became a dominant motif in his art, apparently having been inspired by the fact that his exhibition at the Ferus that year was scheduled to open near Valentine's Day. Each of the paintings was named after a famous film star, this piece presumably having been dedicated to Sophia Loren, so that within the context of *Circa 1958*, works of different styles and media by Ray Johnson, Andy Warhol, and Bengston are all devoted to contemporary celebrities. Over the course of the next few years, Bengston became increasingly involved with enhancing the finish of his works (a 1960s phenomenon in California art often referred to as "finish fetish"). He used spray painting techniques, lacquers, and metallic paints derived from the California custom car and motorcycle culture to achieve gleaming surfaces bearing no evidence of the artist's hand.

Suggested Reading:
Billy Al Bengston: Paintings of Three Decades. Exhibition catalogue. Houston: Contemporary Arts Museum, 1988.

Plate 39

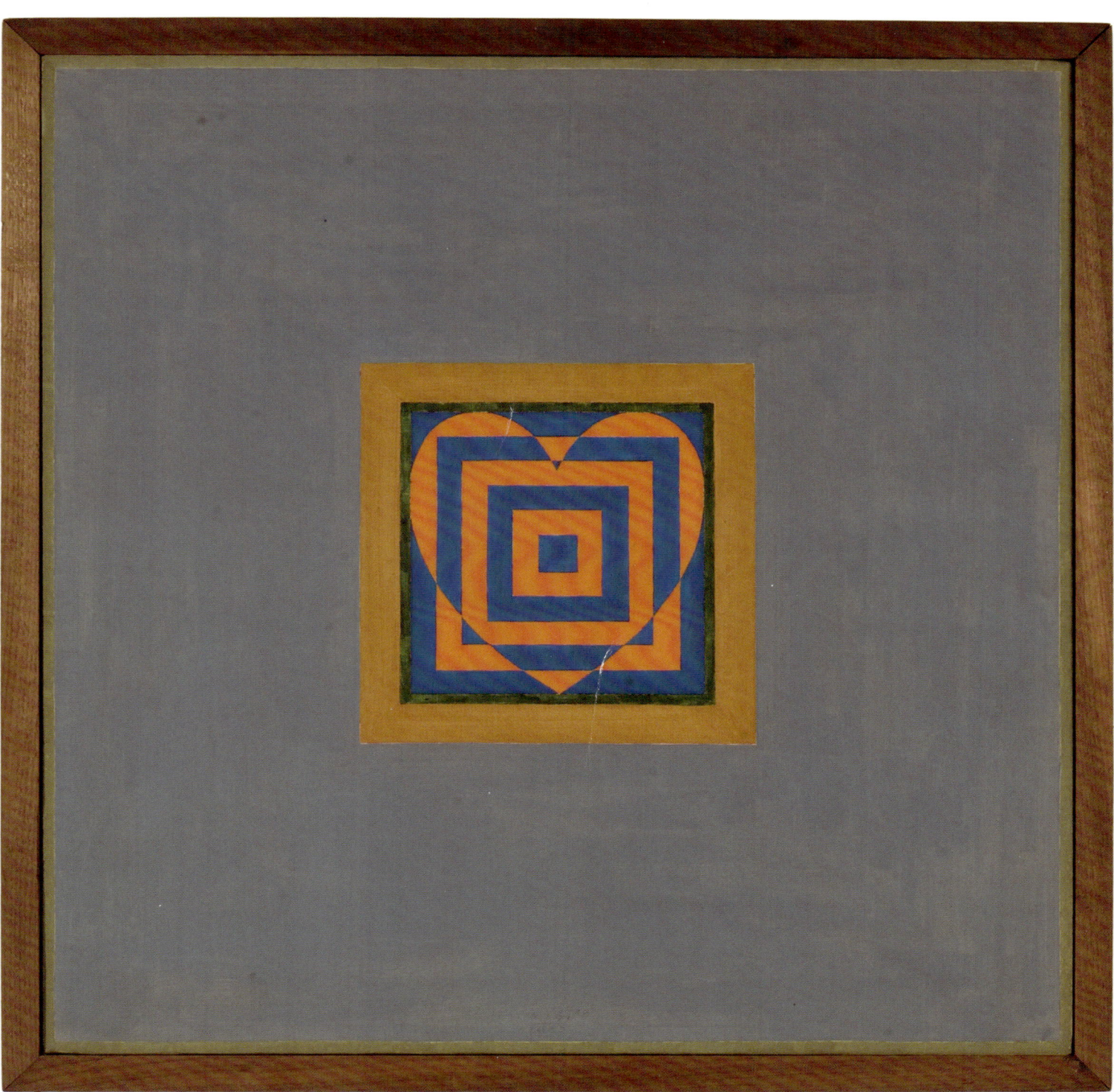

Karl Benjamin
Born in Chicago, Illinois, 1925;
lives in Claremont, California

*Interlocking Forms (Thalo Green,
Raw Umber, Mars Yellow)*, 1958
oil on canvas
40 x 30 inches
The Carl and Marilynn Thoma
Collection

Included in the *Four Abstract Classicists* exhibition presented at the Los Angeles County Museum in 1959, along with Lorser Feitelson and John McLaughlin, whose work is also featured in *Circa 1958*, Karl Benjamin's painting is hardly "classical." It is neither calmly serene nor conservative, as the term implies, but highly animated, infused with a spirit akin to that of jazz music and its improvisations. A self-taught artist, Benjamin began painting in 1950 and soon arrived at a flatly-rendered style in which often quirky, clean-edged shapes abut in complex patterns that engage spatial play, as seen in his 1958 painting *Interlocking Forms (Thalo Green, Raw Umber, Mars Yellow)*. As the title of this work indicates, form is of primary importance to Benjamin's art, with color a close second, the artist's choice of hue being highly individual and intuitive, courting the unexpected. A long-time teacher at the Claremont Colleges in Pomona, California, Benjamin's early paintings were recently featured, together with work by his "hard-edge" colleagues Feitelson and McLaughlin, in the traveling exhibition *Birth of the Cool: California Art, Design and Culture at Midcentury*, which opened at the Orange County Museum of Art in Newport Beach in fall 2007.

Suggested Reading:
Hickey, Dave. *Dance the Line: Paintings by Karl Benjamin*. Exhibition catalogue. West Hollywood: Louis Stern Fine Arts, 2007.

Plate 40

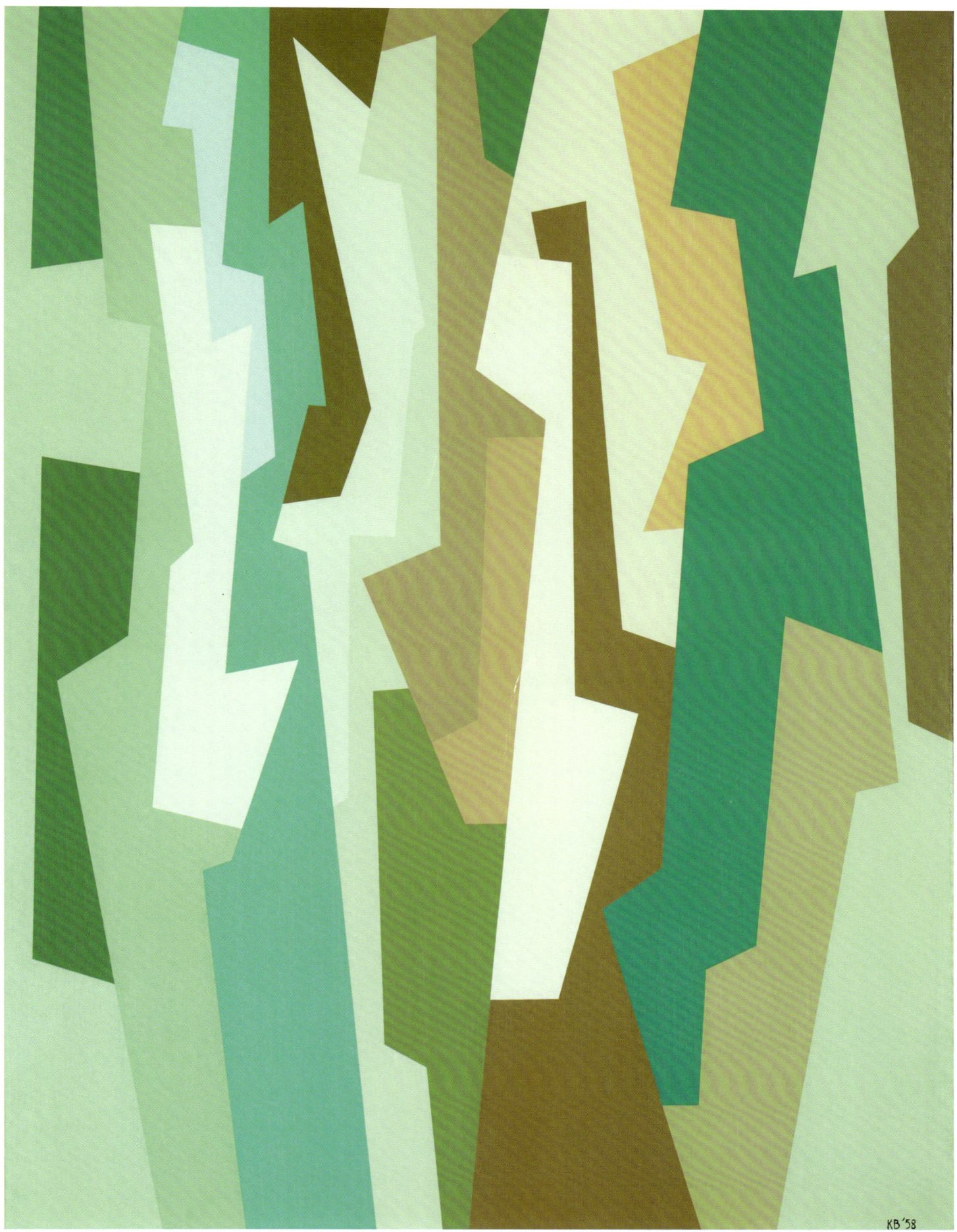

Ronald Bladen
Vancouver, British Columbia,
Canada
1918 – 1988
New York City

Green and Black, 1961-62
painted wood with metal
hardware
45 x 20 1/2 x 7 inches
Linda and James O. Clark

Ronald Bladen attended art school in his native Vancouver before moving to San Francisco for fifteen years, during which time he did metalwork, serving as a welder on ships during the war and making bolts for railroads. In his spare time, he painted and got to know such poets and writers of the Beat Generation as Jack Kerouac and Allen Ginsburg. Upon moving to New York in 1957, he became involved with the Tenth Street scene and had solo shows in 1958 and 1960 at Nicholas Krushenick's Brata Gallery of his paintings, which were rendered in earth tones and evocative of landscape motifs. Although executed in the gestural mode, which was ubiquitous at the time, Bladen's paintings were distinctive in their heavily pigmented nature, the impasto so thick as to rise several inches off the masonite or plywood supports. These paintings were followed by a series of purely abstract reliefs incorporating metal elements that showed Bladen's transition into sculpture.

In *Green and Black* (1961-62), which is typical of the reliefs included in Bladen's solo show at the Green Gallery in 1962, a heavily pigmented all-green panel projects five inches off the wall supported by a concealed wooden armature (four metal bolts seen on the painting's surface attach the panel to this wooden framework). Suspended another five inches in front of the monochrome panel near its bottom edge, held in place by bolts and metal rods, are three progressively shorter, black-painted wooden elements that begin as verticals and then bend diagonally to the right. The repetitive gesture of this trio of elements adds movement to the work and anticipates to Bladen's later work in sculpture, particularly *Three Elements* (1965), a mammoth metal sculpture consisting of three freestanding rhomboids set in a row, each perched at a 65-degree angle. Unlike the work of the other artists associated with Minimalism, which tended to focus upon impersonal boxlike forms, Bladen's sculpture of the mid-sixties retained a gestural aspect and a romantic and heroic character that betrayed his Abstract Expressionist origins.

Suggested Reading:
Berkson, Bill. *Ronald Bladen: Early and Late*. Exhibition catalogue. San Francisco: San Francisco Museum of Modern Art, 1991.

Dreishpoon, Douglas. *Ronald Bladen: Drawings and Sculptural Models*. Exhibition catalogue. Greensboro, NC: The Weatherspoon Art Museum, UNC-Greensboro, 1995.

Plate 41

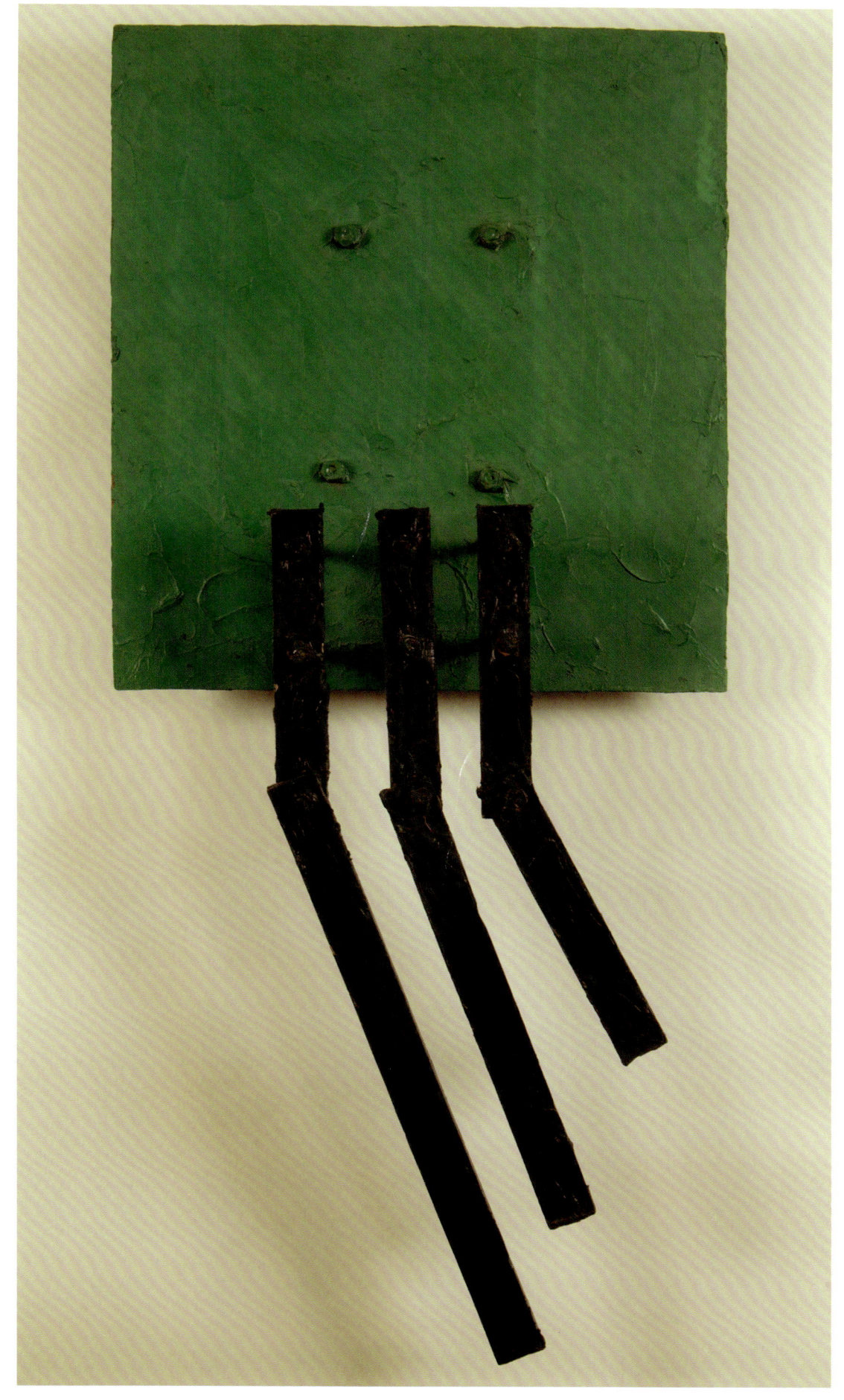

Chryssa

Born in Athens, Greece, 1933;
lives in New York City

Three Arrows, 1960
painted aluminum
72 x 66 x 5 inches
Purchase, with funds from the
Friends of the Whitney Museum
of American Art
Whitney Museum of American
Art, New York, 61.3

Born in Athens, Greece, Chryssa Varda studied in Paris and then briefly in San Francisco, before moving to New York in late 1954. She was immediately struck by the visual dynamics of the urban environment, particularly its signage and the lights of Times Square. She began to produce metal tablets and plaques featuring gridded arrangements of raised letters and works based on newspaper type. Her preoccupation with language and signs soon gave way to large-scale reliefs like the imposing, painted aluminum *Three Arrows* (1960). Here, three intersecting, downward-pointing triangles appear on four abutting panels enclosed in a wooden frame, the "arrows" formed by the arrangement of a series of T-shaped knobs. It is at once an abstract painting and a sign and finds a parallel in the work of Jasper Johns, Robert Indiana, Ed Ruscha, and a number of other artists who were involved with issues of art and language at this same time. In 1962, Chryssa extended her interest in the lights and signs of the city into work in neon, being among the first artists to use emitted light and neon as artistic media.

Suggested Reading:
Hunter, Sam. *Chryssa*. New York: Harry N. Abrams, Inc., 1974.

Varda, Chryssa and Douglas Schultz. *Chryssa: Cityscapes*. London: Thames and Hudson, 1990.

Plate 42

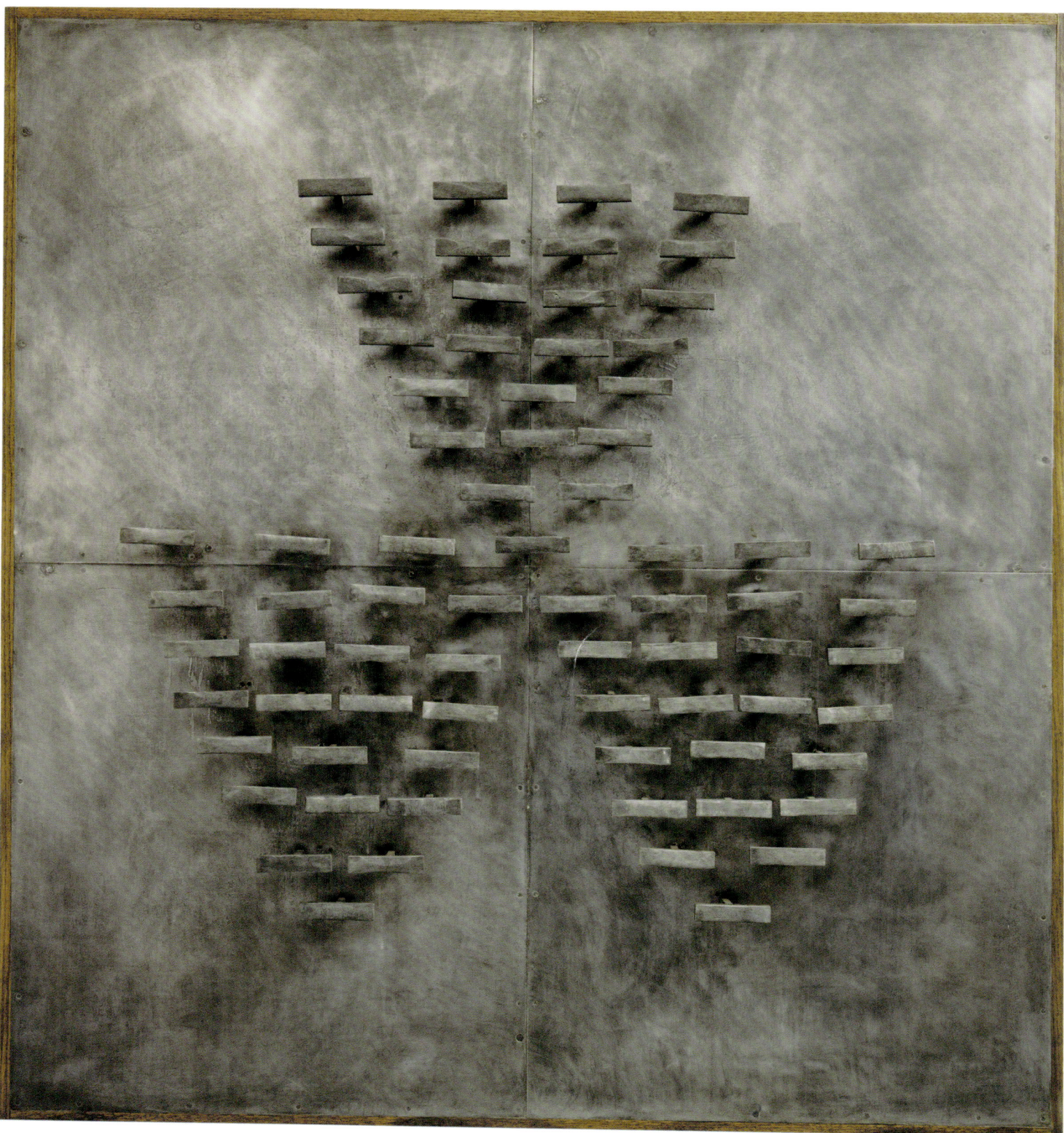

Beauford Delaney

Knoxville, Tennessee
1901 – 1979
Paris, France

Composition, 1958
oil on canvas
58 1/2 x 45 1/2 inches
Courtesy of Michael Rosenfeld
Gallery, LLC, New York,
New York

Born and raised in Tennessee, Beauford Delaney moved to Boston at age sixteen, where he took classes and frequented museums and galleries. By 1930, he had moved to New York. Throughout the 1930s and forties, Delaney exhibited expressionistically rendered portraits, urban landscapes, and interiors while supporting himself through teaching and a variety of other part-time jobs. By the early 1950s, Delaney was living in Greenwich Village and increasingly associated with the group of Abstract Expressionists. While he exhibited Expressionist works, he was reluctant to be linked to a single style, and he continued to work with figurative and abstract subjects throughout his life.

After a fellowship at Yaddo, the artists' colony in Saratoga Springs, New York, personal and professional interests took Delaney to France. In Paris, with its vibrant African communities and numerous African American expatriates, Delaney was fully embraced by the French cognoscenti and soon became a popular and well-known artist in an environment that held little of the racism that he had experienced in New York.

By 1958, Delaney was creating fully abstract paintings. Of particular influence on his development was the work of Claude Monet, whose late *Water Lilies* murals had recently opened to the public at l'Orangerie in Paris. In *Composition* (1958), swirling brush strokes of closely valued colors create a sense of shimmering light and luminosity. Here, Delaney's interest resides in such abstract values as color, light, layering of surface, and movement.

Delaney remained in Paris for the remainder of his life, but for brief travels abroad, including once to New York. Plagued with bouts of depression and alcoholism throughout his life, these grew increasingly worse. Because of his standing as a significant artist, he was cared for by the French government during the final years of his life.

Entry by Emily Kass

Suggested Reading:
Bearden, Romare and Harry Henderson. *A History of African American Artists*. New York: Pantheon Books, 1993.

Plate 43

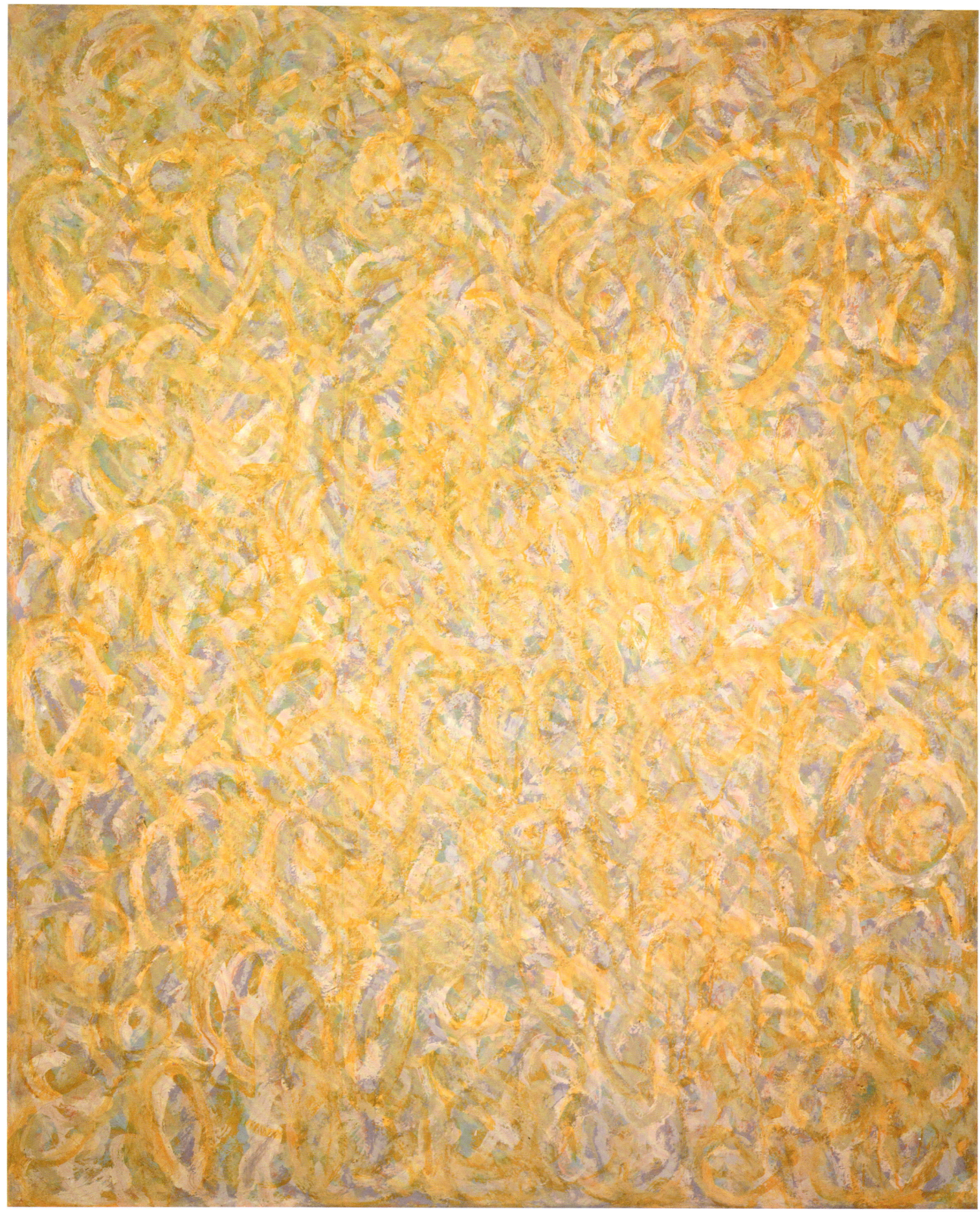

Lorser Feitelson

Savannah, Georgia
1898 – 1978
Los Angeles, California

Dichotomic Organization:
Stripes, 1959
oil on canvas
70 x 70 inches
Feitelson Arts Foundation,
courtesy Louis Stern Fine Arts

Raised in New York and educated both in New York and Paris, Lorser Feitelson moved to Los Angeles in 1928, where, together with his former pupil and future wife the painter Helen Lundeberg, he worked in a Surrealist style. In the mid-forties, Feitelson began to translate the human and other natural forms found in his early paintings into abstract shapes that interacted within evocative, spatially ambiguous compositions. In an extended series of works entitled "Magical Space Forms," the abstract elements grew into large, sharply angled, clearly defined flat planes. Although these paintings made Feitelson a leading figure in Los Angles-based hard-edge abstraction, his true celebrity within the largely unacknowledged Los Angeles art world at the time derived from his hosting the long running, nationally televised, NBC Sunday morning program *Feitelson on Art* from 1956 to 1963.

Feitelson's *Dichotomic Organization: Stripes* (1959) belongs to a series of works of the same title produced 1959-61, each consisting of fields of vertical stripes in bold and unexpected colors. Although stripe paintings had appeared in Feitelson's work earlier, the title of the new series clearly indicates that the artist's interest here was in "dichotomic organization:" the division of the work into two parts. The painting seen in *Circa 1958* offers a studied asymmetry and false mirroring, the left and right halves of the canvas creating psychological tension through disparities in the width, rhythm, spatial orientation, and often boldly clashing colors of the stripes. While wholly and even severely abstract, the work's elongated forms, fluctuations in space, disequilibrium, and palette find points of origin in his Surrealist work.

Suggested Reading:
Lorser Feitelson and the Invention of Hard Edge Painting 1945-1965. Exhibition catalogue. West Hollywood, CA: Louis Stern Fine Arts, 2003.

Plate 44

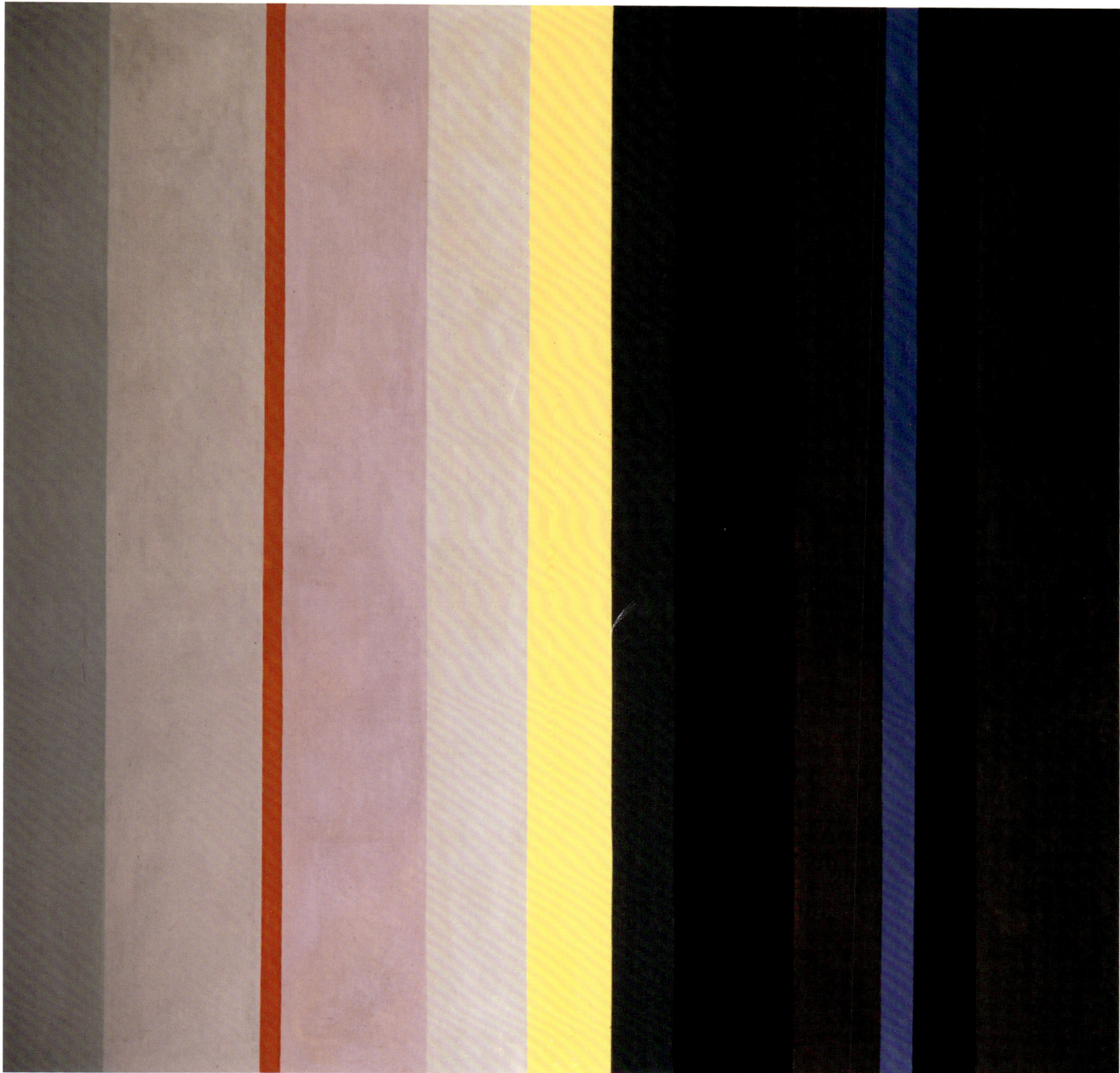

Al Held
New York City
1928 – 2005
Todi, Italy

Untitled, 1959
oil and collage on paper
mounted on canvas
2 panels, overall: 100 3/8 x 98 x
3/4 inches
each panel: 100 3/8 x 49 1/4
inches
Al Held Foundation, Inc.

In the mid-fifties, Al Held was a vigorous, second generation "Action Painter," producing large-scale, heavily textured gestural abstractions in a muted earth-toned palette. In 1959, a dramatic change occurred in his art: his painted gestures began to describe bold, graphically rendered triangles, rectangles, and circles and his color became equally vivid, with black, white, and the primary colors predominating. While the artist's monumental "Taxi Cab" paintings, executed in acrylic paint on enormous sheets of white photographic paper, are generally identified as the watershed works in this regard, *Untitled* (1959), which immediately preceded the "Taxi Cab" series, reveals much about the transition that occurred in his art. Like the "Taxi Cabs," it was painted in Sam Francis' enormous, sky lighted studio, which was lent to Held for a short period when Francis was away, the light, air, and space of the studio providing inspiration.* The surface of *Untitled* is covered with printed papers of varying sorts—sheets of newspaper, comic pages, and whole pages taken from magazines, the advertisements (Air France, Mercedes, Coca-Cola), and photographic reproductions remaining largely visible on the surface below the painted forms. Images of religious icons appear along the painting's central spine. Superimposed upon this papered surface is a veritable frenzy of surface activity that gives form to outlined geometric and quasi-geometric shapes. They are painted in black and white and the primary colors, although bubble gum pink, purple, mint green, and other colors also appear. From this work proceeded the less expressionistic and more controlled "Taxi Cab" paintings, which in turn gave rise to work that was calmer still, Held moving increasingly away from his Abstract Expressionist origins to an art of geometric clarity.

Suggested Reading:
Armstrong, Richard. *Al Held*. New York: Rizzoli, 1991.

*Conversation between Mara Held, the artist's daughter, and Roni Feinstein during a visit to the Al Held Foundation in Boiceville, New York, April 1, 2008.

Plate 45

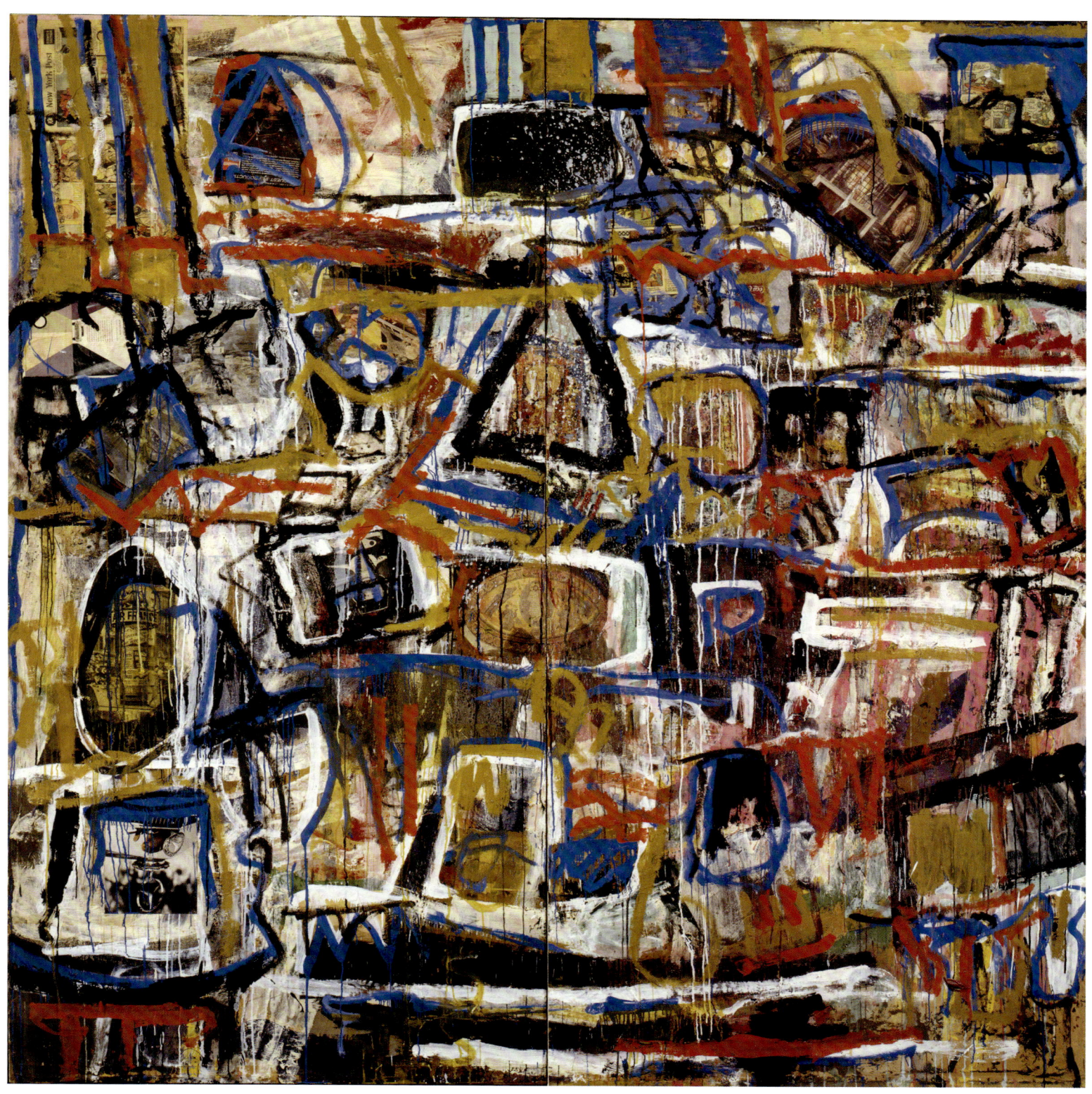

Alfred Jensen
Guatemala City, Guatemala
1903 – 1981
Livingston, New York

Magic 2 and 6, 1960
oil on canvas
27 x 20 inches
Courtesy of Michael Rosenfeld
Gallery, LLC, New York, New
York

Born in Guatemala in 1903, the multilingual Alfred Jensen spent time in Denmark, Los Angeles, Munich (studying briefly with Hans Hofmann), Paris, and elsewhere before settling in New York permanently in 1951. While he first became preoccupied with Goethe's color theory in the late thirties and soon began to make drawings based on his continued investigations into light, color, and information systems, he considered these "research" and not art, painting all the while in a derivative, gestural Abstract Expressionist style. Apparently under the encouragement of his friend, Mark Rothko, in 1957, at the age of 54, Jensen began to create paintings based on his "studies," works that incorporated checkerboards or grids, forms, and prismatic colors not for their own sakes, but as manifestations of arcane numerical and philosophical systems involving time measurement, seasonal change, the calendar, mathematical calculations, and temple architecture. In 1960, Jensen read a book on Mayan hieroglyphics, which brought him back to his childhood in Guatemala and may have influenced the cryptic imagery seen along with dotted forms in *Magic 2 and 6* (1960). As seen here, Jensen painted in oil paint in pure, high key color squeezed directly on to the surface of the painting from the tube. He then spread the paint over the surface within compacted areas, creating a rich, densely textured surface. Although Jensen's investigations were eccentric and highly personal, the geometric and non-gestural nature of his art caused it to be included in exhibitions devoted to Post-painterly Abstraction.

Suggested Reading:
Cathcart, Linda L. and Marcia Tucker. *Alfred Jensen: Paintings and Diagrams from the years 1957-1977*. Exhibition catalogue. Buffalo, NY: Albright-Knox Art Gallery, 1978.

Alfred Jenson's official website, "Alfred Jensen," www.alfredjensen.com.

Plate 46

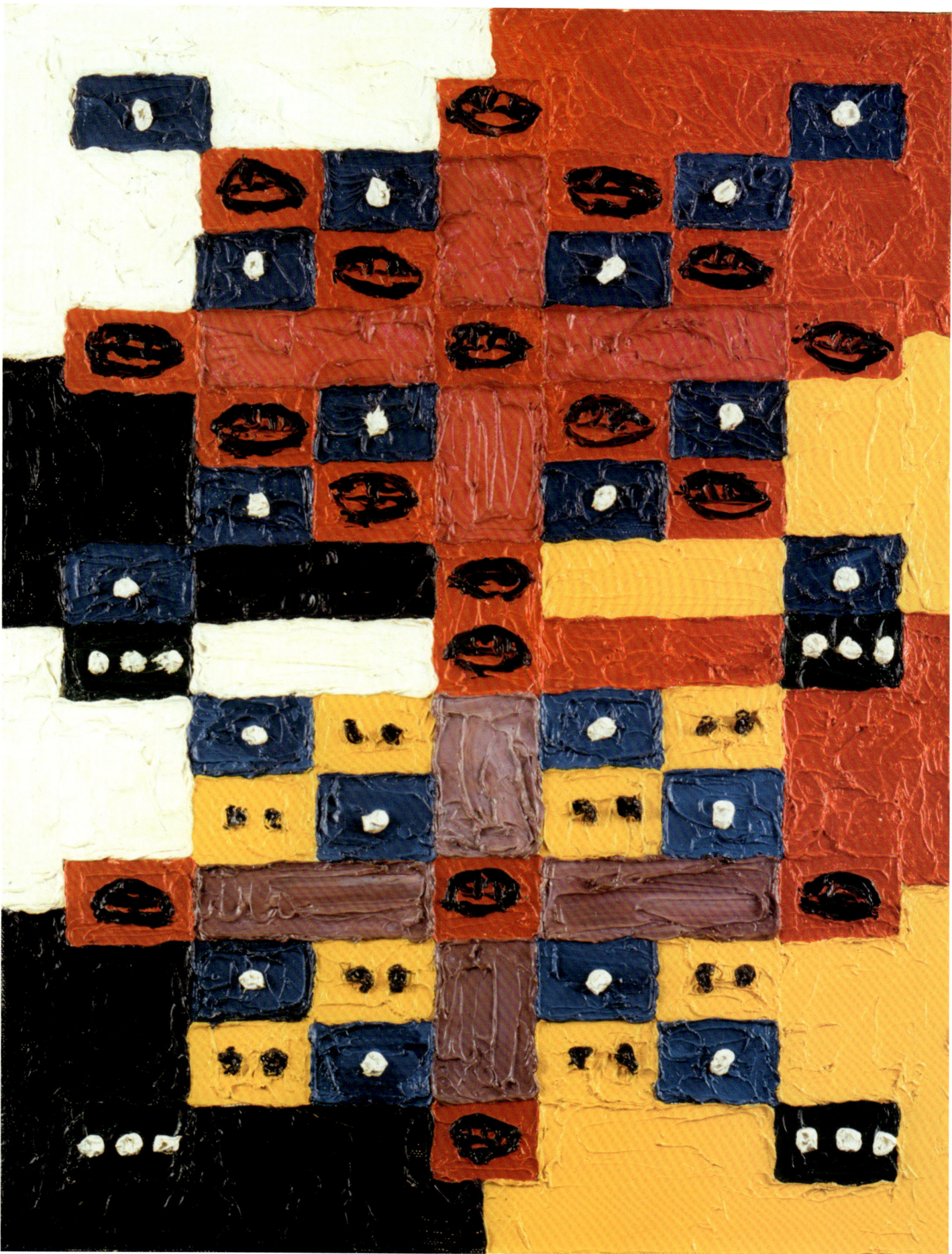

Ellsworth Kelly

Born in Newburgh, New York, 1923; lives in Spencertown, New York

Two Blacks, White and Blue, 1955
oil on canvas, four joined panels
92 x 24 inches
Private Collection

Ellsworth Kelly's *Two Blacks, White and Blue* (1955) was included in the artist's solo show at the Betty Parsons Gallery, New York, in 1956. It consists of four vertically stacked panels that are impersonally rendered in the colors and non-colors indicated by its title. Kelly had begun to create multi-panel works while living in Paris around 1950, the concept appealing to him because it eliminated traditional figure-ground relationships found in painting and asserted that each panel be viewed as a separate entity. Moreover, as Kelly pointed out, "Even though the white is the smallest area in the vertical, it is as strong as the others."* While the clean organization of *Two Blacks, White and Blue* and its palette may recall the abstract painting of the Dutch Neo-Plastic artist Piet Mondrian, Kelly's painting departs from easel painting to participate in and articulate architectural space. Further, while often uplifting the viewer through its purity of concept, Kelly's art is not geared to spiritual expression, but to formal investigation. His elegant and highly innovative art, which was conceived in Paris apart from New York School influence, made him a leading figure in Post-painterly Abstraction, a precursor of aspects of Minimalism and a dynamic force in the art world to the present day.

Suggested Reading:
Bois, Yve-Alain. *Ellsworth Kelly: The Early Drawings, 1948-1955*. Exhibition catalogue. Cambridge, MA: Harvard University Art Museums, 1999.

Waldman, Diane. *Ellsworth Kelly: A Retrospective*. Exhibition catalogue. New York: Guggenheim Museum, 1996; distributed by Harry N. Abrams, Inc.

*Telephone conversation between the artist and Roni Feinstein, March 7, 2008.

Plate 47

Gabriel Kohn

Philadelphia, Pennsylvania
1910 – 1975
Los Angeles, California

Object of the Sea, 1957
oil and plaster on wood
62 x 56 x 19 inches
Private Collection, Courtesy
McKee Gallery, New York

After initial art studies in New York, a stint working as a designer for Paramount Pictures in Los Angeles, and service in the army's camouflage corps, Kohn went to Paris from 1946 to 1952 to study with and then work for Ossip Zadkine, a Russian-born sculptor based in Paris who taught and influenced a number of American direct wood carvers, among them Kohn, George Sugarman, and Sidney Geist (Richard Stankeiwicz, who also studied with Zadkine, pursued a different path). Beginning in the mid-fifties, in addition to the carving he had learned with Zadkine, Kohn also employed the joinery processes of sanding, doweling, gluing, and laminating, techniques derived from carpentry and furniture making. These are slow, deliberate processes, which lack the spontaneity of the open, welded metal construction techniques used by most of his Abstract Expressionist contemporaries, so that although Kohn is often associated with the earlier movement, his large-scale, volumetric sculptures share the formal control and concentrated focus of Post-painterly Abstraction.

Object of the Sea (1957) features a cluster of joined quasi-geometric shapes that is at once abstract and allusive, the work evoking, as per its ambiguous title, a creature or craft of the sea (fins, tails, sails, and rudders being called to mind). Kohn was a fairly prominent figure in the late fifties, having had his first solo show in New York at the Tanager Gallery in 1958 and another one-man show at the Leo Castelli Gallery the following year, both of which were favorably reviewed. In 1961, however, Kohn relocated first to Sarasota, Florida, and then to Los Angeles, effectively removing himself both from the New York scene and art history, his strong, stunning work consequently being little known today.

Suggested Reading:
Livingston, Jane. *Gabriel Kohn, 1910-1975*. Exhibition catalogue. Washington, DC: Corcoran Gallery, 1977.

Plate 48

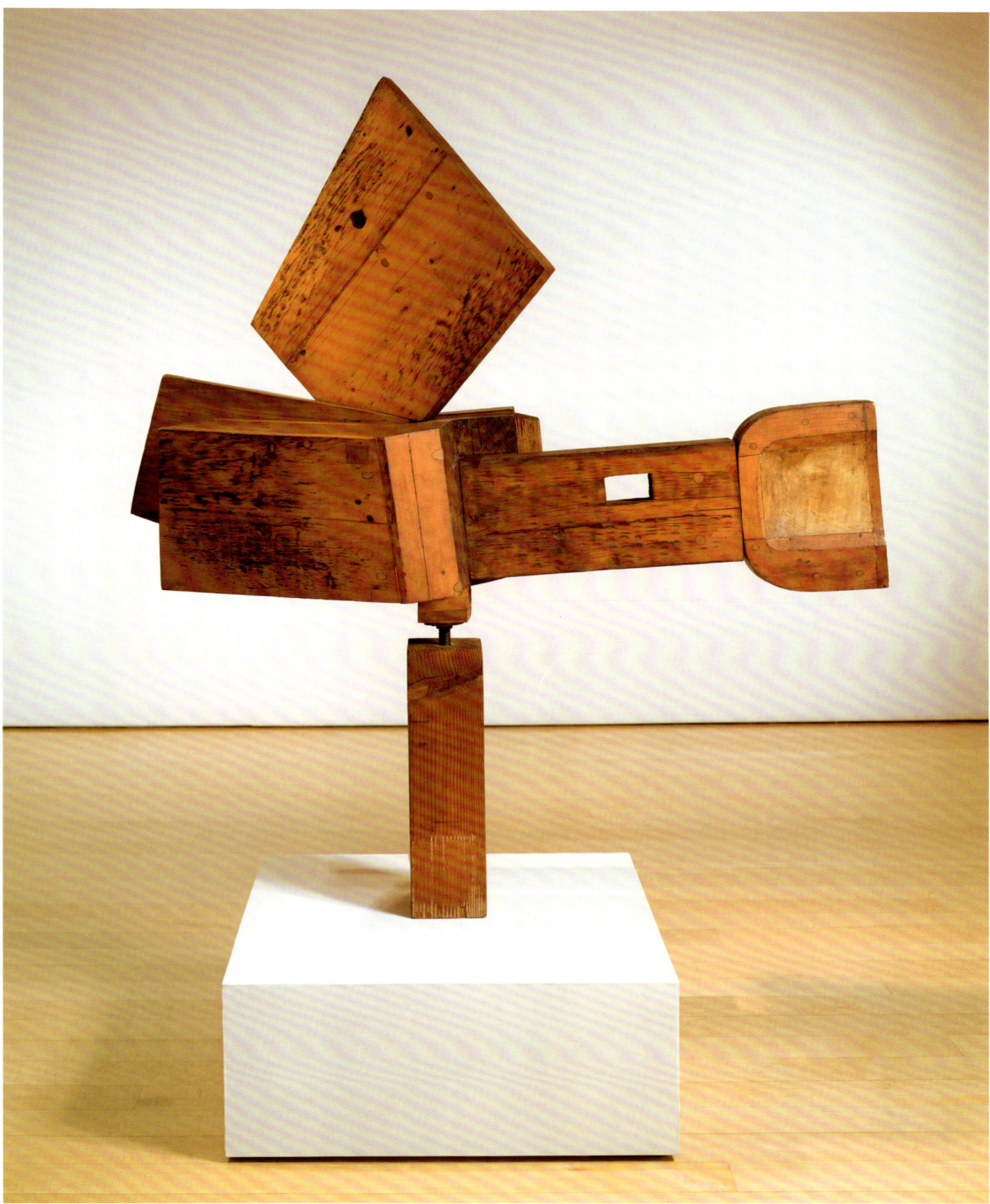

Nicholas Krushenick
New York City
1929 – 1999
New York City

Untitled, 1961
acrylic on linen
30 3/4 x 25 inches
Marianne Boesky Gallery,
New York

Nicholas Krushenick was working in a gestural style influenced by Abstract Expression in 1958, the year in which he and his brother John opened the cooperative Brata Gallery on Tenth Street in New York, which also showed the work of his friends Al Held and Ronald Bladen, who were then painting in a related manner.

By 1961 Krushenick had moved to a flat, graphic style of his own invention which derived influences both from comic books and brand packaging of the time. Thick black outlines were used to define highly animated abstract forms, which were filled in with bright, pure colors. As seen in *Untitled* (1961), the forms seen in Krushenick's art are generally not self-contained, but seem to continue beyond the work's framing edge. Although a mountain range might seem to be suggested, this is a fully abstract work with no correspondences in reality, which makes it all the more remarkable that Krushenick, who was part of Clement Greenberg's *Post Painterly Abstraction* show in 1964, has often been included in books and exhibitions devoted to Pop Art, the sole abstractionist among imagist painters. Krushenick's work is frequently cited as a precedent for the more recent genre of "Comic Abstraction" as represented by the work of artists ranging from Carroll Dunham to Rivane Neuenschwander and Albert Oehlen.

Suggested Reading:
Swanson, Dean. *Nicholas Krushenick*. Exhibition catalogue. Minneapolis, MN: Walker Art Center, 1968.

Plate 49

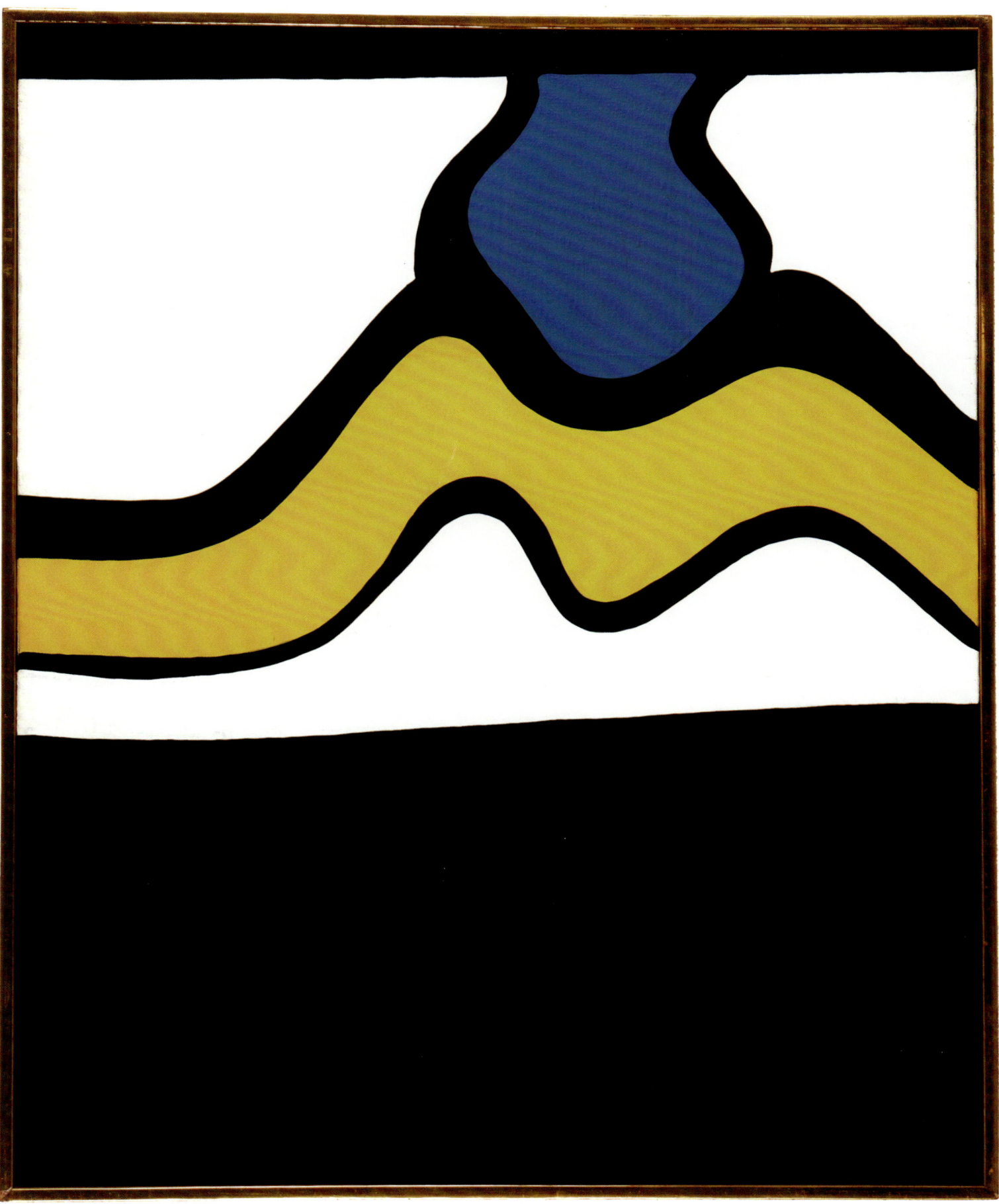

Alexander Liberman
Kiev, Russia
1912 – 1999
Miami Beach, Florida

Yellow Continuum, 1958-59
oil on canvas
four panels, 85 1/2 x 24 7/8
inches overall
The Alexander Liberman Trust,
courtesy Mitchell-Innes & Nash,
New York

Raised in Paris and educated at the Sorbonne and the École des Beaux-Arts, Alexander Liberman and his family fled Paris in 1941 at the time of the Nazi occupation, settling in New York, where he began working for *Vogue* magazine. Liberman spent the rest of his life working for Condé Nast Publications, fostering various art world connections by commissioning projects by leading artists (among them Picasso, Duchamp, Pollock, Rauschenberg, and Johns) for the magazine, while exhibiting his own work in New York galleries. From 1950 until 1963, Liberman created "hard-edge" paintings focused on the form of the circle. In the vertically-stacked four panels of *Yellow Continuum* (1958-59), which were included in Liberman's first solo show at the Betty Parsons Gallery in 1960, the artist explored variations in the spatial reading of a yellow orb set on a white ground when overlapped or adjoined by a series of smaller blue and black dots. While wholly abstract, the solar or planetary reference contained by the work is inescapable and alludes to similar works by early twentieth-century Russian Suprematist and Constructivist artists like El Lizzitsky and Alexander Rodchenko. In 1959, Liberman learned to weld steel and by 1964 carried his spatial concerns and Constructivist vision into the monumentally-scaled sculpture in primary colors for which he is best known.

Suggested Reading:
Rose, Barbara. *Alexander Liberman: Painting and Sculpture, 1950-1950*. New York: Abbeville Press, 1981.

Plate 50

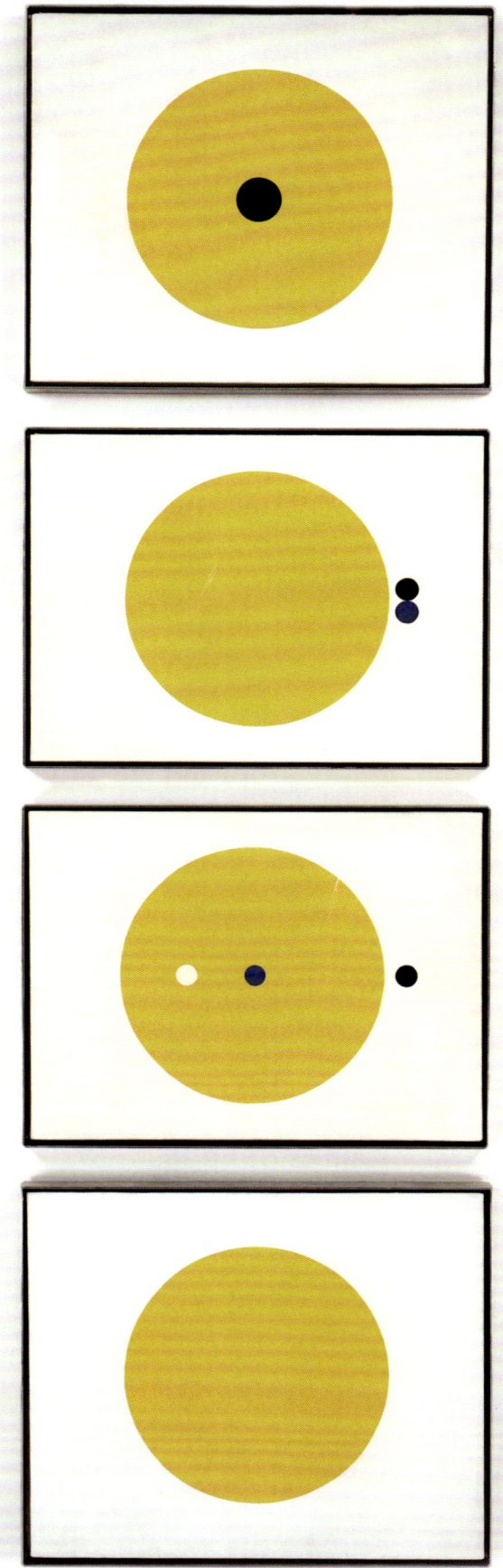

Morris Louis
Baltimore, Maryland
1912 – 1962
Washington, DC

Theta Beta, 1960
acrylic resin paint on canvas
104 5/8 x 233 1/2 inches
Ackland Art Museum, Gift of
Marcella Louis Brenner, 90.87

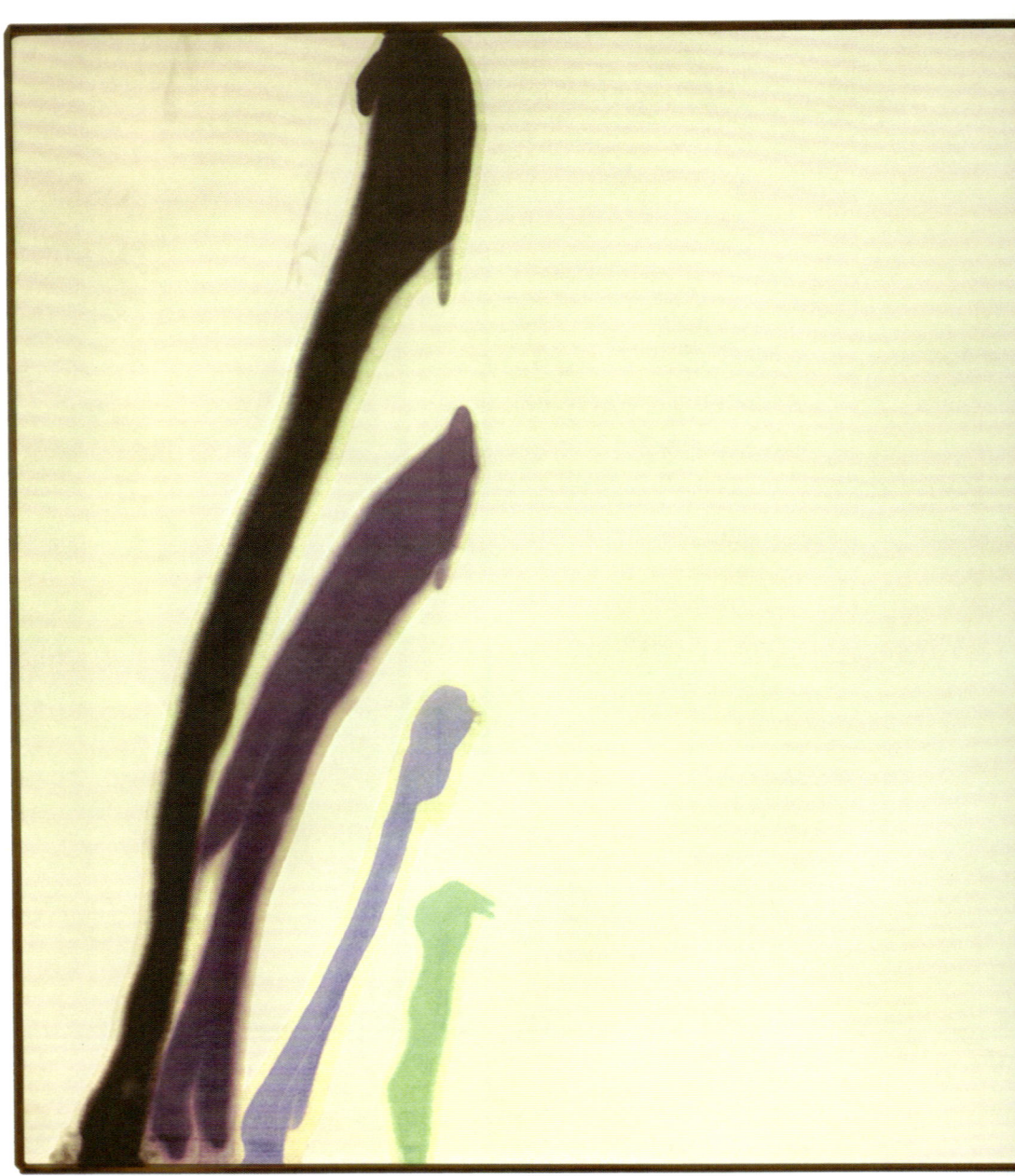

The direction of Morris Louis' work was guided by his exposure in the early fifties to Helen Frankenthaler's "stain painting" technique in which thin pigment is applied to unprimed canvas. Louis, who with Kenneth Noland pioneered the use of staining in Post-painterly Abstraction, worked in series. In his first groups of paintings, the "Veils" and "Florals" (1954-59), great swaths of color were poured so as to overlap, intersect, and blend on the picture surface, while remaining wholly untextured and flat, the weave of the canvas clearly visible. The first exhibition of the "Veils" took place in 1959 at French & Company, New York, whose artistic advisor, the critic Clement Greenberg, was a great champion of Louis'

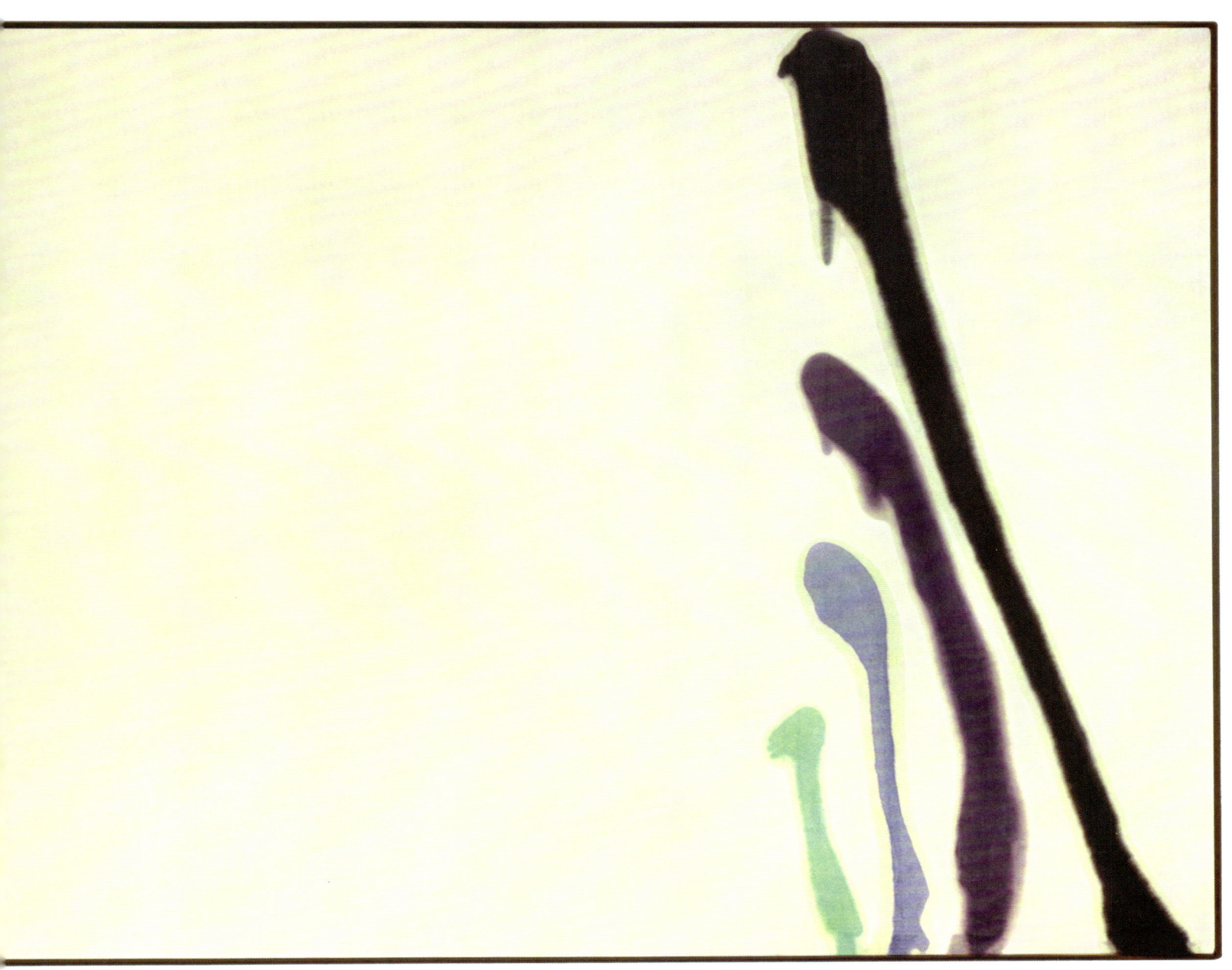

art. In the artist's "Unfurled" series (1960-61), as represented by *Theta Beta* (1960), a few rivulets of stained color appear near the outer edges of a vast expanse of otherwise bare canvas, openness having replaced the density of form and color seen in his earlier work. In *Theta Beta*, lyrical marks dance at the periphery of the viewer's vision, offering a new definition of what a painting can be. In Louis' final series, the "Stripes," straight vertical bands of brilliant color are bunched together on neutral grounds, the artist having returned to centralized (rather than the more radical peripheral) form.

Suggested Reading:
Upright, Diane. *Morris Louis, the Complete Paintings: a Catalogue Raisonné*. New York: Harry N. Abrams, Inc., 1985.

Plate 51

Agnes Martin
Maklin, Saskatchewan, Canada
1912 – 2004
Taos, New Mexico

This Rain, c. 1960
oil on canvas
70 x 70 inches
Collection Emily Fisher Landau,
New York

Agnes Martin moved to New York from New Mexico in 1957 at the invitation of the art dealer Betty Parsons, who a year later gave Martin her first solo show. Martin settled in Coenties Slip in lower Manhattan, where she enjoyed the company of fellow artists Robert Indiana, Robert Rauschenberg, Jasper Johns, and others. Inspired by their Assemblages, she began to incorporate into her compositions found objects, like bottle caps and bolts. By around 1960, however, the landscape watercolors, Surrealistic paintings, and experiments with Assemblage that had been her earlier concerns were supplanted by highly simplified abstractions, as seen in *This Rain* (c. 1960). Although Martin's mature work is generally said to have begun with her use of the grid in 1961, the mood and reductive nature of *This Rain* anticipated the work that was to preoccupy the artist for the rest of her life. Here, two rectangles painted with thin washes of color float one above the other, recalling the paintings of the Abstract Expressionist painter Mark Rothko. However, the square format, reduction of painterly means, muted palette, and Zen-inspired self-restraint of Martin's painting causes her work to serve both as an exemplar of Post-painterly Abstraction and precursor of Minimal Art.

Suggested Reading:
Haskell, Barbara. *Agnes Martin*. Exhibition catalogue. New York: Whitney Museum of American Art, 1993.

Plate 52

John McLaughlin
Sharon, Massachusetts
1898 – 1976
Dana Point, California

K-1957, 1957
oil on canvas
48 x 40 inches
Michael Kohn Gallery, Los
Angeles

Born to a cultivated Boston family before the turn of the century, John McLaughlin developed an early appreciation for Asian art and thought, eventually going to live in Japan for several years and then opening an art gallery in his home city devoted to Japanese prints and antiques. Without having received any formal training, McLaughlin began to devote himself to painting full time when he moved to California in the late forties. His aim was to produce wholly impersonal, formally austere abstractions; *K-1957* (1957) was typical of his work of the mid- to late fifties, which came to be associated with other non-painterly California art.

Although *K-1957*, with its vertical and horizontal lines, rectangles, and play of solid and void, recalls the work of Piet Mondrian, the guiding principle of McLaughlin's art was "equilibrium through opposition," based on the yin-yang of the Taoist East. The meditative mood, quietly evocative color, and studied bilateral symmetry of McLaughlin's art set his paintings apart from those of the Dutch master. The surface of *K-1957* is divided into two uneven "halves," each of which "registers as an imperfect ghost or memory of . . . its other 'half.'"* Geared to studied contrasts of light and dark, McLaughlin's work may be understood to have anticipated the perceptual concerns of Larry Bell, Robert Irwin and others associated with California "Light and Space Art" in the early sixties.

Suggested Reading:
Larsen, Susan C. *John McLaughlin, Western Modernism, Eastern Thought: Essays*. Exhibition catalogue. Laguna Beach, CA: Laguna Art Museum,1996. Distributed by Distributed Art Publishers.

*Prudence Carlson, "Introduction," in *John McLaughlin: Paintings of the Fifites*, exhib. cat. (New York: Andre Emmerich Gallery, 1987).

Plate 53

Kenneth Noland

Born in Asheville, North Carolina, 1924; lives in South Shaftsbury, Vermont

That, 1958–59
oil on canvas
83 x 83 inches
Collection of David Mirvish, Toronto

In October 1959, Noland exhibited fifteen paintings at French & Company in his third solo show in New York. While his previous exhibitions (in 1957 and 1958) had passed with little notice, this show, the first full-scale presentation of his stained circle paintings, was a different matter, as the works—like *That* (1958–59)—burned with great coloristic intensity and made a grand statement testifying to the power of centralized, predetermined forms that ran counter to the prevailing New York School aesthetic. In 1953, Noland had gone with Morris Louis to view Helen Frankenthaler's paintings executed with a stain technique, although it took Noland several years to develop his own characteristic method of direct stain. In his "Circle Painting" series, which occupied him from 1957-63, Noland began in the center and worked outward, with concentric bands of high color in varying widths stained directly onto bare, unprimed, and unsized, canvas. Although these works recall Jasper Johns' "Target" paintings, a more pertinent precedent for Noland were the concentric squares found in the work of his teacher at Black Mountain College, Josef Albers. The gesturally-rendered outer gray circle seen in the radiant *That*, however, does not owe anything to either Johns or Albers, but is a dramatic vestige of the "Action Painting" of the preceding generation.

Suggested Reading:
Agee, William C. *Kenneth Noland: The Circle Paintings, 1956-63*. Exhibition catalogue. Houston: Museum of Fine Arts, 1993.

Plate 54

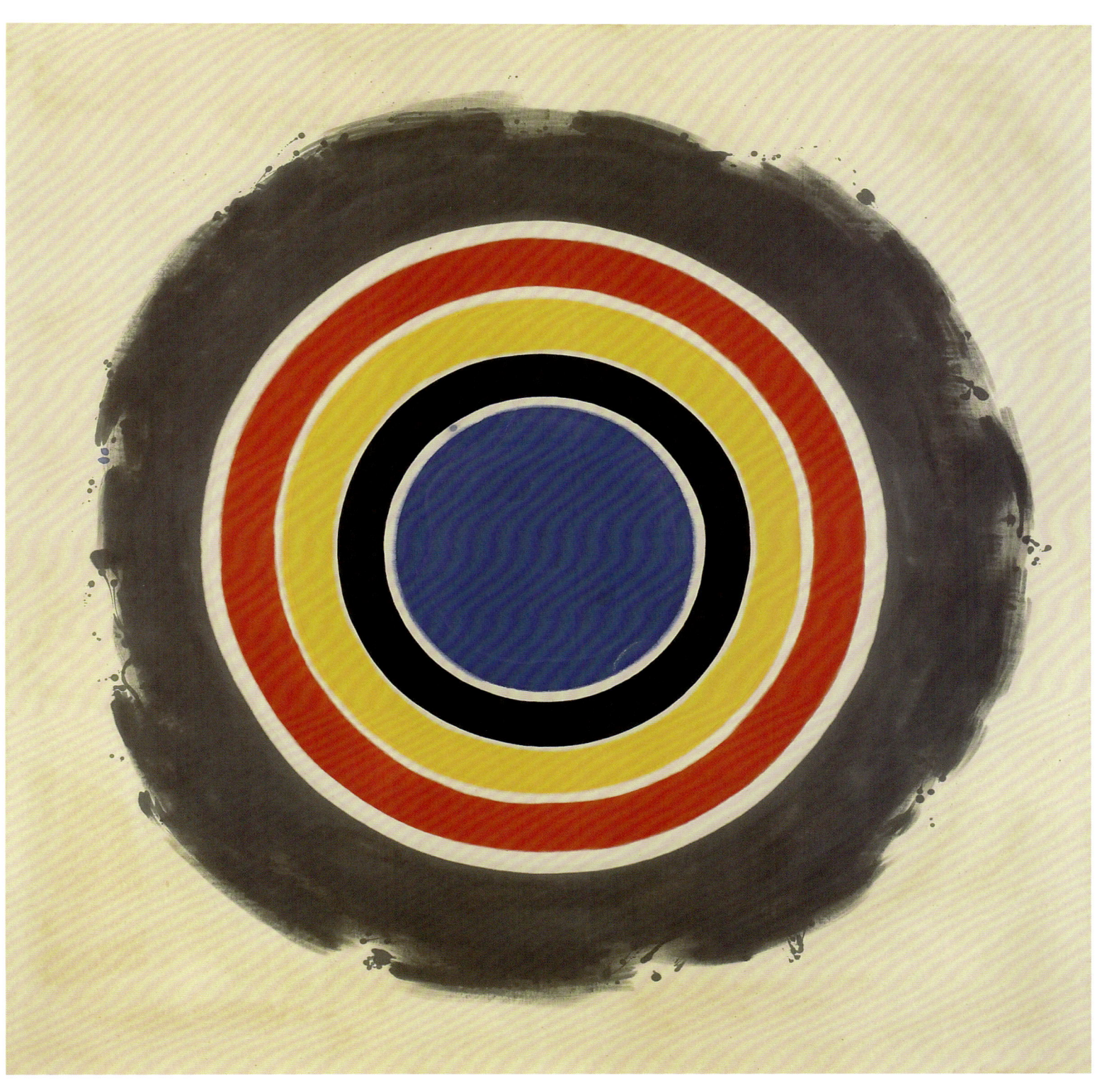

George Ortman
Born in Oakland, California,
1926; lives in New York City

Circle, 1958 (restored by artist)
oil on collaged canvas with
plaster on wood
48 x 48 inches
Courtesy of Mitchell Algus
Gallery and the artist

In New York in the late fifties, George Ortman began to produce works that rejected the "purist" sensibility often attached to geometric abstraction in favor of combining aspects of painting and sculpture. In *Circle* (1958), a square canvas is entirely covered over with overlapping, differently-sized circles of cut-out white canvas. This all-over activated, "bubbling" surface is punctuated by three rows of three, evenly spaced bull's eyes of white, blue, and black. In actuality, these are large white plaster rings enclosing smaller blue-painted wood inserts, which in turn enclose dark holes or voids, resembling the pupil of the eye. While the target-like forms and Ortman's collage technique may call to mind Jasper Johns' early "Targets," whose surfaces were covered with newspaper collage, Ortman's painting-constructions were wholly original creations, their intention seeming to be to make every element of the composition a discrete physical entity. Other work by Ortman created around this time was often more overtly symbolic, with symmetrical arrangements of arrows, geometric forms, and other shapes seeming to embrace a secret sign system or code. Whatever their meaning, Ortman's painted constructions, which were included in such major exhibitions as *Towards a New Abstraction*, presented at the Jewish Museum in 1963, were admired by Donald Judd and other Minimalist artists who began to emerge at that time for their pronounced physicality.

Suggested Reading:
The Renaissance Society at The University of Chicago. "George Ortman," renaissancesociety.org/site/search.html.

Plate 55

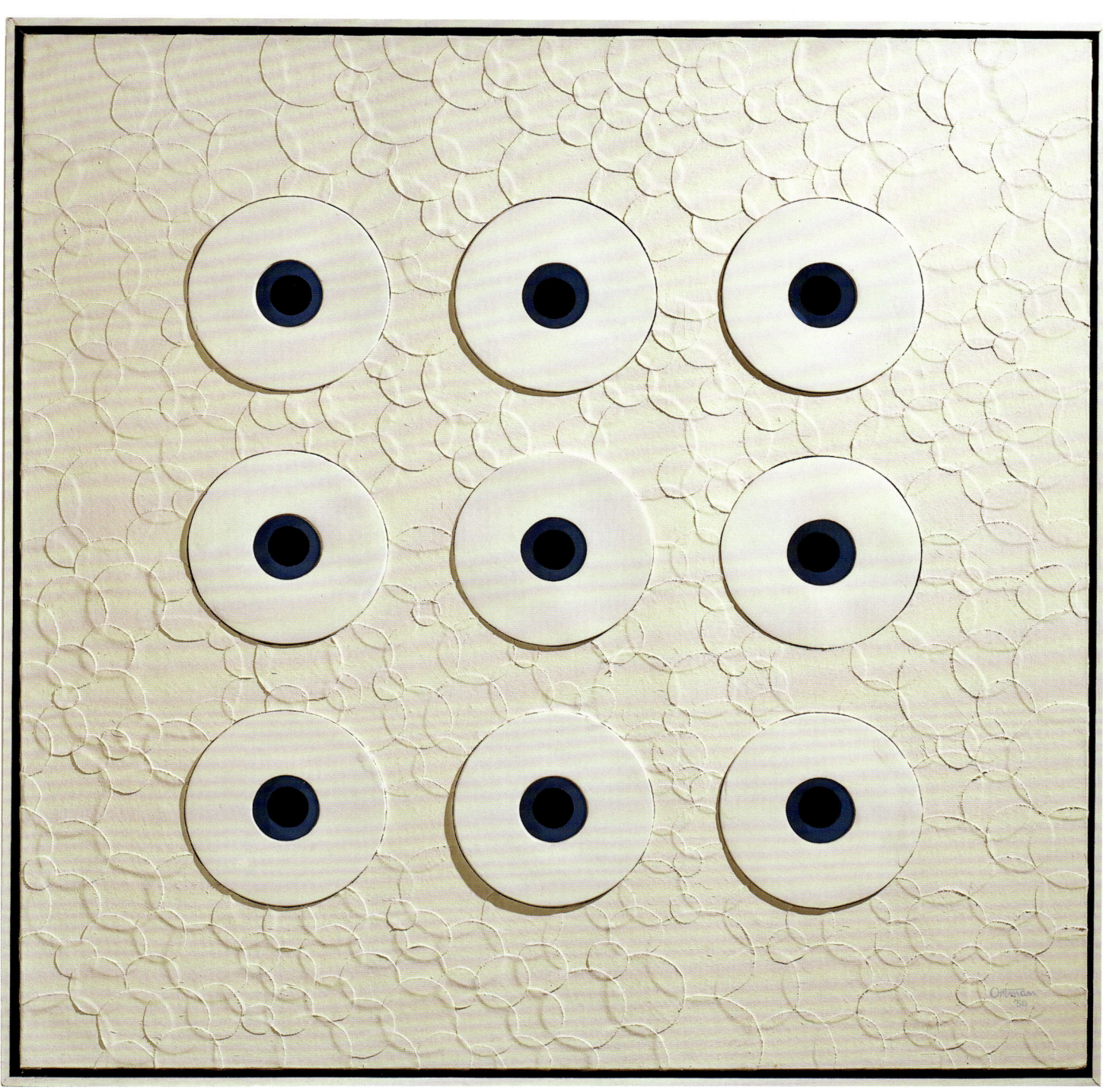

Robert Ryman

Born in Nashville, Tennessee,
1930; lives in New York City

*An all white painting measuring
9 1/2" x 10" and signed twice
on the left side in white umber*,
1961
oil on linen canvas
13 3/4 x 13 3/4 inches
San Francisco Museum of
Modern Art
Purchased through a gift of
Mimi and Peter Haas

Robert Ryman moved from Tennessee to New York in 1952 with the intention of becoming a jazz musician. In 1953, seeking a means of financial support, Ryman became a guard at the Museum of Modern Art, a job he was to hold for seven years. Some time in 1953, without having received any artistic training, Ryman began to make paintings and by 1955, largely influenced by the close values and high degree of abstraction seen in Mark Rothko's work, began to experiment with monochrome, his first apparently having been executed with orange paint. In 1958, he began to paint all-white square monochromes, a practice he has continued to the present day, the artist's *oeuvre* devoted to an ongoing exploration of the seemingly endless permutations involved in using different tones of white paint on various supports.

In 1961, Ryman executed a series of small scale white paintings on unstretched linen canvas, each featuring a few small horizontal accents. *An all white painting measuring 9 1/2" x 10" and signed twice on the left side in white umber* (1961) features, as its wholly literal title indicates, "graphic embellishments" in the form of the artist's signature and the date of execution (RRYMAN61), which appears twice along the left edge, its rhythmic nature having been likened to the beats one might hear in music. Ryman does not consider the incorporation of his signature and the date in a work to be a violation of his purist aesthetic, as these are traditional components of painting. Ryman's stripped-down aesthetic made him a pioneering figure in Minimal Art.

Suggested Reading:
Storr, Robert. *Robert Ryman*. Exhibition catalogue. London: Tate Gallery; New York: Museum of Modern Art, 1993.

Plate 56

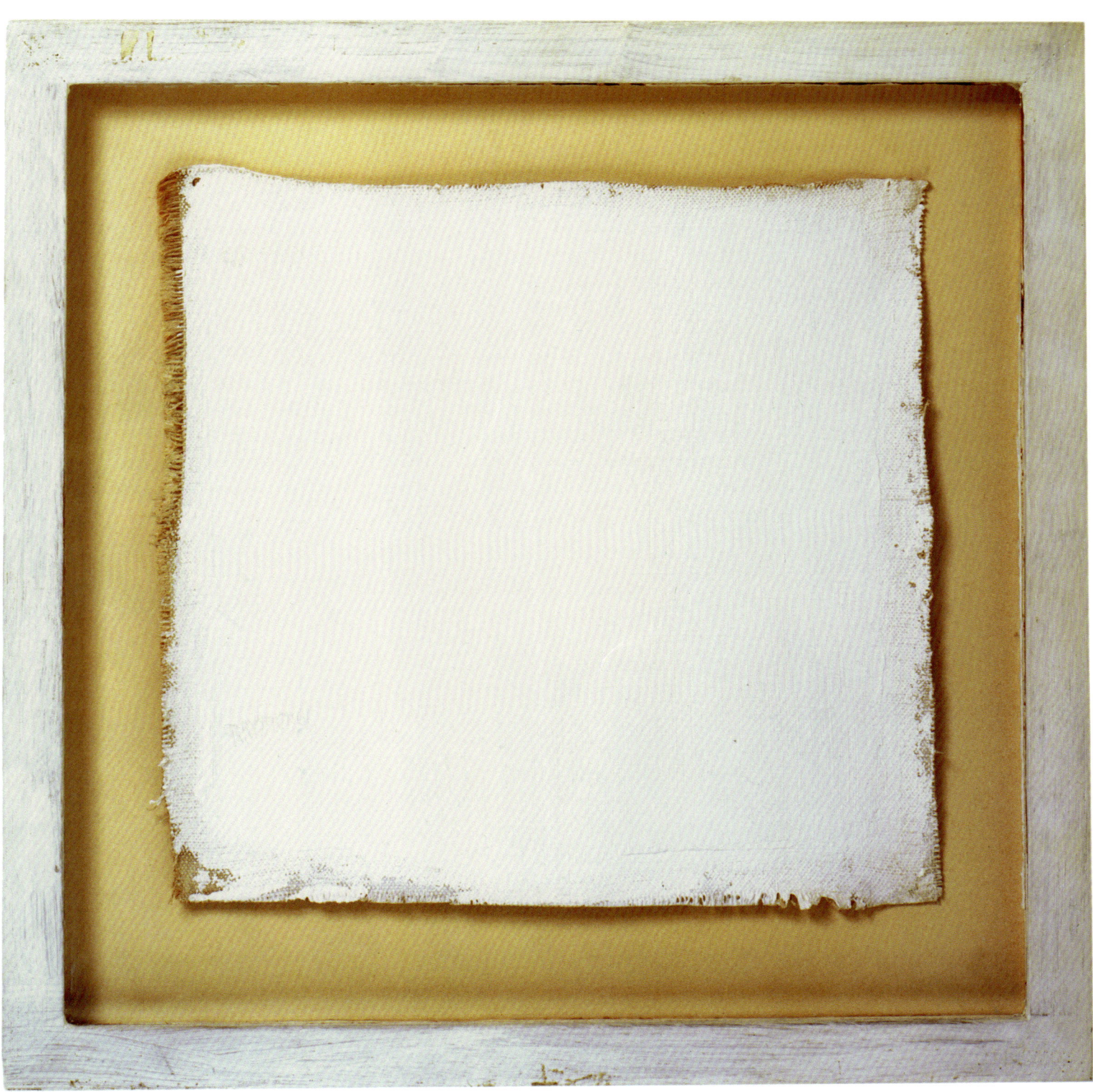

Leon Polk Smith
Chickasha, Indian Territory,
Oklahoma
1906 – 1996
Long Island, New York

Expanse, 1959
oil on canvas
68 x 74 inches
Washburn Gallery, New York

A Native American artist born in Indian Territory, Oklahoma, shortly after the turn of the century, Leon Polk Smith studied art education at Columbia University's Teachers College in the late thirties, at which time he began to paint in a Neo-Plastic style heavily influenced by Piet Mondrian. In 1954, Smith broke free of the straight and diagonal lines of the European-derived manner to produce his first signature paintings consisting of curvilinear forms inscribed within round-format canvases (tondos). This change in his work had been motivated by seeing a sports equipment catalogue filled with line drawings of tennis balls, baseballs and so on, each a circular form with internal definition. After producing an extended series of tondos, Smith returned to square format canvases, producing such works as the imposing, aptly titled *Expanse* (1959). In this crisply rendered work, which caused Smith's work to be labeled "Hard-edge" in the early sixties, a large, irregularly undulating curved white form runs vertically though a black field. The form is distinctly organic in nature and swollen in feel, with both the white "figure" and the black "ground" reversing in the viewer's eye to read as silhouettes and evoke bodily references.

Suggested Reading:
Ratcliff, Carter. *Leon Polk Smith: American Painter*. Exhibition catalogue. Brooklyn, NY: Brooklyn Museum of Art, 1996.

Plate 57

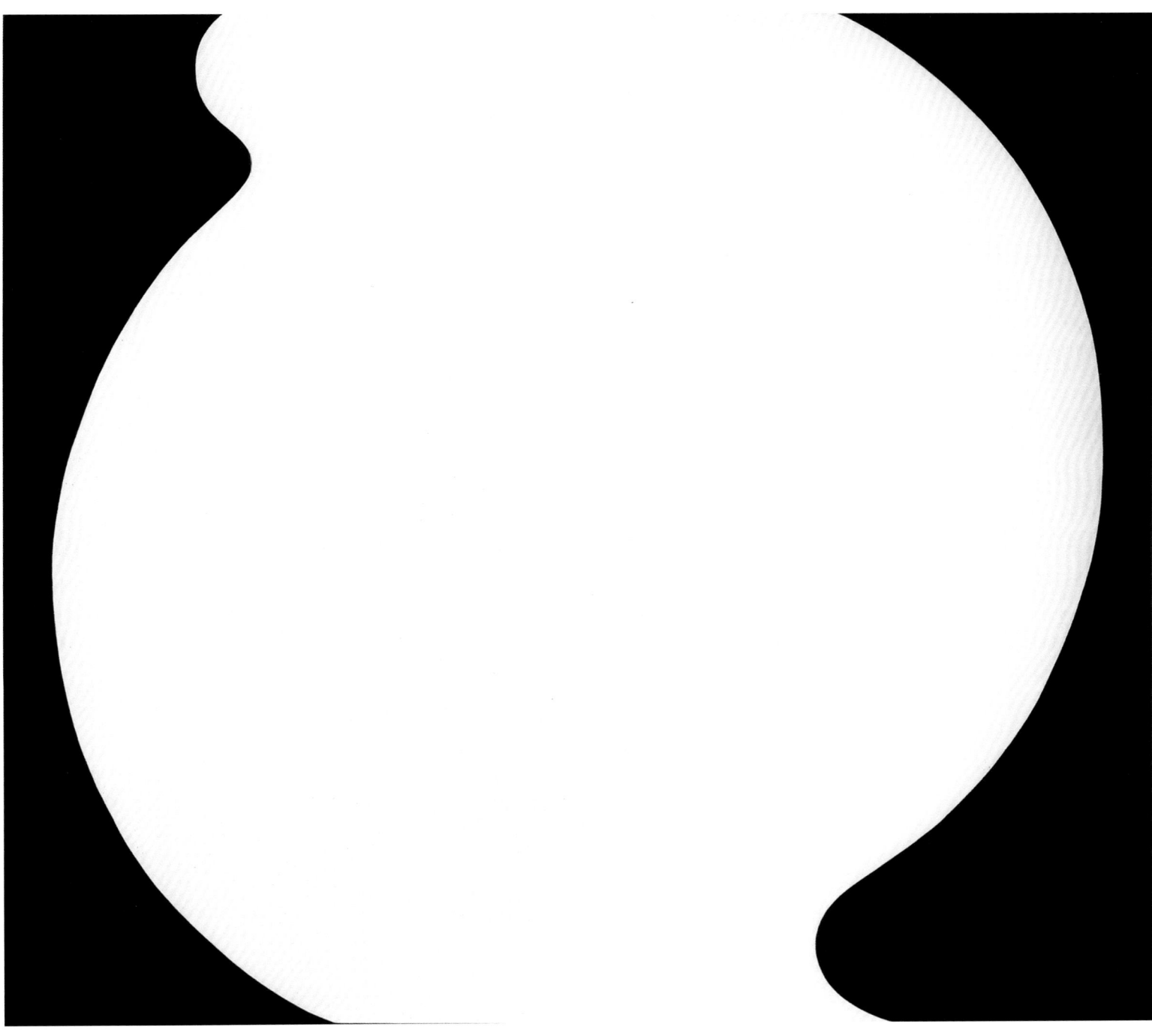

Tony Smith

South Orange, New Jersey
1912 – 1980
New York City

Spitball, 1961
granite
12 1/8 x 14 1/2 x 15 inches
Montclair Art Museum.
Museum Purchase; Prior gift of
Harry A. Astlett

Tony Smith began his career as an architect, studying at the New Bauhaus headed by Laszlo Moholy-Nagy in Chicago, working for Frank Lloyd Wright, and then launching an independent architectural practice in 1940. In 1946, Smith also began teaching art at New York University and became close friends with many of the Abstract Expressionists, especially Mark Rothko and Barnett Newman, with whom he shared a spiritual conception of art.

In 1961, Smith abandoned architecture for sculpture, and began to create such works as *Spitball* (1961), which was based on a cardboard model. While a finished work in and of itself, this small-scale granite sculpture is a model (or *maquette*) for a steel version of the piece of the same date that was fabricated in an edition of three. One is currently installed on the campus of Case Western Reserve University in Cleveland, Ohio, and measures 11 feet 6 inches x 14 feet and weighs almost 800 pounds.

Smith described his sculptures as "presences," seeking to imbue their modular forms, which are often based on the tetrahedron, with a life force as they "unfold" through space. Dramatic and physically imposing when seen on monumental scale, his sculptures thus combine the geometric with the anthropomorphic. Although Smith's emergence as a sculptor coincided with early Minimal Art, which shared his use of geometric and modular forms, industrial materials, and factory fabrication, Smith's sculpture stands at some distance from this "cool," unemotional art. True to its Abstract Expressionist heritage, Smith wanted his art to be "a conduit for spiritual things."

Suggested Reading:
Storr, Robert. *Tony Smith: Architect, Painter, Sculptor*. Exhibition catalogue. New York: Museum of Modern Art, 1998. Distributed by Harry N. Abrams, Inc.

Plate 58

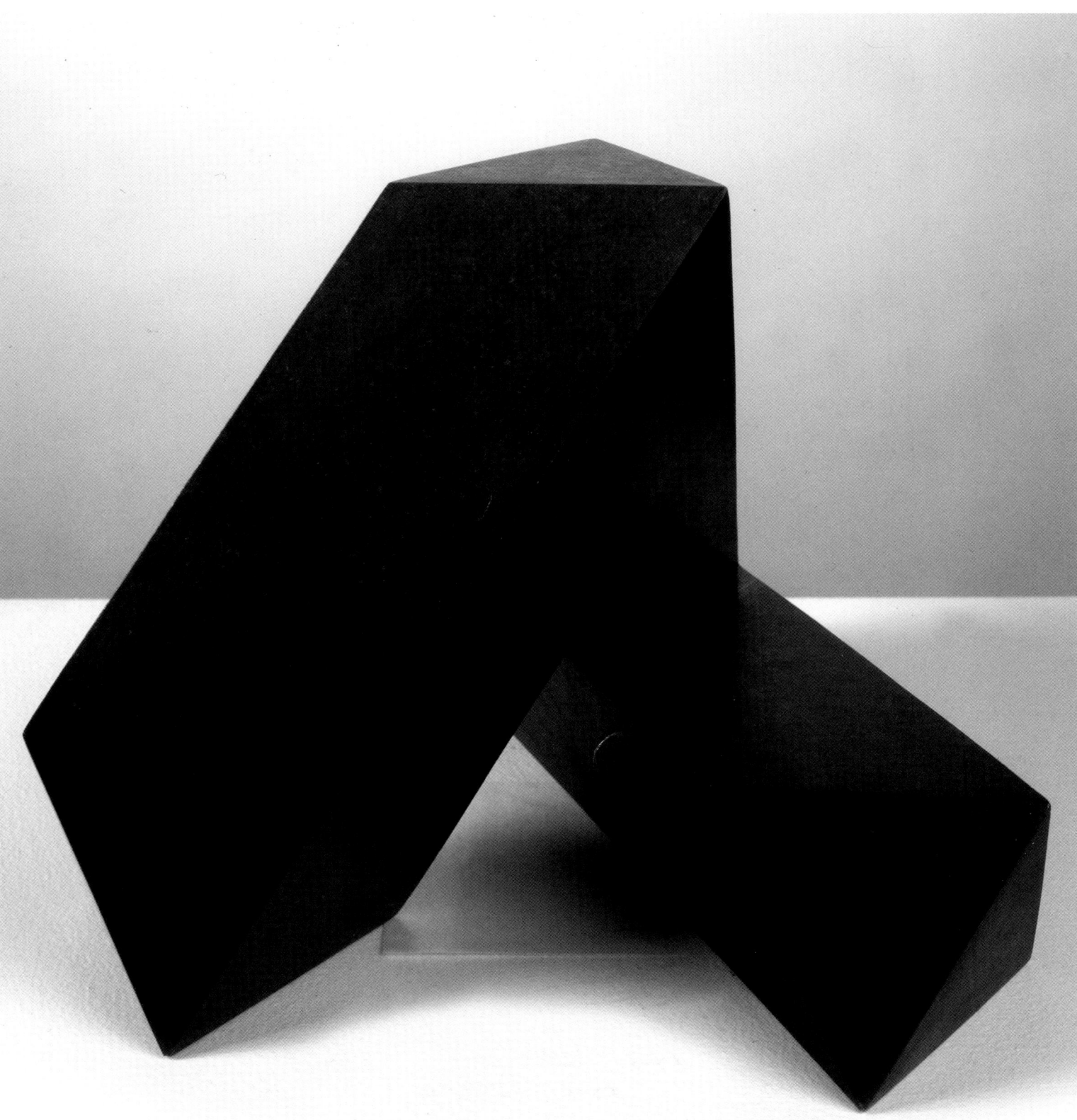

Frank Stella
Born in Malden, Massachusetts,
1936; lives in New York City

Blue Horizon, 1958
enamel and oil on canvas
72 x 72 inches
David Winton Bell Gallery,
Brown University, Gift of
Lawrence Rubin

Frank Stella received his first formal art training in the early fifties while attending Phillips Academy in Andover, Massachusetts, a private high school, where he studied under Patrick Morgan, who had been a pupil of Hans Hofmann in Munich. Stella then enrolled in Princeton University, where he studied art history with William C. Seitz, who had written his dissertation on Abstract Expressionism and later curated the 1961 exhibition, *The Art of Assemblage*, at The Museum of Modern Art (Princeton did not offer formal art classes until Stella's junior year at the school). Although Stella had committed himself to abstract painting while still in high school, in 1957, he executed several Assemblages of cardboard and wood, some of them made in collaboration with his friend Darby Bannard. A year later, while still attending Princeton, he visited Jasper Johns' first solo show at the Leo Castelli Gallery, which directed the course of his future art.

Inspired by Johns' *Flag*, Stella started to create paintings filled with repetitive bands of stripes. *Blue Horizon* (1958), a monochrome painting dominated by a pattern of horizontal stripes, was among the later works in this series, painted after Stella's college graduation and move to New York City. A series of vertical bands interrupt the horizontal flow of the work on its right side (which are actually *pentimenti*, or underpainting), the poor coverage, and encrusted nature of the work's surface having resulted from the combination of cheap non-art enamel paints and unsized cotton duck (the pattern of the drips reveal that the vertical bands were actually painted as horizontals, but that the canvas was then turned onto its side). While the broad, somewhat meandering gestures of the stripes, the all-over composition, and the work's scale all look back to Abstract Expressionism, the predetermined and unitary nature of the design and reliance on monochrome anticipate Stella's series of "Black Paintings" (1958-60) (page 12, fig. 10), whose inclusion in The Museum of Modern Art's exhibition, *Sixteen Americans* of December 1959, launched Stella's unparalleled career.

Suggested Reading:
Cooper, Harry and Megan R. Luke. *Frank Stella 1958*. Exhibition catalogue. Cambridge, MA: Fogg Art Museum, Harvard University Art Museums; London: Yale University Press, 2006.

Plate 59

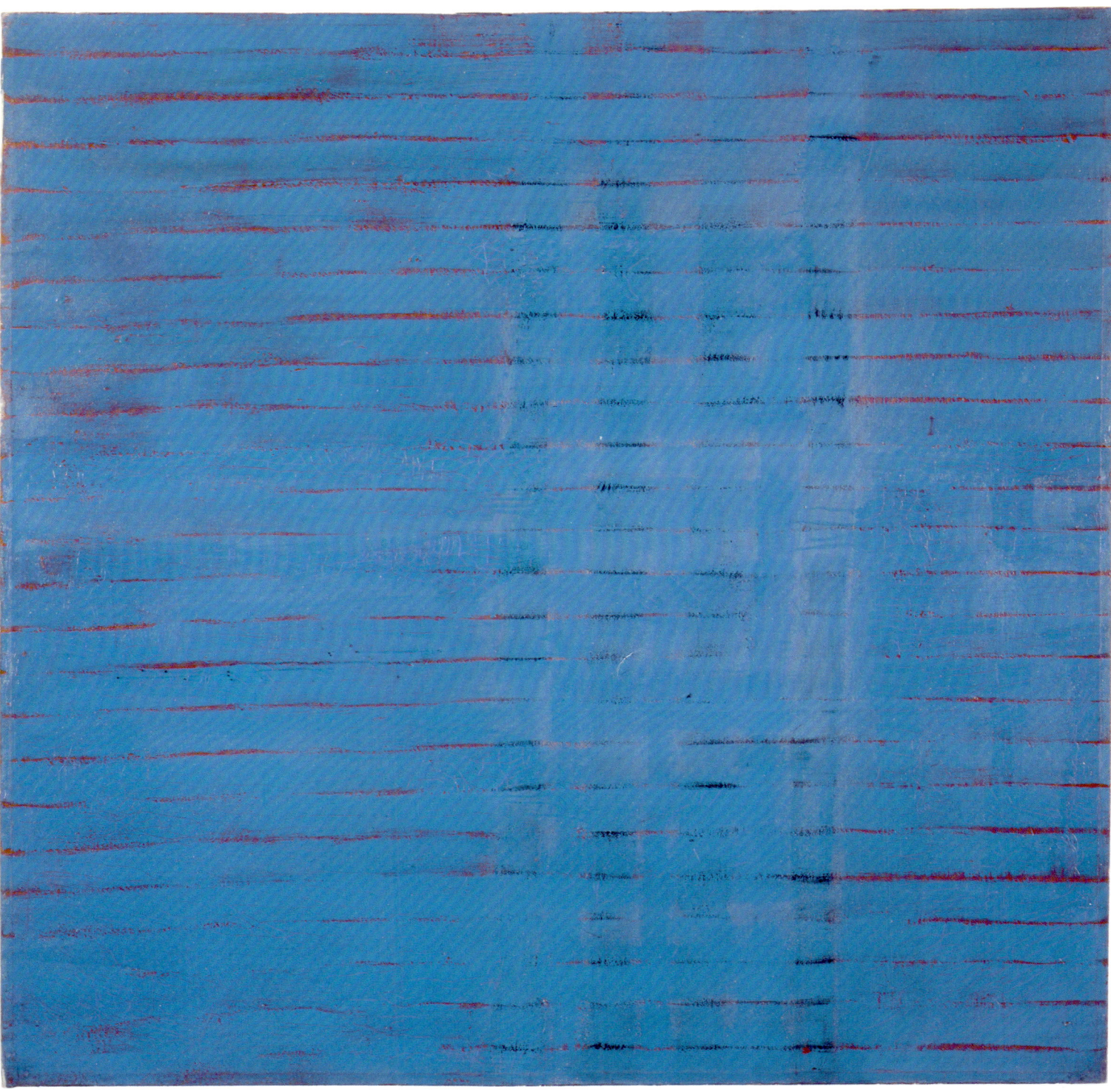

Myron Stout

Denton, Texas
1908 – 1987
Provincetown, Massachusetts

Untitled (No. 3-1956), 1957
oil on canvas
26 x 18 inches
Carnegie Museum of Art,
Pittsburgh
Gift of Leland Hazard, 58.33

After teaching art in Hawaii during World War II, Myron Stout moved to New York in the late forties and soon, like his friend and teacher Hans Hofmann, began dividing his time between New York City and Provincetown, Massachusetts, where he settled permanently in 1954. At the moment when the artists of the New York School were transforming the scale and character of painting, producing grand, expansive, heroic works, Stout developed a personal aesthetic devoted to intimately-sized, highly concentrated, seemingly simple, but painstakingly worked abstractions. As seen in *Untitled* (1957), these were black-and-white paintings, each of which typically featured a single, strongly defined organic shape. Here, tension exists between the irregular shape, which seems to want to extend its "arms" outward, and the framing edge of the canvas that confines it. The clarity, precision, and impersonal nature of Stout's work, developed in the early fifties, anticipated the emergence of Post-painterly Abstraction later that decade.

Suggested Reading:
Schwartz, Sanford. *Myron Stout*. Exhibition catalogue. New York: Whitney Museum of American Art, 1980.

Plate 60

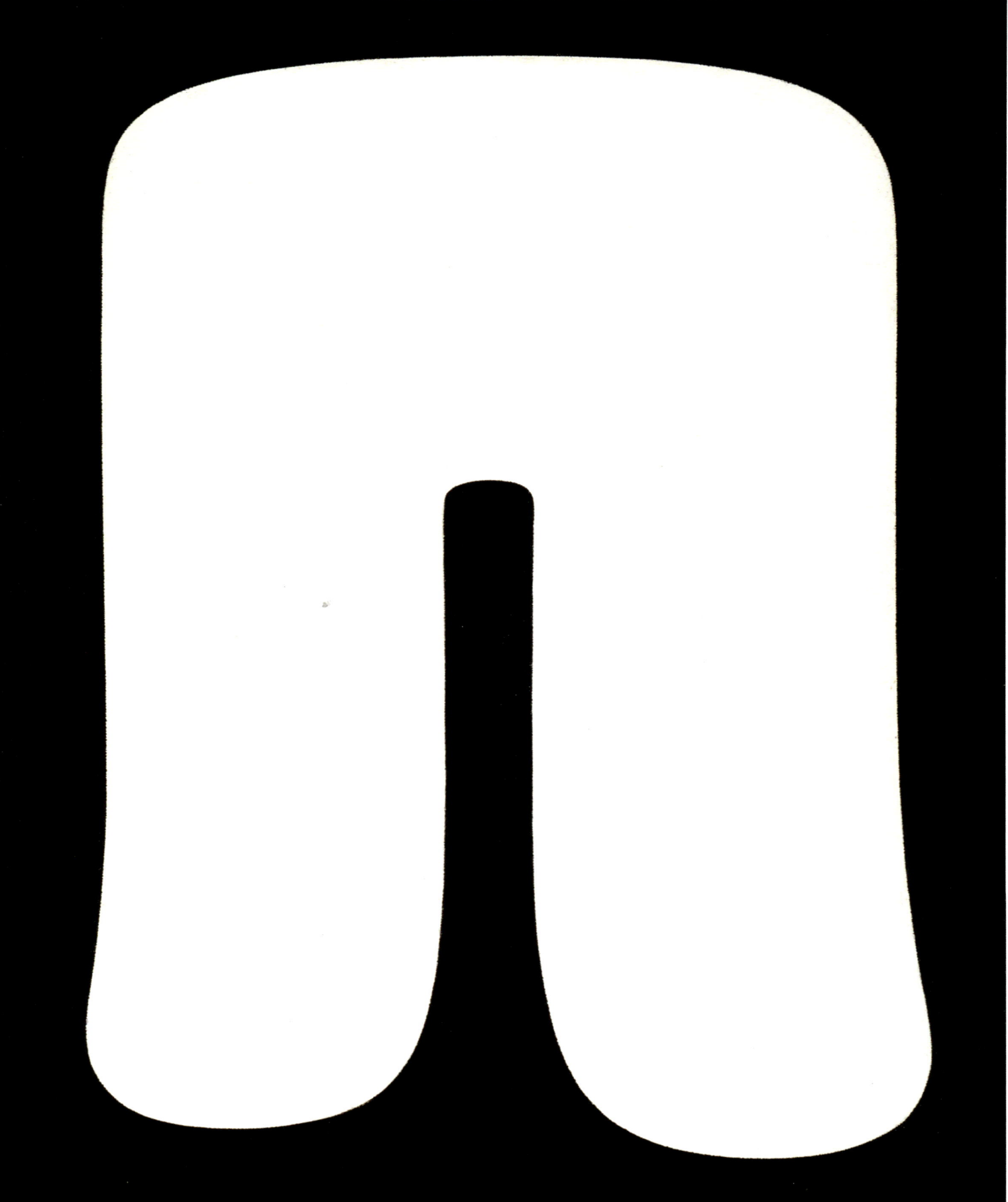

Alma Thomas
Columbus, Georgia
1891 – 1978
Washington DC

Yellow and Blue, 1959
oil on canvas
28 x 40 inches
Courtesy of Michael Rosenfeld
Gallery, LLC, New York,
New York

Born in Columbus, Georgia, Thomas' family moved to Washington DC when she was a teenager. She pursued a career in teaching, one of the few professions open to educated Black women in the early twentieth century. In 1924, she became the first graduate of the newly formed Fine Arts Department at Howard University and later, earned a master's degree from Columbia University. In 1943, Alma Thomas helped found the Barnett Aden Gallery in Washington. For many years she was a fixture on the Washington art scene, attending gallery and museum openings, and befriending many artists who later became associated with the Washington Color School, such as Morris Louis and Gene Davis.

In 1957 and 1958, with retirement on the horizon, Thomas began to study with Expressionist painter Jacob Kainen at American University and began to experiment with abstraction and the more expressive possibilities of color. *Yellow and Blue* (1959), is one of Thomas' first abstract paintings. Blocks of dense color are juxtaposed as Thomas tentatively explores the relationships between warm and cool colors. Jagged black brush strokes create a web or grid, locking the colors in place. The canvas is heavily painted with loaded brush and palette knife.

Within a very few years the planes of color would be replaced by mosaic-like strokes in vividly hued patterns, and the black lines supplanted by areas of underlying primed canvas. While the loosely geometric elements of her paintings, saturated colors, and expressive use of blank canvas are sometimes linked with the Washington Color School Painters, her work is singular for its joyful and emotional content within a tightly controlled vocabulary. In 1972, at over 80 years old, Alma Thomas became the first African American woman artist to be given a solo exhibition at the Whitney Museum of American Art.

Entry by Emily Kass

Suggested Reading:
Foresta, Merry A. *A Life in Art: Alma Thomas 1891 – 1978*. Exhibition catalogue. National Museum of American Art, 1981; Fort Wayne Museum of Art.

Alma W. Thomas: A Retrospective of the Paintings. San Francisco: Pomegranate Communications, 1998.

Plate 61

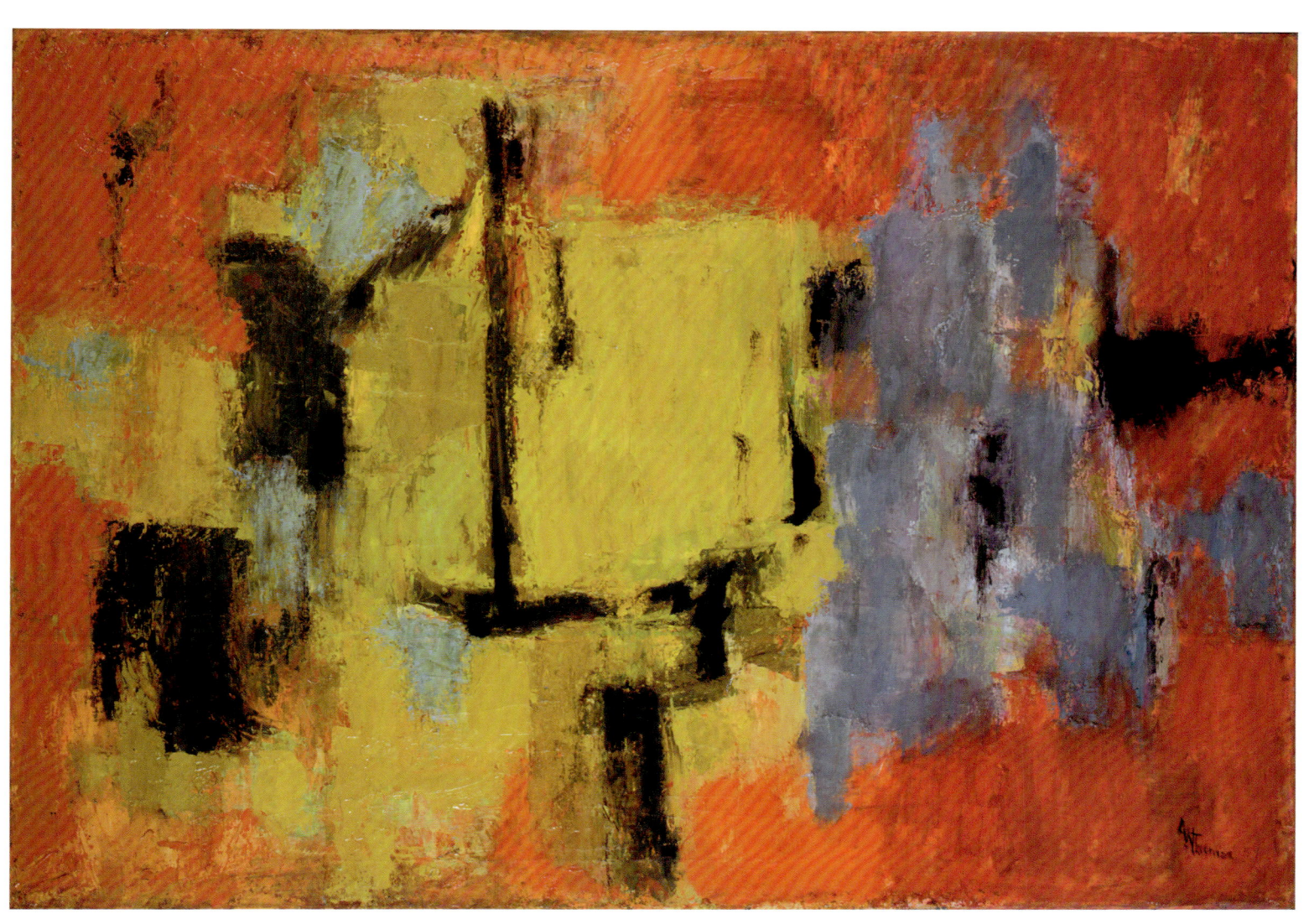

Jack Youngerman

Born in Louisville, Kentucky, 1926; lives in Bridgehampton, New York

Coenties Slip, 1959
oil on canvas
81 x 68 inches
Whitney Museum of American Art, New York, 69.94
Gift of Governor Nelson A. Rockefeller

Jack Youngerman studied at the University of Missouri and the University of North Carolina at Chapel Hill, before taking advantage of the GI Bill and going to Paris to attend the École des Beaux-Arts. He stayed in Paris for almost ten years, became close friends with his compatriot Ellsworth Kelly, and married the actress Delphine Seyrig, who had performed in the film "Last Year in Marienbad." In Paris, he discovered Matisse's late paper cutouts, Hans Arp's prints and collages, and Wassily Kandinsky's woodcuts, whose impact upon his painting continued well after he moved to New York in 1956 at the urging of art dealer Betty Parsons, who presented his first solo show in America at her gallery in 1958. In New York, Youngerman took up residence in Coenties Slip, where Kelly, Agnes Martin, Lenore Tawney, and Richard Anuszkiewicz were among his neighbors.

Coenties Slip (1959) was typical of his work of this time. Although from a distance the work seems to present a floral motif—an orange flower with black shadows set against a white ground—upon approach the image breaks apart into a landscape of crags and fissures, the thickly textured surface calling attention to itself and its assertive handling. The myriad jagged forms engage in a dynamic play of figure-ground, positive-negative reversals. What appears to be the passive white "ground" at the bottom of the piece, for example, actually extends upward like a lapping wave or stalagmite, commanding a place on the picture surface. While affirming Youngerman's European roots, the work's charged energy, abstract forms, and evocations of things in nature also recall the work of such early American modernists as Georgia O'Keeffe and Arthur Dove. Having amalgamated a variety of influences independent of New York School sources, Youngerman arrived at a dramatic style of painting apart from personal expression.

Suggested Reading:
Waldman, Diane. *Youngerman*. Exhibition catalogue. New York: Solomon R. Guggenheim Museum, 1986.

Plate 62

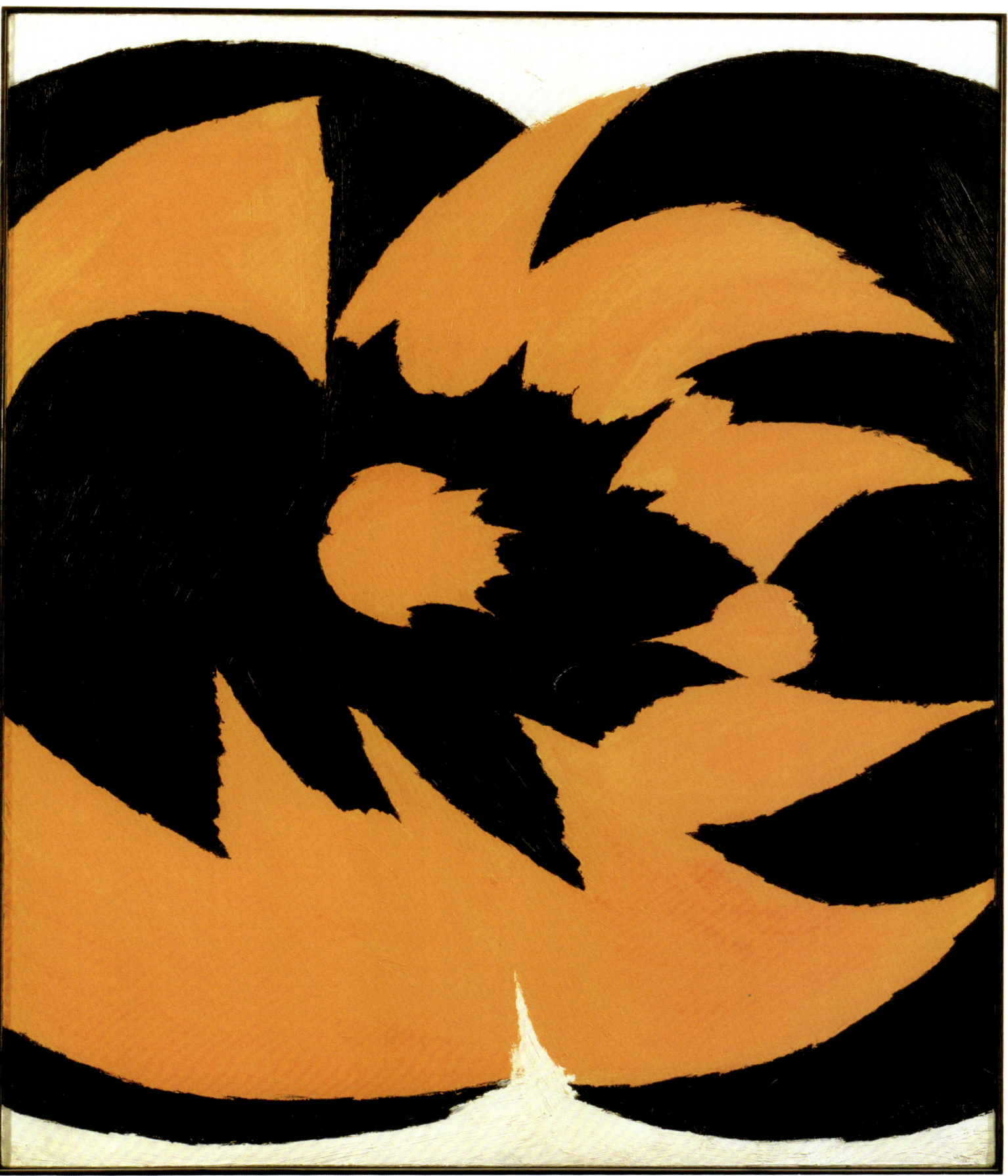

SELECTED BIBLIOGRAPHY

Alloway, Lawrence. *Eleven from the Reuben Gallery*. New York: Solomon R. Guggenheim Museum, 1965.

———— and Allan Kaprow. *New Forms-New Media*. New York: Martha Jackson Gallery, 1960.

Armstrong, Elizabeth, ed. *Birth of the Cool: California Art, Design, and Culture at Midcentury*. Newport Beach: Orange County Museum of Art; Munich: Prestel Art, 2007.

————, ed. *In the Spirit of Fluxus*. Minneapolis: Walker Art Center, 1993.

Chassman, Neil A. *Poets of the Cities of New York and San Francisco, 1950–1965*. New York: E. P. Dutton, 1974.

Crow, Thomas. *The Rise of the Sixties: American and European Art in the Era of Dissent*. New York: Harry N. Abrams, Inc., 1996.

Feinstein, Roni. *The "Junk" Aesthetic: Assemblage of the 1950s and early 1960s*. New York: Whitney Museum of American Art, 1989.

Ferguson, Russel, ed. *Hand-Painted Pop: American Art in Transition, 1955–62*. Los Angeles: The Museum of Contemporary Art; New York: Rizzoli International, 1992.

Forty Years of California Assemblage. Los Angeles: Wight Art Gallery, University of California, Los Angeles, 1989.

Geldzahler, Henry. *New York Painting and Sculpture: 1940–1970*. New York: E.P. Dutton & Co., Inc., in association with The Metropolitan Museum of Art, 1969.

Gettings, Frank. *Different Drummers*. Washington, DC: Smithsonian Institution Press in association with the Hirshhorn Museum and Sculpture Garden, 1988.

Glimcher, Mildred, ed. *Indiana, Kelly, Martin, Rosenquist, Youngerman at Coenties Slip*. New York: Pace Gallery, 1993.

Greenberg, Clement. *Art and Culture: Critical Essays*, Boston: Beacon Press, 1971

Grenier, Catherine, ed. *Los Angeles, 1955-1985: Birth of an Art Capital*. Paris: Centre Pompidou, Panama Musées, 2006.

Gumpert, Lynne and Pepe Karmel. *New York Cool: Painting and Sculpture from the NYU Art Collection*. Exhibition catalogue. New York: Grey Art Gallery, New York University, 2008.

Halberstam, David. *The Fifties*. New York: Villard Books, 1993.

Hapgood, Susan, ed. *Neo-Dada: Redefining Art, 1958-1962*. New York: American Federation of Arts in association with Universe Publishing, 1994.

Haskell, Barbara. *Blam! The Explosion of Pop, Minimalism, and Performance, 1958–1964*. New York: Whitney Museum of American Art, 1984.

Hendricks, Geoffrey, ed. *Critical Mass: Happenings, Fluxus, Performance, Intermedia and Rutgers University, 1958—1972*. New Brunswick, NJ: Mason Gross Art Galleries, 2003. Distributed by Rutgers University Press.

Houston, Joe, ed. *Optic Nerve: Perceptual Art of the 1960s*. Columbus Museum of Art in association with London: Merrell, 2007.

Kleeblatt, Norman L., ed., *Action/Abstraction: Pollock, de Kooning, and American Art, 1940-1976*. The Jewish Museum, New York, in association with Yale University Press, 2008.

Madoff, Steven Henry. *Pop Art: A Critical History*. Berkeley: University of California Press, 1997.

Marter, Joan, ed. *Off Limits: Rutgers University and the Avant-Garde, 1957–1963*. New Brunswick, New Jersey: Rutgers University Press, 1999.

Miller, Dorothy Canning. *Sixteen Americans*. New York: The Museum of Modern Art, 1959. Distributed by Doubleday.

Plagens, Peter. *Sunshine Muse: Contemporary Art on the West Coast*. New York, Frederick A. Praeger, 1974.

Rosenzweig, Phyllis. *The Fifties: Aspects of Painting in New York*. Washington, DC: Smithsonian Institution Press in association with the Hirshhorn Museum and Sculpture Garden, 1980.

Russell, John and Suzi Gablik. *Pop Art Redefined*. New York: Frederick A. Praeger, 1969.

Sandler, Irving. *American Art of the 1960s*. New York: Harper & Row, 1988.

———. *New York School: Painters and Sculptors of the Fifties*. New York: Harper & Row, 1978.

———. *A Sweeper-Up After Artists: A Memoir*. New York: Thames & Hudson, 2003.

Seitz, William C. *Art in the Age of Aquarius: 1955–1970*. Washington, DC: Smithsonian Institution Press, 1992.

———, ed. *The Art of Assemblage*. New York: The Museum of Modern Art, 1961. Distributed by Doubleday.

Stich, Sidra. *Made in USA, An Americanization in Modern Art: The '50s & '60s*. Berkeley: University Art Museum, University of California, 1987.

Wilkin, Karen and Carl Belz. *Color as Field: American Painting, 1950-1975*. New York: American Federation of Arts; New Haven: Yale University Press, 2007.

Wingate, Ealan, Lisa Kim, and Erin Wright, eds. *Ferus*. New York: Gagosian Gallery, 2002.

EXHIBITION CHECKLIST

Richard Anuszkiewicz
American, born 1930
Circle Unretained, 1957
oil on canvas, 36 x 32 inches
Collection of the artist, courtesy Jacobson Howard Gallery

Darby Bannard
American, born 1934
Greenstone, 1960
alkyd resin on canvas, 67 x 61 inches
Collection of the artist, courtesy Jacobson Howard Gallery

Romare Bearden
American, 1911 – 1988
Jacob and the Angel Tree, 1961
collage of printed papers (magazine stock), 13 x 9 inches
The Estate of Nanette Bearden

Larry Bell
American, born 1939
Untitled, 1961
mirror, wood, paint, 12 x 12 x 5 inches
Courtesy of the artist

Billy Al Bengston
American, born 1934
Sophia, 1960
oil on canvas, 21 x 21 inches
Courtesy of Samuel Freeman

Karl Benjamin
American, born 1925
Interlocking Forms (Thalo Green, Raw Umber, Mars Yellow),
1958
oil on canvas, 40 x 30 inches
The Carl and Marilynn Thoma Collection

Wallace Berman
American, 1926 – 1976
Untitled, 1956–57
collage on canvas: ink and shellac on torn parchment paper on
primed canvas, 19 1/2 x 19 1/2 inches
Private Collection

Ronald Bladen
Canadian, 1918 – 1988
Green and Black, 1961-62
painted wood with metal hardware, 45 x 20 1/2 x 7 inches
Linda and James O. Clark

Lee Bontecou
American, born 1931
Flit, 1959
welded iron, canvas, wire, and black velvet, 65 x 65 inches
Anonymous Gift, courtesy of the Herbert F. Johnson Museum of
Art, Cornell University

George Brecht
American, born 1926
Three Chair Events, 1961
three chairs in differing contexts, dimensions variable
Realized in 2008 with permission of the artist

John Chamberlain
American, born 1927
Nutcracker, 1958
painted steel, 47 x 39 x 30 inches
Private Collection, courtesy Allan Stone Gallery, New York

Chryssa
American, born 1933
Three Arrows, 1960
aluminum, 72 x 66 x 5 inches
Whitney Museum of American Art, New York
Purchase, with funds from the Friends of the Whitney Museum
of American Art, 61.3

Bruce Conner
American, 1933 – 2008
Walkie-Talkie, 1959
mixed media, 32 7/8 x 11 1/4 x 13 1/4 inches
Hirshhorn Museum and Sculpture Garden, Smithsonian
Institution, Washington, DC
Joseph H. Hirshhorn Purchase Fund, 2008

Beauford Delaney
American, 1901 – 1979
Composition, 1958
oil on canvas, 58 1/2 x 45 1/2 inches
Courtesy of Michael Rosenfeld Gallery, LLC, New York,
New York

Jim Dine
American, born 1935
Study for *The Car Crash: Man in Woman's Costume and
Woman in Man's Costume*, 1960
ballpoint pen, ink, chalk, watercolor, colored pencil, pencil, and
cut-and-paste paper on paper, 16 3/4 x 21 3/4 inches
The Museum of Modern Art, New York, Gift of the Artist,
122.1965

Lorser Feitelson
American, 1898 – 1978
Dichotomic Organization: Stripes, 1959
oil on canvas, 70 x 70 inches
Feitelson Arts Foundation, courtesy Louis Stern Fine Arts

Red Grooms
American, born 1937
Policewoman, 1959
wood and metal on wood, 45 x 29 x 10 inches
University at Buffalo Art Galleries, Gift of David K. Anderson,
2000

Al Held
American, 1928 – 2005
Untitled, 1959
oil on collage on paper mounted on canvas, 2 panels, overall
100 3/8 x 98 3/4 x 3/4 inches
Al Held Foundation, Inc.

Robert Indiana
American, born 1928
Eat, 1962
graphite on paper, 25 1/8 x 19 1/16 inches
Ackland Art Museum, purchased with the aid of funds from the
National Endowment for the Arts and the Ackland Associates,
77.20.1

Alfred Jensen
American, 1903 – 1981
Magic 2 and 6, 1960
oil on canvas, signed, 27 x 20 inches
Courtesy Michael Rosenfeld Gallery, LLC, New York, New York

Jess
American, 1923 – 2004
The Hang'd Man: Tarot XIII, 1959
magazine reproductions on window shade in wooden frame,
with screen door, 80 x 30 1/2 inches
Krannert Art Museum and Kinkead Pavilion, University of Illinois,
Urbana-Champaign, Purchase John Needles Chester Fund

Jasper Johns
American, born 1930
Flashlight II, 1958
papier-mâché and glass, 3 x 8 3/4 x 4 inches
Estate of Robert Rauschenberg

Ray Johnson
American, 1927 – 1995
Movie Star with Horse, 1958
mixed-media collage, 16 5/8 x 13 1/2 inches
Frances Beatty and Allen Adler

Ray Johnson
American, 1927 – 1995
Untitled (James Dean in the Rain), c. 1955-1958
mixed-media collage, 15 1/2 x 11 3/4 inches
Estate of Ray Johnson, Richard L. Feigen & Co., New York

Allan Kaprow
American, 1927 – 2006
Untitled, 1959
stepladder, chicken wire, newspaper, and tape, dimensions variable
Realized in 2008 with permission from the artist's estate, courtesy of Hauser and Wirth, London

Ellsworth Kelly
American, born 1923
Two Blacks, White and Blue, 1955
oil on canvas, four joined panels, 92 x 24 inches
Private Collection

Edward Kienholz
American, 1927 – 1994
John Doe, 1959
free-standing assemblage: oil paint on mannequin parts, child's perambulator, toy, wood, metal, plaster, and rubber, 39 1/2 x 19 x 31 1/4 inches
The Menil Collection, Houston

Gabriel Kohn
American, 1910 – 1975
Object of the Sea, 1957
oil and plaster on wood, 62 x 56 x 19 inches
Private Collection, Courtesy McKee Gallery, New York

Nicholas Krushenick
American, 1929 – 1999
Untitled, 1961
acrylic on linen, 30 3/4 x 25 inches
Marianne Boesky Gallery, New York

Alexander Liberman
American, 1912 – 1999
Yellow Continuum, 1958–59
oil on canvas, four panels, overall 85 1/2 x 24 7/8 inches
The Alexander Liberman Trust, courtesy of Mitchell-Innes & Nash, New York

Roy Lichtenstein
American, 1923 – 1997
The Bad Man, 1956
oil on canvas, 22 5/8 x 18 5/8 inches
Mr. Eric B. Schnurer, West Chester, Pennsylvania

Morris Louis
American, 1912 – 1962
Theta Beta, 1960
acrylic resin paint on canvas, 104 5/8 x 233 1/2 inches
Ackland Art Museum, Gift of Marcella Louis Brenner, 90.87

Robert Mallary
American, 1917 – 1997
Untitled, undated
mixed-media resin, 91 x 45 1/2 x 6 3/4 inches
Private Collection, courtesy Allan Stone Gallery, New York

Marisol
French, born 1930
The Large Family Group, 1957
painted wood, 37 x 38 x 6 1/2 inches
The Corcoran Gallery of Art, Washington, DC, Gift of Mr. and Ms. C. M. Lewis

Agnes Martin
American, 1912 – 2004
This Rain, c. 1960
oil on canvas, 70 x 70 inches
Collection of Emily Fisher Landau, New York

John McLaughlin
American, 1898 – 1976
K-1957, 1957
oil on canvas, 48 x 40 inches
Michael Kohn Gallery, Los Angeles

Robert Morris
American, born 1931
Box with the Sound of Its Own Making, 1961 (recreated by the artist in 1993)
walnut box, speaker, audio recording, 9 1/2 x 9 1/2 x 9 1/2 inches
Collection of the artist

Louise Nevelson
American, 1899 – 1988
Distant Cathedral, 1955
wood painted black, 47 x 24 x 18 inches
Courtesy PaceWildenstein

Kenneth Noland
American, born 1924
That, 1958–59
oil on canvas, 83 x 83 inches
Collection of David Mirvish, Toronto, Canada

Claes Oldenburg
American, born 1929
The Old Dump Flag, 1960
wood, 8 3/4 x 10 3/4 inches
Courtesy of Claes Oldenburg and Coosje van Bruggen

Claes Oldenburg
American, born 1929
Left-Handed Flag, 1960
wood and nails, 17 1/2 x 12 7/8 inches
Courtesy of Claes Oldenburg and Coosje van Bruggen

Claes Oldenburg
American, born 1929
Heel Flag, 1960
heel, nails, wood, and rope, 13 1/4 x 14 1/2 inches
Courtesy of Claes Oldenburg and Coosje van Bruggen

Yoko Ono
Japanese, born 1933
Painting to Hammer a Nail, 1961/1966/2008
molded wood frame, oak and plywood, paint, mirror foil, hammer, chain, and nails, dimensions variable
Realized in 2008 with permission from the artist

George Ortman
American, born 1926
Circle, 1958 (restored by the artist)
oil on collaged canvas with plaster on wood, 48 x 48 inches
Courtesy of Mitchell Algus Gallery and the artist

Robert Rauschenberg
American, 1925 – 2008
Painting with Grey Wing, 1959
Combine: oil, printed reproductions, unpainted paint-by-number board, typed print on paper, photographs, fabric, stuffed bird wing, and dime on canvas, 31 3/4 x 21 1/2 x 2 1/2 inches
The Museum of Contemporary Art, Los Angeles
The Panza Collection

Robert Rauschenberg
American, 1925 – 2008
Slow Fall, 1961
Combine: oil, metal, fabric, newspaper, nineteenth-century nail on board with crushed can, string, cola can, lead weight, nail, and milk carton, 56 1/2 x 21 x 12 inches
The Museum of Contemporary Art, Los Angeles
The Panza Collection

James Rosenquist
American, born 1933
Coenties Slip Studio, 1961
oil on shaped canvas, 34 x 43 inches
Collection of the artist

Ed Ruscha
American, born 1937
E. Ruscha, 1959
oil on canvas, 45 1/4 x 45 1/4 inches
Courtesy of Ed Ruscha

Robert Ryman
American, born 1930
*An all white painting measuring 9 1/2" x 10" and signed twice
on the left side in white umber*, 1961
oil on linen canvas, 13 3/4 x 13 3/4 inches
San Francisco Museum of Modern Art
Purchased through a gift of Mimi and Peter Haas

Lucas Samaras
American, born 1936
Pin Box, 1963
construction with box, pins, glass, jar, and wool, 12 x 19 x
10 3/4 inches
The Robert B. Mayer Family Collection, Chicago

George Segal
American, 1924 – 2000
The Legend of Lot, 1958
plaster, wood, chicken wire, wood base, and oil on canvas,
overall 74 x 96 x 66 inches; painting 72 x 96 inches; figure 72
inches high
Courtesy of the George and Helen Segal Foundation, Inc. and
Carroll Janis, Inc.

Leon Polk Smith
American, 1906 – 1996
Expanse, 1959
oil on canvas, 68 x 74 inches
Washburn Gallery, New York

Tony Smith
American, 1912 – 1980
Spitball, 1961
granite, 12 1/8 x 14 1/2 x 15 inches
Montclair Art Museum. Museum Purchase; Prior gift of Harry A.
Astlett

Richard Stankiewicz
American, 1922 – 1983
Railroad Urchin (1959-20), 1959
steel, 51 x 41 x 20 inches
Zabriskie Gallery

Frank Stella
American, born 1936
Blue Horizon, 1958
enamel and oil on canvas, 72 x 72 inches
David Winton Bell Gallery, Brown University, Gift of Lawrence
Rubin

Myron Stout
American, 1908 – 1987
Untitled (No. 3-1956), 1957
oil on canvas, 26 x 18 inches
Carnegie Museum of Art, Pittsburgh; Gift of Leland Hazard,
58.33

Lenore Tawney
American, 1907 – 2007
Bound Man, 1957
wool, silk, linen, goat hair; discontinuous weft brocade, woven,
91 x 36 inches
Museum of Arts & Design, New York
Purchased by the American Craft Council, 1958

Alma Thomas
American, 1891 – 1978
Yellow and Blue, 1959
oil on canvas, signed, 28 x 40 inches
Courtesy of Michael Rosenfeld Gallery, LLC, New York,
New York

Andy Warhol
American, 1928 – 1987
The Gilded Lilly, c. 1956
ink, gold and silver foil on paper, 22 x 27 inches
The Robert B. Mayer Family Collection, Chicago

Tom Wesselmann
American, 1931 – 2004
Portrait Collage #7, 1959
mixed media and collage on board, 8 x 10 inches
The Estate of Tom Wesselmann

Tom Wesselmann
American, 1931 – 2004
Portrait Collage #16, 1960
mixed media and collage on board, 8 1/2 x 11 1/2 inches
The Estate of Tom Wesselmann

Jack Youngerman
American, born 1926
Coenties Slip, 1959
oil on canvas, 81 x 68 inches
Whitney Museum of American Art, New York, Gift of Governor
Nelson A. Rockefeller, 69.94

CREDITS

Image Credits

Plate 1
Art © Romare Bearden Foundation / Licensed by VAGA, New York, NY

Plate 2
Art © Wallace Berman Estate / Image courtesy of The Menil Collection, Houston

Plate 3
Art © Lee Bontecou / Image courtesy of Knoedler & Company, New York

Plate 4 a, b, c
Art © George Brecht / Photograph by Peter Geoffrion

Plate 5
© 2008 John Chamberlain / Artists Rights Society (ARS), New York / Image courtesy of Allan Stone Gallery

Plate 6 a, b
Image courtesy Gallery Paule Anglim, San Francisco / Photograph by Lee Stalsworth

Plate 7
© 2008 Jim Dine / Artists Rights Society (ARS), New York

Plate 8
© 2008 Red Grooms / Artists Rights Society (ARS), New York / Image courtesy of Keystone Film Productions, Inc.

Plate 9
© 2008 Morgan Art Foundation Ltd. / Artists Rights Society (ARS), New York / Photograph by Peter Geoffrion.

Plate 10
Image courtesy Gallery Paule Anglim, San Francisco

Plate 11
Art © Jasper Johns / Licensed by VAGA, New York, NY / Image courtesy of Robert Rauschenberg Collection.

Plate 12
© Courtesy of the Estate of Ray Johnson at Richard L. Feigen & Co. / Image courtesy of Ali Elai, Camerarts

Plate 13
© Courtesy of the Estate of Ray Johnson at Richard L. Feigen & Co. / Image courtesy of Ali Elai, Camerarts

Plate 14
Photograph by Peter Geoffrion

Plate 15 a, b
© Nancy Reddin Kienholz, courtesy of L.A. Louver Gallery / Photograph by George Hixon, Houston

Plate 16
© Estate of Roy Lichtenstein / Photograph courtesy of The Roy Lichtenstein Foundation

Plate 17
© Estate of Robert Mallary / Photography courtesy of Allan Stone Gallery

Plate 18
Art © Marisol Escobar / Licensed by VAGA, New York, NY

Plate 19
© 2008 Robert Morris / Artists Rights Society (ARS), New York / Photograph by Jesse Levinson

Plate 20
© 2008 Estate of Louise Nevelson / Artists Rights Society (ARS), New York / Photography courtesy of PaceWildenstein, New York, NY

Plate 21
© Claes Oldenburg / Photograph by Dorothy Zeidman

Plate 22
© Claes Oldenburg / Photograph by Nathan Rabin

Plate 23
© Claes Oldenburg / Photograph by Dorothy Zeidman

Plate 24
© Yoko Ono / Photograph by John Bigelow Taylor

Plate 25
Art © Rauschenberg Estate / Licensed by VAGA, New York, NY

Plate 26
Art © Rauschenberg Estate / Licensed by VAGA, New York, NY

Plate 27
Art © James Rosenquist / Licensed by VAGA, New York, NY / Photography courtesy of James Rosenquist

Plate 28
© Ed Ruscha / Photography courtesy of Ed Ruscha

Plate 29
© Lucas Samaras, courtesy PaceWildenstein, New York / Photograph by Michael Tropea

Plate 30
Art © The George and Helen Segal Foundation / Licensed by VAGA, New York, NY

Plate 31
Courtesy Zabriskie Gallery and the estate of the artist

Plate 32
Art © Estate of Lenore Tawney / Photograph by Ed Watkins, 2007

Plate 33
© 2008 Andy Warhol Foundation for the Visual Arts / (ARS), New York / Photograph by Michael Tropea

Plate 34
Art © Estate of Tom Wesselmann / Licensed by VAGA, New York, NY / Photograph by Jeffrey Sturges, New York, NY

Plate 35
Art © Estate of Tom Wesselmann / Licensed by VAGA, New York, NY / Photograph by Jeffrey Sturges, New York, NY

Plate 36
Art © Richard Anuszkiewicz / Licensed by VAGA, New York, NY / Image courtesy Jacobson Howard Gallery

Plate 37
© Darby Bannard / photograph courtesy of the artist

Plate 38
© Larry Bell

Plate 39
© Billy Al Bengston / Photograph courtesy of Samuel Freeman

Plate 40
© Karl Benjamin

Plate 41
© Estate of Ronald Bladen LLC / Photograph by Adam Reich Photographics

Plate 42
© 2008 Chryssa / Photograph by Jerry L. Thompson

Plate 43
© Estate of Beauford Delaney / Courtesy of Michael Rosenfeld Gallery, LLC, New York, NY

Plate 44
© Feitelson Arts Foundation / Courtesy Louis Stern Fine Arts

Plate 45
Art © Al Held Foundation / Licensed by VAGA, New York, NY

Plate 46
© 2008 Estate of Alfred Jensen / Artists Rights Society (ARS), New York / Photograph courtesy of Michael Rosenfeld Gallery, LLC, New York, NY

Plate 47
© Ellsworth Kelly

Plate 48
Private Collection, Courtesy McKee Gallery, New York, NY / Photograph by Richard P. Goodbody Inc., NY

Plate 49
Photo courtesy of Marianne Boesky Gallery, New York, NY

Plate 50
The Alexander Liberman Trust / Courtesy of Mitchell-Inness & Nash, New York, NY / Photograph courtesy of Mitchell-Innes & Nash

Plate 51
© Morris Louis / Photograph courtesy of the Ackland Art Muesum

Plate 52
© 2008 Agnes Martin / Artists Rights Society (ARS), New York / Photograph courtesy of Collection Emily Fisher Landau, New York, NY

Plate 53
Photography courtesy Michael Kohn Gallery, Los Angeles

Plate 54
Art © Kenneth Noland / Licensed by VAGA, New York, NY

Plate 55
Courtesy of Mitchell Algus Gallery and the artist / Photograph by Sheldan Collins

Plate 56
© Robert Ryman / courtesy PaceWildenstein, New York / Photograph by Ben Blackwell

Plate 57
Art © The Leon Polk Smith Foundation / Licensed by VAGA, New York, NY / Photograph courtesy of Washburn Gallery, New York

Plate 58
© 2008 Estate of Tony Smith / Artists Rights Society (ARS), New York

Plate 59
© 2008 Frank Stella / Artists Rights Society (ARS), New York

Plate 60
Art © Washburn Gallery, New York / Photograph © 2007 Carnegie Museum of Art, Pittsburgh

Plate 61
Public Domain / Photograph courtesy of Michael Rosenfeld Gallery, LLC, New York, NY

Plate 62
Art © Jack Youngerman / Licensed by VAGA, New York, NY / Photo credit: Jerry L. Thompson

Fig. 1
© 2008 The Willem de Kooning Foundation / Artists Rights Society (ARS), New York

Fig. 2
Art © 2008 Barnett Newman Foundations / Artists Rights Society (ARS), New York / Digital Image © The Museum of Modern Art / Licensed by SCALA / Art Resource, NY

Fig. 3
Art © Jasper Johns / Licensed by VAGA, New York, NY / Magazine © 1958 *ARTnews*, LLC, January

Fig. 4
Art © 2008 Jim Dine / Artists Rights Society (ARS), New York / Photograph © Estate of Fred W. McDarrah

Fig. 5
Photograph © Robert McElroy / Licensed by VAGA, New York, NY

Fig. 6
Photograph © Patricia Faure

Fig. 7
Photograph © Robert McElroy / Licensed by VAGA, New York, NY

Fig. 8
Art © Estate of Ad Reinhardt / Artists Rights Society (ARS), New York / Digital Image © The Museum of Modern Art / Licensed by SCALA / Art Resource, NY

Fig. 9
Collection of the artist, on extended loan to the National Gallery of Art, Washington, DC / Photograph courtesy of the National Gallery of Art

Fig. 10
Art © 2008 Frank Stella / Artists Rights Society (ARS), New York / Photograph courtesy of Collection Walker Art Center, Minneapolis, © Estate of Hollis Frampton

Fig. 11
Photograph © Hans Namuth

Fig. 12
Art © Rauschenberg Estate / Licensed by VAGA, New York, NY / Photograph: Kay Harris

Lenders

Ackland Art Museum, The University of North Carolina at Chapel Hill

Mitchell Algus Gallery

Richard Anuszkiewicz

Darby Bannard

The Estate of Nanette Bearden

Frances Beatty and Allen Adler

David Winton Bell Gallery, Brown University

Larry Bell

Marian Boesky Gallery

George Brecht

Carnegie Museum of Art

Linda and James O. Clark

The Corcoran Gallery of Art

Feitelson Arts Foundation, courtesy Louis Stern Fine Arts

Samuel Freeman

Hauser and Wirth

Al Held Foundation, Inc.

Jacobson Howard Gallery

Carroll Janis, Inc.

Herbert F. Johnson Museum of Art, Cornell University

Hirshhorn Museum and Sculpture Garden, Smithsonian Institution

The Estate of Ray Johnson, courtesy Richard L. Feigen & Co.

Estate of Allan Kaprow, courtesy of Hauser and Wirth

Michael Kohn Gallery

Krannert Art Museum and Kinkead Pavilion, University of Illinois, Urbana-Champaign

Emily Fisher Landau

The Alexander Liberman Trust, courtesy of Mitchell-Innes & Nash

The Robert B. Mayer Family Collection

McKee Gallery

The Menil Collection

David Mirvish

Montclair Art Museum

Robert Morris

Museum of Arts & Design

The Museum of Contemporary Art, Los Angeles The Panza Collection

The Museum of Modern Art

Claes Oldenburg and Coosje van Bruggen

Yoko Ono

George Ortman

PaceWildenstein

Estate of Robert Rauschenberg

Michael Rosenfeld Gallery, LLC

James Rosenquist

Ed Ruscha

San Francisco Museum of Modern Art

Mr. Eric B. Schnurer

The George and Helen Segal Foundation, Inc.

Allan Stone Gallery

The Carl and Marilynn Thoma Collection

University at Buffalo Art Galleries

Washburn Gallery

The Estate of Tom Wesselmann

Whitney Museum of American Art

Zabriskie Gallery

Ackland National Advisory Board

Mr. James-Keith Brown
Chair

Mrs. Erwin P. Boyd
Dr. J. Kenneth Chance
Mr. C. Perry Colwell
Ms. Shirley Drechsel
Ms. Beatrice Cummings Mayer
Ms. Elizabeth Kenan Morton
Ms. Paula Davis Noell
Ms. Josephine Ward Patton
Dr. Sheldon Peck
Ms. Katharine Lee Reid
Mr. Herbert F. Shatzman
Ms. Gayle Sheppard
Mr. John LeRoy Townsend III
Mr. Charles J. Wolfe Jr.
Ms. Catherine R. Williams

Ex Officio:
Dr. Carol Tresolini

Emeritus:
Dr. Charles W. Millard III
Mr. Robert Myers
Mr. James R. Patton Jr.
Mrs. Ann Bondurant Young

Ackland
Exhibition Staff

Emily Kass, Director

Carolyn Wood, Assistant Director for Art and Education
Timothy Riggs, Curator of Collections
Barbara Matilsky, Curator of Exhibitions
Carol Gillham, Assistant Curator for Collections
Chris Huber, Assistant Curator for Exhibitions
Lauren Sanford, Curatorial Assistant
Anita Heggli, Registrar
Scott Hankins, Assistant Registrar
Lyn Koehnline, Conservator
Joe Gargasz, Chief Preparator
Andrew Nagy, Preparator
Kirby Sewell, Preparator
Carolyn Allmendinger, Director of Academic Programs
Beth Shaw McGuire, Senior Museum Educator
Leslie Balkany, Museum Educator
Betty Carr, Education Assistant
Kate Arpen, Museum Graduate Intern
Erica Longenbach, Patton-Boggs Intern

Suzanne Rucker, Administrative Manager
Nancy Thacker, Administrative Secretary
Stephanie Brown, Museum Housekeeper
Debbie Pulley, Security Guard Supervisor
James Britt, Security Guard
Reggie Edwards, Security Guard
James Glover, Security Guard

Amanda Hughes, Director of External Affairs
Jocelyn Arem, Coordinator of Public Programs and Special Projects
Kate Baker, Executive Assistant for Advancement
Nic Brown, Director of Communications
Kyle Fitch, Director of Annual Giving
Corey Reece, Internet/Technology Coordinator